FINDING FRAN

BOOKS BY LOIS W. BANNER

In Full Flower: Aging Women, Power, and Sexuality
(1992)

American Beauty
(1983)

Elizabeth Cady Stanton
(1979)

Women in Modern America
(1974)

coeditor
Clio's Consciousness Raised
(1974)

FINDING FRAN

HISTORY AND MEMORY
IN THE LIVES OF TWO WOMEN

Lois W. Banner

COLUMBIA UNIVERSITY PRESS

NEW YORK

COLUMBIA UNIVERSITY PRESS
Publishers Since 1893
New York   Chichester, West Sussex
Copyright © 1998 by Lois W. Banner

Library of Congress Cataloging-in-Publication Data
Banner, Lois W.
Finding Fran : history and memory in the lives of two women / Lois W. Banner.
p.   cm.
Includes bibliographical references.
ISBN 0–231–11216–5 (cloth : alk. paper)
1. Banner, Lois W. 2. Durkee, Noura. 3. Feminists—California—Biography.
4. Women in Islam. 5. Lama Foundation.   I. Title.
HQ1413.B36A3   1998
305.4'092'2—dc21   98–23608

Casebound editions of Columbia University Press books are printed on permanent and
durable acid-free paper.
Printed in the United States of America
c 10 9 8 7 6 5 4 3 2 1

Columbia University Press gratefully acknowledges permission to use the following
photographs:
Climbing the Chilkoot Pass. Courtesy of Special Collections Division, University of
Washington Libraries; negative no. Hegg 97;
Columbia (statue of Alma Mater). Photo copyright (c) Fred Knubel;
Lois Banner and her children, c. 1983. Photo copyright (c) Diana Waler/*People Weekly*;
and The masjid al-hara, Makkah. Photo courtesy of UPI/Corbis-Bettmann.

For Melba Parkes Wendland (1906–1952)
and
Lydia Murray Huneke Moss (1905–1996)

CONTENTS

ACKNOWLEDGMENTS

Without the generosity of many individuals, this book could not have been written. Marilyn (Mimi) Abers, Fran's college roommate and my friend for over
thirty years, has been involved with it from the beginning. She accompanied me
to Santa Fe, New Mexico, in 1991 and to Alexandria, Egypt, in 1993, where she
took photographs for me and helped me to focus my interviews. Moreover, she
provided me with insight into Fran and their years at Stanford. My thanks also
to Stanley Burstein of the Classics Department of California State University,
Los Angeles, for helping me to identify the position of Fran's grandfather,
Augustus Taber Murray, in the turn-of-the-century field of classics. Elizabeth
Davenport of the University of Southern California, an Episcopal priest, aided
me in understanding the structure and rites of the Episcopal Church.

Rosalie Bean Kane, a member of my high school class and a friend ever
since, provided me with a file of our student newspaper and helped me to
understand our student culture, while expressing amusement that I took the
"popularity system" so seriously. I also thank Gladys Waddingham, now
deceased, for her conversations with me as well as for authoring many volumes on Inglewood's history when in her eighties and nineties. "Mrs.
Waddingham" was my Spanish teacher in high school and the last living member of my mother's cohort of teachers there. Pianist George Malloy of New
York City, who studied piano with my mother in the 1940s, helped me to
understand her musical talent and that of my uncle.

A number of individuals helped me to reconstruct my years as a graduate student at Columbia University. I thank my fellow (and sororal) students William Chafe, Linda Kerber, Regina Morantz-Sanchez, Barbara Sicherman, and Carroll Smith-Rosenberg for their interviews with me. Professors Robert Cross, William Leuchtenberg, and Alden Vaughan wrote long and searching responses to the questions I posed to them in writing.

My brothers, Paul and John Wendland, and my sister, Lila Myers, preserved the family papers that I would have thrown out years ago. They allowed me to use those papers, and they shared their memories of our childhood with me. I am greatly indebted to Noura's natal family, especially to her brother Albert Huneke and her sister, Betty Huneke Buckman. They assembled Noura's letters and other Huneke family papers and shared them with me. They also talked about their childhood with me.

Without the great generosity of Fran's first husband, Hans (Siddiq) von Briesen, and his wife, Sakina, I doubt I would have tried to find Fran. In interviews at their home in Santa Fe in the summer of 1991, they first told me what had happened at Lama, and they gave me Noura's address in Alexandria. I salute all they have done to keep the Lama Foundation healthy over the years, and I especially praise them for the herculean task of fund-raising they have spearheaded since the forest on the Lama property and many of its buildings burned down in the massive forest fire in the Sangre de Christo mountain range in the spring of 1995.

Without the support of Siddiq and Sakina, I doubt that the residents and guests whom I met at Lama in the summer of 1993 would have so willingly shared their impressions of the community and its early leaders with me. I thank those individuals at Lama who spoke openly to me, implicitly trusting that I would not violate their confidences. Because I have wanted to serve them well, I have kept their identities largely anonymous.

I am grateful to Tasnim Fernandez, my Sufi teacher in Los Angeles, for her wisdom and kindness in guiding me through the mazes of Sufi doctrine and for putting up with my resistances and inconstancies. As an interpreter of spiritual doctrines she has few peers; as a leader of the Dances of Universal Peace she inspires peace and joy. I also appreciate the loving support of my fellow Sufi Order mureeds, especially David Holbert, Tom Clover, and Paul and Muhiya Judy Warren.

My thanks to all those individuals who read the many versions of this manuscript over the years and who forced me to delve deeply into painful areas of memory and personality. They include Elinor Accampo, Judith

Grant, Cynthia Hogue, Helen Horowitz, Mary Kelley, Elaine Tyler May, Azade-Ayse Rorlich, and members of my "girl gang" in Los Angeles: Wini Breines, Ellen DuBois, Alice Echols, and Alice Wexler. I also acknowledge the friendship and support for nearly forty years of my college sorority sisters Barbara Bates, June Barlow Johnson, Patricia McBroom, Lourdes Miranda, and Rosemary Rau-Levine. I thank Lila Karp for the intellectual stimulation and personal support she provides me as well as for all she has taught me about second wave feminism. I thank my agent, Nikki Smith, for her faith in me over the years, and Ann Miller, my editor at Columbia University Press, for her wisdom and care in dealing with my story.

Entering my life in the middle of this project, John Laslett, now my husband, has given me extraordinary love and support. He has shown me that personal relationships formed in midlife can have a special richness and that there is truth in the aphorism: "The third time is the charm."

To my daughter, Olivia, as always, I extend my love and thanks. A brilliant scholar and writer in her own right, once again, as before, she took over a manuscript of mine when my energy was flagging and helped me to shape it into its final form. I hope that plunging so deeply into my story, which is also her story, has proven to be as therapeutic for her as it has been for me. To Noura's daughters Fatima and Saida I hope that I can always be the "auntie" I became in Alexandria and that my telling of your mother's story will help you to better understand her. Finally, I thank Nuridin Durkee for putting up with me.

To Noura Durkee, what can I say? Noura/Fran, in allowing me to tell your story, in placing your life in my hands, you have given me a great gift. I have tried to respond to that gift by telling your story with affection and honesty. Thank you for allowing me to find you.

A Note on Word Usage

Throughout this manuscript, I follow the more recent transliterations of Arabic words for Muslim institutions and practices. Thus I use *masjid*, rather than *mosque*, for Muslim houses of worship; *Makkah*, rather than *Mecca*, to designate Islam's holy city; *Ka'abah* for *Cabah*; and *Qur'an* rather than *Koran*.

FINDING FRAN

Abiquiu, New Mexico
August 1994

It's a cool summer's evening in this isolated desert region midway between Santa Fe and Taos. Noura and I sit on the soft, intricately patterned Middle Eastern rugs that cover the floors of this house, in which she once lived. Leaning on pillows, we talk about our past and our present and why we have come together here, in these mesas covered with scrub brush, near Georgia O'Keeffe's Ghost Ranch. I think of O'Keeffe's bleached animal skulls, so appropriate to Abiquiu's aridity—its beige and copper hues, its arroyos and canyons. We could be on the moon—or in Saudi Arabia—another desert landscape important in Noura's life.

We drink coffee, although I might prefer wine to relax. But Noura is a strict Muslim, and she abides by Islam's prohibition against alcohol. Incorporating Islam throughout her life, she follows the simple lifestyle of Muhammad, the Arab who founded Islam in the seventh century c.e. She cooks Middle Eastern food—lamb, chicken, vegetables—and places it in mounds on a large brass tray. There is little furniture in the house. Seated on a carpet, we eat from the tray, communally.

The pictures on the walls contain Arabic calligraphy in black and gold. The words come from the Qur'an, from phrases that honor Allah. This isn't the art one would expect in the home of Noura and her husband, Nuridin. American by birth, both were once artists in the Western tradition; in the 1950s and 1960s New York galleries displayed Nuridin's work and museums purchased it. But calligraphy suits the home of this devout couple. The most sacred form of Muslim art, it celebrates Islam's reverence for the words of the Qur'an, and it respects the religion's prohibition of the idolatry of portrayals of Allah in art and—by extension—of the human form, since humans can share in God's majesty, through divine grace.

Near the house, a large masjid dominates the landscape. Nuridin supervised building the structure, following the design of Hassan Fathy, a renowned Egyptian architect. The masjid is the center of a Muslim community that Noura and Nuridin founded in 1980 as an outpost of Islam in America, a religious and educational center where East would meet West and their own lives be fulfilled. They called it Dar-al-Islam, the territory of Islam, the abode of the faithful. They left it some ten years later.

What am I doing here? I'm a professor of U.S. history and gender studies at the University of Southern California in Los Angeles. A feminist and atheist for most of my adult life, I'm dressed in shorts and T-shirt, engaged in conversation with this Muslim woman who covers her body with clothing and wears a scarf carefully arranged to hide every hair on her head, even during the heat of the day. To an outsider, we must present a curious picture. We are in Abiquiu together because Noura and Nuridin have sold this house that they owned, and Noura has traveled from her home in Alexandria, Egypt, to pack up and move their possessions. I have come from Los Angeles to help her and to continue interviewing her for this book. I began those interviews the year before in Alexandria; we will continue them in Abiquiu.

This isn't our first meeting. Forty years ago, we were best friends in high school. Noura's name was then Fran. Like me, she was a schoolgirl with her mind on books and boys. It was the 1950s, the era when post–World War II prosperity and Cold War fears brought a return to patriarchal nuclear families. We lived with our families in Inglewood, a suburb of Los Angeles, where we attended the local high school. (My last name was then Wendland, and hers was Huneke.) Then inseparable, we coped with the standard 1950s high school culture revolving around football players and prom queens, while we fantasized about a future together in New York City after college. We never expected that our lives would turn out so differently.

Why did our lives take such different paths—mine to feminism and hers to Islam? That is the major question this book addresses. The answer at first seems simple: sixties radicalism swept me to feminism and an academic career and Fran to religious spirituality. In 1969 she left mainstream society to move to the Lama Foundation, a spiritual community in the mountains near Taos, New Mexico. That same year, while finishing a Ph.D. at Columbia University and teaching at Douglass College of Rutgers University, the state university of New Jersey, I encountered the new feminism then appearing. In 1972, while I was planning the first national conference in women's history, Fran left the Lama Foundation to become an art editor and illustrator for Pir Vilayat Inayat Khan, head of the Sufi Order in the West, an ecumenical and Westernized offshoot of Islam. In 1976, when Fran made the profession of faith to Islam and took the name Noura, I was writing a biography of Elizabeth Cady Stanton, the nineteenth-century U.S. woman's rights leader.

Yet cultural trends and historical timing explain only part of our stories. Our families and our early environment in Inglewood also influenced us. Thus my narrative begins with our childhoods. I tell the story of my upbringing first because mine is the authorial voice in this work and because Fran and I didn't become friends until high school. Soon after we met there my mother died, and I became attached not only to Fran but also to her mother, Lydia. When we went to different colleges (Fran to Stanford and I to UCLA), our friendship suffered. We became close again in the early 1960s when, after college, we both moved East: I to New York City to work for a Ph.D. and Fran to Rochester, New York, following her graduate student husband.

When Fran moved to Lama in 1969, however, our relationship was put on hold. As a feminist academic, living in a suburban nuclear family, I didn't seem any longer to have much in common with Fran, who was living in a small community and exploring religious spirituality. For the next twenty-four years, we neither saw nor corresponded with one another.

After all those years, why did I decide to find Fran? Not surprisingly, I was intrigued by her profession of Islam. It seemed to me so extreme, so against the American grain. Given our similarity when young, I was puzzled that we took such different life paths. Didn't the feminism of the 1960s influence her? In my case it changed my life. Without its influence, I doubt I would have become a scholar or remained in university teaching. How could Fran, my independent friend, not have been touched by feminism?

I address these questions both by comparing Fran and me and by telling our separate stories. Many readers should find my story familiar, for feminism profoundly influenced many women of my generation. But how many Westerners are familiar with Islam? Friends of mine who meet Noura are perplexed by her scarf and her religious phrases. I understand their reaction. For when I discovered that Fran was Muslim, I was dismayed. Knowing nothing about Islam, I identified it with fanatical shaykhs, holy wars, and swarthy Middle Eastern men kidnapping their children from their American wives. These were the stereotypes presented by the media, and I accepted them.

Even after Noura described her faith to me, I didn't understand it. For the word "Islam" means submission, and "Muslim" one who submits. How could the Fran I'd known—independent, questioning, stubborn—submit to anyone or anything? When Noura told me that through submission she found freedom, I was even more perplexed. The best explanation I could then muster was that freedom doesn't have the same meaning to everyone. In fact, my appraisal wasn't that far off. But I had to learn much more to correct my stereotypical views of Islam.

Before I visited Noura in Alexandria, she recommended that I read the autobiography of Jehan Sadat, the wife of Anwar al-Sadat, the president of Egypt who won the Nobel Peace Prize. Reading that book was a first step toward understanding Noura. A devout Muslim, Jehan Sadat was a social reformer and a feminist. In addition to taking on public duties as the president's wife and private ones as a wife and mother, she studied for a Master's degree in Arabic Literature at the University of Cairo. She also spearheaded women's projects: family planning clinics, daycare centers, production cooperatives.

Like Jehan Sadat, Noura holds feminist beliefs. She supports a woman's right to education, work, and pay equal to that of men. On the issue of abortion, she has ethical objections, but she supports the notion of a woman's right to her body and thus to choice in the matter. Throughout her adult life, Noura has been a wife and mother as well as a working woman. She founded nursery and elementary schools. She illustrated and published books; she studied the Arabic language and the Muslim religion at the postgraduate level at a Saudi Arabian university in Makkah, and she studied the Qur'an and Arabic calligraphy with professors at the renowned Al-Azar University in Cairo. At present she teaches English as a Second Language and writes and illustrates children's books for three Muslim publishers from her home.

In professing Islam, she became Sufi as well as Muslim, and that orientation is important in understanding her. Sufism is the mystical, esoteric path within Islam, traceable to Muhammad and his companions. Much modern Islam is legalistic, focused on interpreting laws and directives for every aspect of behavior. In general, these laws are drawn from the Qur'an, the revelations of Allah to Muhammad over a period of twenty-three years, as well as from the hadith, the sayings of Muhammad observed and recorded by his followers, and the sunnah, the practices of Muhammad during his life. Muslim Sufis follow the law, but they also stress a direct connection between God and humans. "God is closer to you than your jugular vein" is an oft-quoted Sufi—and Muslim—saying.

Sufi mysticism involves a spiritual journey toward union with the divine. Sufis call that interior path *tariqa* and the pilgrim the *salik*; over the centuries many Sufi commentators have elaborated on the stages of repentance, self-denial, and illumination on the path. Many Eastern religions possess a concept of such a journey and its goal in enlightenment. Yogis call the final state of self-awareness *samadhi*; Buddhists *vimokka*; Kabalists *en sof*; Muslims *tawhid*. Christian mystics call it the grace of God, or *contemplatio*. Dante's *visio beatifica* in the *Divine Comedy* encompasses it.

When I left Alexandria, still puzzled by Noura's profession of Islam, I decided to follow her path. The Lama Foundation still exists, and I lived there for several weeks during the summer of 1993. I also sought out the Los Angeles branch of the Sufi Order in the West. (The Sufi Order permits non-Muslims to participate.) Like many participant observers, I became part of the groups I was studying. In the end, I joined the Sufi Order.

In retrospect, I can see that during my life I have undergone several conversions: to academic rationality when in college; to feminism in the 1960s; and, recently, to a mystical belief system. But in taking up new commitments, I haven't abandoned older ones. I remain an academic devoted to critical investigation and a feminist devoted to the equality of men and women. I don't cover my head, and I don't pray five times a day or fast at Ramadan, as Islam requires. I don't follow Islamic law; I'm not a Muslim. What the Sufi Order has given me is a spirituality I thought I'd lost when in 1960 I left my family in Los Angeles for graduate school in New York City and fled my past, never expecting that one day I would come back.

Once I returned to Los Angeles and encountered my past on the streets I traveled and the places I went to, I couldn't avoid it. As an historian, I wanted to learn what I could about its truth through critical investigation, not solely through the imprecision of memory. But the "truth" of my past involved not just finding out about my family, my high school, and my childhood community. It also involved finding Fran. For she and her mother, Lydia, played major roles in shaping me.

This memoir combines biography, autobiography, and social and oral history. In writing it, I've delved into my memory and that of Noura. I've investigated both my family papers and hers. I've talked to family members and friends of both of ours, especially mine at Columbia and hers at Lama. To understand our early lives, I researched the history of Inglewood as well as our family backgrounds. To provide a cultural context, I read in depth about such subjects as the history of the university, the feminist movement, sixties spirituality and communalism, and Islam.

As this work proceeded, Noura became involved with its production, especially as we realized that our memories of our early years differed and we tried to understand the meanings of those differences. Noura read early drafts of the book. This reading stimulated her memory and helped her to reconstruct her own life story. We spent many hours discussing what I had written, and I rewrote the manuscript in light of those conversations. What I've written about her life often combines our recollections so seamlessly that I couldn't differentiate between them, and I often tell her story through my voice. Sometimes the narrative about her life is so much hers that I include it as quoted passages after her name, especially in the chapters on Lama and on Dar-al-Islam.

In this book I am sympathetic to Noura's espousing sixties spirituality and communalism, as well as her taking up Islam, partly because of my affection for her. Yet my sympathy has also been aroused by my frustration over current historical interpretations unfairly hostile to these movements. Many feminists dismiss spirituality as irrelevant, and academics and popular writers alike scorn the communal movement of the sixties as the work of irresponsible hippies. Where appropriate, I recast those movements in a positive light. I also stress the importance of the Lama Foundation within the communal movement, as well as Noura and Nuridin's role in that community and in Dar-al-Islam. With regard to Islam, my goal has been to explain Noura's profession of faith to non-Muslims. As many as one billion individuals worldwide profess Islam, while it is estimated that Islam will soon outgrow Judaism as the largest non-Christian religion within the

United States. Westerners need to understand its attraction to a gifted and educated woman such as Fran.

Moreover, in teaching women's history for over twenty years, I have become increasingly concerned by my students' lack of awareness of second wave feminism and of how it reshaped possibilities for women; that concern has motivated me to tell my own story. Adopting the media's characterization of feminists as a small group of man-hating "braburners," students who enter my classes have no realization of my generation's life trajectories nor of the sexism we encountered in attempting to forge careers. As the backlash against feminism grows, popular books are written from this same negative perspective. Many of their authors overlook the complexities of the feminist movement and its transformative effect on lives. Overlooking its many narrative threads and how it unfolded differently in specific locales and in individual personalities, they present a caricature not a true picture.

Above all, this book explores two women's experiences during the post–World War II eras of gender traditionalism in the 1950s and of social ferment in the 1960s. Our differing lives illustrate the power and complexities of those decades, how each could impact on two lives so uniquely. In addition, this book is about a friendship. It shows how childhood bonds can remain strong, even if unrealized, throughout a lifetime. We can exist as phantoms in each other's memories, until with a twist of fate, those phantoms become real humans again. Noura would say that there has been an inevitability to our friendship, that Allah knew its progression from its beginning to the present, knew all its twists and turns, knew that our paths, so different, would be reconciled in the end. Although I don't agree with her interpretation, I accept it as a viable point of view.

I

MY STORY
1944–1952

CHAPTER ONE

The House on Hillcrest

Today I went back, as I do occasionally, to look at the house in which I grew up. I drove from my home in Santa Monica, near the beach, south over the Baldwin Hills, where tracts of vacant land still stand amid Los Angeles urban sprawl. I continued to the city of Inglewood and the intersection where Hillcrest Boulevard begins. On a corner of the intersection still stands the Inglewood Woman's Club, where my grandmother played bridge and I soloed with my mother's children's chorus. My childhood home, large and imposing, is one block away.

In 1944, when I was five, my family moved into the house. We were an extended group, ten in number. There were my mother and father and my three siblings: my sister, four years older than me, my brother, two years my elder, and a second brother, born soon after we moved in. My maternal great-grandmother and grandparents lived with us, and their son, my uncle, moved in between each of his four marriages. With so many family members ranging so widely in age, we were nothing on the order of Freud's oedipal family of mother, father, and child. Indeed, all my relatives in that house influenced me, each contributing to what I became.

And so did that house. To me it was a place for fantasy, even while it was the site where my family fashioned a common and daily life. Moreover, the street and the city where it was located also were part of the physical and mental geography of my childhood world—as they were part of Fran's.

Understanding the house, the street, and the city is important to knowing me—and that understanding is also important to knowing Fran.

I don't know why that street was named Hillcrest or called a "boulevard." I've looked through city records, but they don't provide an answer. It isn't on the crest of a hill. Although it's wide, with a tree-filled center divider, it's suburban, not urban.

In 1888 fourteen men, led by Daniel Freeman, a wealthy Canadian emigrant, drew up the plans for Inglewood. They located it on Freeman's land. A decade earlier he'd purchased two of the huge ranchos into which Mexican rulers had divided Southern California early in the nineteenth century. Freeman's property stretched from the outskirts of downtown Los Angeles to the ocean; it included nearly 25,000 acres. A sometime entrepreneur, in the mid-1880s Freeman persuaded the owners of the area's developing railroad system to build a station on his land. That made it ideal for urban settlement at a time when migrants were flocking to Southern California and speculators were founding cities throughout the region.

Shortly before the city's founding, Freeman built a Victorian mansion on a forested, gated, and multi-acre estate not far from what would be the center of the city, and he laid out a racetrack in front of the estate for his personal use. The land across from the track was perfect for the homes of the city's elites. When the track was later turned into a city street, the name Hillcrest Boulevard was probably chosen because it sounded upper class.

The founders of Inglewood wanted to create a noteworthy place, an elite cultural center in an Edenic setting. They adopted the sylvan name Inglewood, laid out parks, built a hotel, projected a "Freeman" college. But their plan never worked. The depression of the 1890s hit Los Angeles and precipitated a decline in migration and in land prices. The hotel, failing to draw a clientele, was torn down; the college was never built. The boom of the 1880s turned into a bust; for some years it was possible that, like other Los Angeles satellite cities launched during the boom, Inglewood might disappear—or become a stop on the train line between downtown Los Angeles and the cities along the beach. My home, among the first on the tract of land across from the Freeman estate, wasn't built until the 1920s.

Yet land was plentiful. In 1905 some enterprising residents established a large cooperative poultry farm and another group a cemetery; for a time chickens and burials sustained Inglewood. In the 1920s the city attracted small manufacturing plants, and the incorporation of other small cities such as Torrance and Hawthorne out of Freeman's land provided a supportive economy. In the 1930s a large commercial horseracing track was built not far from my house, while the city airport, originally a plowed-over beanfield for local flying buffs, was expanded to serve the metropolitan region. Today, as Los Angeles International (LAX), it's one of the largest airports in the nation.

As LAX grew, aircraft companies built plants near it, and they attracted as workers "Okie" migrants from the Dust Bowl, especially with the expansion of the industry during World War II. These newcomers swelled Inglewood's population, making the city mostly lower middle and working class. There were well-to-do lawyers and merchants and clubs such as Rotary and the Elks. In the late 1940s a tract of middle-class, split-level homes was built not far from my house. But the parents of my childhood friends were mostly working-class mail carriers and factory workers. By the 1950s small stucco houses built for them dominated Inglewood's residential architecture; my block on Hillcrest contained the largest houses in the city.

Since the 1960s Inglewood's population has become mainly African-American. But no Blacks lived there when I was a child, for municipal ordinances prohibited their presence in the city after sundown. When 1960s civil rights laws overturned those codes, Blacks moved in. Yet even after a half century of changes in the class and race composition of the city, traces of the founders' original design remain, as well as early buildings funded by Freeman and his family. Their Victorian mansion was torn down in the 1970s, but the Woman's Club still stands. So does a large Episcopal church, built in 1915 and located across an alley behind my Hillcrest house. Designed in light stucco and in English Gothic style by the same architect as the National Cathedral in Washington, D.C., its straight lines point to the sky. One Inglewood historian calls it "the finest example of pure Gothic architecture west of the Mississippi."

In the church's courtyard still stands a large tree my sister and older brother and I climbed as children. Yet we never went inside the church. For we were Lutherans, not Anglicans, and our fundamentalist Missouri Synod prohibited us from entering any church but our own. I never experienced the rites of that Episcopal church nor encountered its congregation. Fran and her family attended that church, but I didn't know them then. They lived crosstown, in a large house near the airport in the midst of the aircraft workers' homes. Not until later would I meet Fran; not until recently would I learn how that church and its religion influenced her.

If I were to stand near that Episcopal church long enough, I might hear its bells chiming the hours, as I did in my childhood. But my visits there are brief, because I don't want to hear the bells. In my memory their tones are morbid, announcing death. For beginning in 1949, when I was ten, one by one the adults I loved the best in my family died, shattering my childhood world.

With its Gothic lines and light stucco exterior, my childhood home looks as though it should be the rectory for the Episcopal church. Yet a cupola over the enclosed entrance gives it the appearance of a castle. It's a fantasy structure, one of those architectural flights typical of Los Angeles, where flamboyant houses have long served as visual markers of material success in this city of tropical landscapes and Hollywood dreams. My elders first heard about the house in the 1930s from my mother's gynecologist, its owner and original builder. He told my mother it was a replica of a country house he'd seen on a vacation in England.

As when I lived there, several large stucco houses of nondescript design still flank my house. Down the block are some one-story "California" bungalows with wide porches and screened windows to catch breezes in the warm climate. There are a few houses in the Spanish Revival style common to Southern California, with terra cotta tiled roofs, Moorish arches, and walls resembling adobe. Several 1930s bungalow courts still remain, as do some small apartment buildings constructed when Inglewood grew in population during World War II.

Such types of houses on Hillcrest Boulevard indicate the failure of any expectations that my block might be an upper-class enclave. Indeed, when I lived there, the residents I knew were elderly widows of modest means and children I played with whose families seemed to just get by. In a modest frame house lived Bunola Kay, an unmarried, would-be actress in her late forties who gave singing lessons to children like my siblings and me and fashion counseling to adult women. Next to her, in one of the large stuccos, lived a banker and his family. In another was a divorcée making do on meager alimony and child support payments.

Across the street from my childhood house still stood Daniel Freeman's estate, with a chain link fence and forest of trees surrounding a dark, late-Victorian mansion, even larger than my house. But Freeman and most of his family had died years before. His main descendant and heir was his wid-owed daughter, Grace Freeman Howland, who lived as a recluse on the estate with her servants. Years before, the story went, her father and her husband had unexpectedly died. Emotionally crippled, she retreated to her house and rarely left it. My grandmother, liking to claim upper-class con-nections, proudly asserted that our two houses both stood at the center of Freeman's old rancho, as though this joint location gave our family special status. But Mrs. Howland, as we called her, wasn't an acquaintance of ours. She liberally dispensed charity, giving away so much of her inheritance that she was called "Inglewood's Lady Bountiful." But she rarely had visitors or left her home.

This was the late 1940s, but the Levittown model of identical tract homes for middle-class nuclear families, which historians identify as typi-cal of postwar suburbia, doesn't resemble what I experienced. Just as my family was neither nuclear nor exactly middle-class, architectural styles as well as age, types of families, and social class mingled on that Hillcrest block.

Like the exterior, the interior of my Hillcrest house seemed fashioned for people of wealth. The living room was so large that my mother's baby grand piano seemed dwarfed in its expanse. A fireplace, constructed of what my elders called "the finest Italian marble" dominated one wall; large paned windows flooded the room with light. The wallpaper, intact when we moved in, was embossed velvet, off-white, with a fleur-de-lis design; my siblings and I loved to run our fingers over it to feel its luxury. Dark red velvet drapes hung at the windows; the floors were of hardwood, pegged and grooved oak. The moldings were rare cherrywood, and sliding cherry-wood doors could close off the living room from the front hall and the hall from the dining room. That house could hold several meetings at the same time.

The house had been built with servants in mind. Above the garage on the back of the property was a large room to house a live-in couple, with a buzzer system in the main structure to summon them from the kitchen to the other rooms of the house. When we moved in, my elders quickly deactivated the system, since my siblings and I buzzed it incessantly, irri-tating them no end. But they would have removed it anyway, since they would never have hired servants. Although I regarded our house as a man-sion, they seemed to think of themselves as poor.

They furnished the house with what they'd acquired over the years from cheap furniture stores and the Salvation Army. In the living room an inherited antique table stood next to two overstuffed chairs in faded burgundy damask and a sagging couch in dark green brocade. Faded floral rugs covered the floors, doilies the tables, antimacassars the backs of the sofa and chairs. Still-lifes and landscapes painted by my grandmother and framed in imitation gilt hung on the walls, with a portrait of Jesus by an obscure artist over the mantle.

Our elders contended that, with four children in the house, to replace the furniture with up-to-date pieces would be a waste of money. More than thrift, however, determined their decorating scheme. When they finally indulged in some new chairs, what they bought looked exactly like the ones replaced, only newer. My family's church friends furnished their homes in the same style. Their living rooms also contained faded floral rugs, antimacassars and doilies, overstuffed sofas and chairs in dark green and burgundy, and a portrait of Jesus on a wall.

The thriftiness of that style was partly a holdover from the Depression when, like many Americans, my family and their friends lived on limited incomes and developed penny-pinching habits. But the sturdiness of that furniture, with its lower middle-class look, also connected them to their past. It invoked their roots in the folk, not the elites. It announced their ancestry among German peasants who came to farms in Wisconsin and Minnesota in the mid-nineteenth century and in the next generation to low-level semiprofessional jobs in the city of Spokane. In the early 1920s my parents—along with their parents—migrated to Los Angeles.

That decorating style also displayed my family's religious piety. As members of the most conservative Lutheran denomination, our lives were saturated with religion. We went to Sunday service every Sunday, and we children went to Sunday school after the service and to parochial school during the week. At home we prayed before meals and at bedtime, and we held family devotions every evening after dinner. My father was president of our congregation for many years as well as a leader in regional Missouri Synod groups. His obituary in the Synod newspaper in 1979 when he died at eighty-two called him "a Lutheran patriarch for Southern California." My mother was our church's organist, and my family celebrated her piety. My grandmother told the story of how, in a college biology class, my mother answered an exam question about the creation of the world not with the expected argument from Darwinian evolutionism but with the verse from Genesis: "God created the world in six days, and he rested on the seventh." The first family member to graduate from college, breaking new ground in family upward mobility, my mother risked flunking an exam to remain faithful to her religion.

Our Lutheranism was harsh and patriarchal. A capricious God the father constantly tested our belief in him because we couldn't be trusted to remain faithful. We were all born with "original sin," all evil by nature, because Adam and Eve in the Garden of Eden had followed Satan and violated God's command against eating the forbidden apple. Heaven and hell were the carrot and stick held out to insure our belief. If we followed the commands of our Lutheran God, set down in the Bible and interpreted in our creeds, and if we believed in him as a triune God—Father, Son, and Holy Ghost—after we died he would reward us with eternal life in heaven. But if we gave in to Satan and didn't believe, we would burn forever in the fires of hell. It was standard fundamentalist dogma, softened by the hope that Jesus Christ, the son of God who died on the cross for our sins, might intervene to save us—but we could never be certain that he would.

Every evening we children memorized a passage from the Bible to recite the next morning in school. Although I no longer remember most of those verses, I can still recollect a few, mostly gloomy ones about the omnipotent harshness of our God. "Whom the Lord loveth, he chasteneth, and scourgeth every son whom he receiveth." Or: "I the Lord thy God am a jealous God, visiting the iniquities of the fathers upon the children unto the third and fourth generation." Then there were the passages about heaven being preferable to earth, this "vale of tears," and about the resemblance of human life to Christ's suffering on the Cross. "For me to live is Christ, to die is gain." Not the cheeriest pictures to paint for children.

But I also have positive memories of my childhood religion, memories relating to the security of belief and the appeal of piety. At the age of eight I announced to my family that I was giving up any thoughts of marriage to become a deaconess—the Lutheran version of a Catholic nun, according to my father. The impulse didn't last long, but for a few days I had visions of dedicating myself to God and of being absolutely certain of his grace. And later, when I was in high school and even though my faith was waning, I could watch a sunset over the Pacific Ocean, with red and orange streaks in a darkening sky, and imagine that I saw God and his angels coming down from heaven to lift me up to join them for eternity.

Despite their severe religion, my elders weren't fictive kin to the

"American Gothic" painted by Grant Wood—the gaunt and scowling couple who with their pitchfork and barn have come to symbolize the stern folk who settled the Midwest. Without much evidence of guilt, my elders stretched their creed all the time to accommodate behavior such as gambling and card playing, which was anathema to stricter Lutherans. I can't imagine that they could have done otherwise and maintained any family peace, with all those people with their distinctive personalities and their versions of the American Dream living in that house that looked like a castle, with its velvet embossed wallpaper, cherrywood moldings, and a fireplace made of the finest Italian marble.

The Hollywood film business and the thriving music industry in Los Angeles brought both sides of my family to Southern California; religion had nothing to do with it. My father, Harry, a sometime journalist in Spokane who'd attended a year of college at the local state university branch, was twenty-two when he came to Los Angeles with his parents. Hoping for a career as a screenwriter, he instead wound up in advertising. My mother, Melba, a child piano prodigy, was eighteen when she came to Los Angeles from Spokane with her parents and her younger brother, Eddie, also a promising musician. Melba attended the University of Southern California on a scholarship. After a brief attempt on the concert stage, she became a high school music teacher and a part-time church organist.

Melba and Harry hadn't known each other in Spokane; they met in the mid-1920s at a Lutheran event. Married in 1929, they moved to Inglewood because the local high school hired Melba as a teacher. Once she had children and continued to work, her parents, Charlie and Lillian, moved in to help with the housework and childcare, and Eddie joined them between his marriages. During Melba's childhood in Spokane her family had lived in the home of my widowed great-grandmother, Magdalena, and they replicated that arrangement in Inglewood. In 1944 Lena, now eighty-five, joined them from Spokane. With Eddie's presence and the expected birth of my younger brother, the bungalow we lived in was too small. Thus they bought the house on Hillcrest.

Why did they buy a mansion when they could have made do with something less elegant? Behind their backs their friends wondered how they afforded what an Inglewood historian calls one of the "grandest" houses in the city. On the contrary, they claimed that it hadn't been expensive because during the war no one wanted to take on such a large house.

Besides, my father was doing well at work; they had extra money from Charlie's and Lillian's jobs on a wartime night shift at one of the aircraft factories; and my mother's gynecologist, who owned the house, offered it to her at a good price.

Over the years my mother and this doctor had become close, for he played a major role in her life. After she suffered a series of miscarriages and couldn't seem to carry a baby to term, he suggested that she adopt a child. Following his advice, my elders adopted my sister Lila and, to everyone's surprise, that solved the problem. Melba soon became pregnant with my older brother Paul, then with me, and finally with my brother John. Melba often talked about the Hillcrest house with her doctor, and she fantasized owning it. When he offered it to her, she jumped at the chance to buy it.

Yet my elders didn't attempt to fashion an upper-class lifestyle appropriate to our mansion. Content with their shabby decor and with friendships formed through the church and the high school, absorbed in their varied activities and the complexities of dealing with each other, they didn't choose to meet and entertain community leaders, put on teas and cocktail parties, or host charity events. Simply owning that house was enough for them.

With my mother working, my grandmother Lillian was our household manager. But aside from childrearing, she didn't seem to like domestic tasks. She did the chores quickly so that she could go to church, play bridge, or paint pictures—which she actually sold in local art shows and to friends, even though her paintings were mainly scenes she copied from greeting cards. For the most part, she didn't require us children to help with the housework, although Charlie and Lena weren't excused. Fearful of her wrath, they obeyed her commands, but they grumbled behind her back and, like her, they also hurried through their chores. As a result, our house was often untidy, until Lillian suddenly noticed the messiness (usually because company was coming) and demanded that we all pitch in to clean up.

Lillian served us a meal every evening, but she didn't seem to like cooking any more than cleaning. Her cuisine was simple, fast, and tasteless: an overdone roast with boiled potatoes and canned vegetables; hamburger meat, canned mushrooms, and cooked rice fried together and called goulash. We ate lots of canned sauerkraut, cole slaw, potato salad, hot dogs, and boiled cabbage; we smothered almost everything with catsup or gravy.

We never ate fish, any meat but chicken or beef, nor such vegetables as broccoli or eggplant. These foods were for Italians and Catholics, Lillian told us, not Germans like us.

The hygiene of my family, like its cuisine, often seemed to come from some distant, honored past. We each took a bath only once a week, on Sunday evening, resorting the rest of the time to what my grandmother called a "sponge bath," with soap and a washcloth. In the bedroom that Lena and Lillian shared stood a chamber pot. Despite my occasional protests that the pot was disgusting, they used it during the night and emptied it each morning. Lena raised chickens in our backyard. When Lillian wanted to serve one for dinner, Lena killed it by wringing its neck with her bare hands. Lillian and Lena weren't squeamish. When serious illness later struck, they changed bandages and emptied vomit buckets and bedpans without a murmur. They would put a hospital bed for the invalid in the dining room near the kitchen, so that they could cook and clean while doing nursing tasks.

Photos of the aging Lena and Lillian (and even of my mother) show them with shapeless, overweight bodies, molded by years of doing no regular physical exercise and of eating heavy meals and sugary desserts. They coated fruit with sugar; they ate a lot of candy and ice cream. Their favorite salad was flavored jello with canned fruit. They added marshmallows, coconut, and whipped cream for guests and called it ambrosia.

Lillian and Lena rinsed their hair with bluing to rid it of the yellow of aging, to make it stark white. They had it cut close to their heads and permed in tiny curls: they looked like Shirley Temples with wrinkled faces. They were always ladylike. They wore gloves and hats to church and downtown, and they never flopped on floors or slouched in chairs. Lillian often chided me on my posture. Stand straight and tall, she would say to me; look like you are upper-class. The message was ambiguous, as was my family's lifestyle, rooted in hopes for the future and affection for the past, in an identification with their lower-middle-class Lutheran peers and in an imagined association with the upper-class Mrs. Howland.

Her Freeman mansion was always across the street, with its somber exterior hidden by the forest of trees that surrounded it beyond a chain link fence. The house and its mysterious recluse fascinated my sister and older brother and me. We rode our bicycles on the sidewalk outside it; we peered through the fence to see what was inside. One day we decided to climb the fence. As we lowered ourselves to the ground on the other side, a white-haired woman suddenly appeared. She frightened and embarrassed us when she identified herself as Mrs. Howland. To our surprise, she didn't chide us. Rather, she seemed to find our trespassing amusing, although she made us promise never to do it again. She invited us into the house and gave us a tour.

The mansion was grand, filled with dark wood wainscotting, oriental rugs, and mahogany antiques. An interior courtyard contained a pond filled with gold carp. We sat down on chairs in the courtyard, and a servant brought us tea in an ornate silver tea service. Mrs. Howland served the tea; I can still hear her cultured voice asking us if we wanted one lump of sugar or two. She answered our questions and asked about our lives. Mrs. Howland wasn't withdrawn, as we expected a recluse to be. Instead, she was warm, with an air of wealth and position and the ability to put one instantly at ease. I'd never met anyone like her. It seemed to me that for a moment I'd entered an elegant space, one of ornate silver tea services and deferential servants far removed from my chaotic family. I never saw her again, but I never forgot the experience. Perhaps my grandmother was right about the appeal of the upper class.

My great-grandmother Lena missed her life in Spokane, and she had difficulty with us children, with our sassy, modern attitude. She had raised Lillian and Melba strictly, but Melba insisted on more leniency with us and Lena didn't approve. When the other adults were away, she would insult us in stentorian tones with German words which I distinctly remember as "shloplese" and "drechhommel." Those words sounded to me like "sloppy" and "dreadful," and I didn't like them at all. But I didn't understand Lena's German. Although my elders had learned German before English and spoke it among themselves, they never taught it to us children.

Lena could be stern, but she could collapse into depression. I remember her sitting in her rocking chair on the back porch, rocking back and forth, with tears streaming down her cheeks and her German Bible in her hands, praying to her God in German to let her die. Yet she also happily made afghans and gossipped with the elderly widows on our block. She chopped cabbage for coleslaw, and she claimed to have lived so long because she had eaten it every day of her life. Exhibiting flashes of determination, she boasted that her father had fought in the Civil War and had spoken with Abraham Lincoln. She claimed that as a child she hid in the cellar of her home in Minnesota to escape Indians on the warpath. Lena was a large woman, nearly six feet tall. She lived to be ninety-five, outliving most of the other adults in my family.

Like Lena, Lillian was often harsh and unyielding. In these traits she was the opposite of Charlie, who was playful and gentle. As a married couple, Lillian and Charlie didn't seem well suited. Although they tried to restrain themselves in our crowded house, they bickered a lot; and Lillian slept in a room with Lena and not one with Charlie. Even then I realized that Lillian tried to control Charlie and that he didn't like her overbearing manner. He might give in to her for a time, but she could never completely dominate him. Unlike the rest of my elders with German backgrounds and surnames such as Krause and Wendland, Charlie was a Parkes from Wales. He didn't speak German and he wasn't especially religious, although he put up a front for Lillian. Most of all, he liked going to Hollywood musicals, a staple of the 1950s screen, so that he could, as Lillian scornfully put it, "look at the women's bare legs." He also liked sports: he watched boxing matches on TV and jabbed his arms along with the fighters. He had a passion for horseracing—and so did my uncle and even my mother. Together the three of them often went to the racetrack near our house.

Lutheran devotional tracts were always scattered on tables in our living room, but so were race track sheets, containing betting odds and information about horses and jockeys. Bookies demanding payment for gambling debts sometimes telephoned for Charlie and Eddie. Those calls were never for my mother, for she drew the line at gambling, although she read the racing sheets and placed fantasy bets. (One season her winnings on paper totaled nearly two thousand dollars—a sum so large that she couldn't help boasting about it.)

The adults in my family formed shifting coalitions. With regard to the horseracing, Melba sided with Charlie and Eddie, although she scolded them when the bookies called. My grandmother and my father—both especially pious—disliked the horseracing expeditions, although they hesitated to challenge Melba, whose paycheck was crucial to the family income. In return, Melba was a partner with my father at church, while she gave Lillian free rein in the household. But she also honored her gentle father and her magnetic brother, and she shared their infatuation with horseracing.

Like her, Eddie was a musician: in the 1940s he played trumpet in the MGM studio orchestra. Handsome and debonaire, with an air of Hollywood insouciance, he breezed in and out of our house, and I heard my elders whisper about the liquor on his breath. He loved the fast Hollywood nightlife—drinking and gambling, going to clubs, romancing beautiful women, perhaps taking drugs. He was always in scrapes, always running up debts. He had difficulty remaining married, and he never went to our church. In hushed tones my elders called him an "alcoholic," but they gave him the room above the garage and tried to reform him. When reproving church members scolded Lillian about Eddie's many wives, she always retorted: "At least he marries them."

Melba's identification with Charlie and Eddie had limits. Early in her life, she decided to marry a devout Lutheran, someone without their moral flaws. My father, a church leader who constantly quoted from the Bible, fit the bill. Harry was intensely polite and without much sense of humor, while Charlie and Eddie told jokes all the time. But their carefree personalities could be dangerous, leading to drinking and carousing. "High living and careless living are an abomination to me." Harry expressed those sentiments in a letter to my mother shortly after they met. The only other man she considered marrying, my grandmother told me, was a Lutheran minister.

Melba also respected my father's ambition to succeed in advertising, a profession they both considered key to American prosperity as well as infused with spiritual dynamism. Bruce Barton's 1924 best seller, *The Man That Nobody Knows*, persuaded them of that: they accepted Barton's notion that Jesus Christ was not only a religious prophet but also the world's first supersalesman. In Barton's view, Christ forged a major religion through personal persuasion, providing a model for businessmen for centuries to come. "He picked up twelve men from the bottom ranks of business and forged them into an organization that conquered the world." That's what Barton—and my father—believed.

I hesitate to conclude that this rationalization for a profession that might be seen as crass turned my father into a hypocrite. Mostly he wrote copy for farm and garden products familiar to him from his childhood in a farming suburb of Spokane. Still, even as a child I was puzzled by the loud, pounding advertisements on radio and TV he composed for his client "Wild Man Pritchard." A used car dealer with many Los Angeles franchises, Pritchard promised cars at outrageously low prices. Such hucksterism didn't seem exactly Christian to me.

Advertising was a volatile business, and my father, not always employed, probably did what was necessary to survive in it. Such job insecurity, combined with his ambition, turned him into what we today call a "workaholic." Always at his job, he came home to retreat to his study or to go to church meetings. He often seemed to me a stranger who had wandered into our family. In fact, because he was too busy at work he hadn't gone with Melba and Lillian in 1935 to the Lutheran orphanage in Iowa where they chose my sister. But my mother didn't seem to mind his absences. For there were tradeoffs: he left most family decisions to her; he didn't complain when she moved her family in; he didn't try to stop the racetrack attendance and the gambling; he was proud of her career and her musical ability. When some conservative church members tried to censor her for holding a square dance in our backyard for my sister's sixteenth birthday, my father, as church president, stopped them.

I never liked my father; I never had much of a relationship with him. With his formality and his Bible quoting, he seemed to me to deliver sermons when he spoke, and I had to listen to enough of those in church. I preferred my sensuous uncle and my sweet grandfather, with their jokes and their playfulness, and my conscious identification was with them, not with Harry. They easily gave kisses and hugs; my father was stiff and polite. Anyway, he was often out. He left the childrearing to the women in the house, while he largely abdicated the paternal role to my mother's male relatives.

For a time Harry's workaholism seemed to pay off, when his "Wild Man Pritchard" campaigns generated large advertising revenues. With success seemingly in hand, my father opened his own advertising agency and the family bought the house on Hillcrest. My mother wrote proudly in her diary that "if ever there was a self-made man in America, it's my husband, Harry" and "in my husband and my children I'm the luckiest woman alive." Two years later my father went bankrupt when Pritchard's business failed and the car dealer couldn't pay his advertising bills.

Harry's ambition was characteristic of my family. A success drive propelled them—a drive that went beyond the desire for achievement into a preoccupation with fame. There was my mother's brief career as a concert pianist, in addition to Eddie's attempt in his early twenties to become a trumpet player-band leader on the order of Tommy Dorsey or Eddie James. When Lillian sold her paintings, my elders called her the next "Grandma Moses," and they weren't simply flattering her. Why else would they buy that grand house on Hillcrest when something large, without its elegance, would have sufficed? That house was more than a financial bargain or a whim of my mother's. It symbolized their dreams of success and announced that they had arrived.

Why was my family so ambitious? In the case of my father, I found the answer in family memories and several autobiographical stories he wrote when a young journalist in Spokane. His parents' unhappy marriage was the main reason. His father, John, a low-level engineer, bounced from job to job, and he invested his savings in stocks that proved worthless. In response, my grandmother Alvina spent her time reading her Bible and complaining about her health. John had extramarital affairs; Alvina doted on my father, their only child. In return, Harry resolved to make up for his father's failings by achieving major success.

What about Eddie and Melba? Did their parents' unhappy marriage shape them, too? Family memories in this case are meager, and I had only newspaper clippings and family photos and momentos in the scrapbooks my grandmother kept from which to reconstruct her family's past. In addition, she told me stories about that past. Most of her stories were about Charlie, and mostly they celebrated him. She described how he went on the 1898 Gold Rush to Alaska, and she told me she eloped with him there in 1905. Above all, she praised him for having returned to Alaska in 1908 as secretary to a federal judge who closed down the gambling halls and houses of prostitution that to her were a terrible moral blot in frontier Alaska.

In these stories she gave me the impression that Charlie's Alaska adventures were major feats. In summing up his life, Lillian always used the same phrase: "He packed supplies over the Chilkoot Pass." As a child I didn't understand that phrase. In my mind I conjured up frozen wastelands and precipitous cliffs. I visualized my grandfather, alone with a pack, striving to reach the faraway gold fields where a fortune lay. He was an adventurer braving fierce nature to reach the Yukon, the land of his dreams. "Packing supplies over the Chilkoot Pass" to me meant triumph and the height of human endurance. The glamour of climbing the pass and of crossing unknown distances remained fixed in my mind. It was a master memory toward achievement.

Yet when I was in high school and beginning to date, Lillian told me a different story about Charlie. In this tale she never loved him, and she married him impulsively. She was eighteen, finished with school, and bored in Spokane. He was passing through on his way to Alaska. She met him in a cafe where she was a waitress and he was her customer. He wooed her with stories of his exploits in Alaska and offered her the excitement of going there with him. She accepted at once. However, a few years after they married, she continued, she fell in love with another man. But she didn't have the nerve to run off with him. Instead, she confessed to Charlie. Asserting marital privilege, he demanded sex, and she gave in. As a result, as she put it, he "made me pregnant with Eddie." Expecting Charlie's child, she stayed with him.

Lillian's story surprised me, but I didn't pay attention to it then. I couldn't imagine my grandmother, with her aging body and stern demeanor, involved in such volatile emotions. I was an adolescent, preoccupied with my own problems. I didn't want to hear about my elders' past.

Were Lillian's stories of Charlie's achievements true? How could I reconcile them with her rejection of him? Did they help to explain the family ambition? I decided to use my skills as an historian to find out what had really happened in Alaska. So I went there, following a trail that eventually led me to a large Justice Department file in the National Archives in Washington, D.C. In that file I found documents that told me the truth. Charlie did pack supplies over the Chilkoot Pass. He and Lillian did elope to Alaska in 1905. He did serve as secretary to a federal judge who went to Alaska in 1908 to close down the gambling halls and houses of prostitution. Those parts of Lillian's stories did happen. But the truth is that much more happened to them there that she didn't tell me. What she concealed from me were a series of failures and, finally, Charlie's involvement in illegal activities that cost him his job and almost landed him in jail.

Charlie's adventures began in 1898 when extravagant newspaper reports of gold strikes in the Klondike lured him, along with tens of thousands of other young men, to Alaska and to the Chilkoot Pass. The pass, one of the few openings through the mountains that fringe Alaska's southern coast, leads to Canada and the Yukon. But the Chilkoot is no easy crossing. It culminates in a fifteen-hundred-foot trail over a nearly perpendicular cliff. The cliff is so steep that in 1898 climbers couldn't use pack animals on it; they had to carry their own supplies. In photographs of their climbing the pass, they look like a chain of ants on a field of white. Charlie Chaplin recreated that chain in the opening frames of his 1925 movie, the *Gold Rush*. By then the Chilkoot climb had long been a symbol of the 1898 Gold Rush.

Climbers with money hired human packers, and the packers were mostly Eskimos. Anglos scorned these natives. By extension, the few Anglo men who hired out for the work also met with contempt, and they probably packed for others because they were out of money. Charlie later never earned much money, and he wasn't above gambling his salary away. For him, climbing the Chilkoot Pass wasn't a glorious feat. He was a natural athlete who later won bicycle races in Seattle; he probably packed supplies because, lithe and strong, he was up to the task—and he was broke. Nor did he find any gold in the Klondike, since almost no one who went there in 1898 did. Long before then prospectors and trading companies had staked claims to all the mining land. Most of the newcomers went back home. Within a year the Chilkoot Trail was deserted.

Once he returned from the Yukon, Charlie wisely settled down and learned typing and accounting. Many secretaries were then still male, and management was open to them. His training completed, Charlie found employment in Valdez, Alaska, as secretary to the president of the Copper River and Northwestern Railway. The railway, a conglomerate owned by the New York Guggenheim Syndicate, was involved not only in transportation but also in mining the region's rich copper deposits. When Charlie met Lillian in Spokane, he was no longer with the railroad, but he had an equally promising job as secretary to the president of the Valdez bank. Charlie and Lillian eloped to Seattle and took the steamer to Valdez.

In 1905 Valdez was the commercial center of southern Alaska, but it was still a frontier town. Lillian must have soon encountered Valdez's large red light district, the largest of any town in Alaska. It must have shocked her, offending her Lutheran morality. So would her discovery of Charlie's employment problems, which were common knowledge in Valdez. He hadn't voluntarily left the railroad; he was fired for "divulging confidential information." She may have guessed what I suspect: he was involved in the doubledealing endemic to the exploitation of Valdez's copper, as everyone from individual miners to the Guggenheim syndicate tried to seize a share of the region's wealth.

Such a scenario explains why not only the railroad president but also subsequent employers fired Charlie for spying and why he always found new positions. An engaging man, he could draw confidences out of others. But he was weak-willed and easily led. If problems arose, he could be fingered as the "fall guy." Even if this wasn't the case, he was stupid and talked too much.

In the summer of 1906 Charlie was fired from his bank position, again for "divulging confidential information." In the midst of this disgrace, Lillian gave birth to my mother, and she projected a fantasy of achievement on her baby. She named my mother Melba after the famed Australian soprano, Nellie Melba, whose meteoric rise from obscurity to stardom in opera was a staple of the day's tabloids. A soloist with her church's choir in Spokane, Lillian must have felt a bond with Nellie Melba, who had fled the Australian bush country, leaving behind a husband and a baby, to carve out a glamorous life in Europe. My grandmother also was living in the provinces with a husband who had disappointed her and a baby she probably hadn't anticipated when she impulsively married a stranger. But unlike Nellie Melba, Lillian didn't have the courage to leave—then or later.

Returning to Spokane, she, Charlie, and the baby moved in with Lena. I doubt Charlie wanted to live with his stern mother-in-law. But Lillian insisted and, given his disgrace, he could hardly refuse. Yet their Alaska saga had only begun.

Charlie was granted a third chance in Alaska. In the fall of 1907 Silas Reid, the new federal judge for Alaska's Third Circuit, covering Valdez and Fairbanks in the far North, hired Charlie as his personal secretary and court stenographer. Reid, from Oklahoma, gained his appointment through political connections. As his court assistants he hired cronies from Oklahoma who knew nothing about Alaska, while Charlie knew a great deal. Contacts in Valdez warned Reid about my grandfather, but he discounted the warnings as motivated by political factionalism. Given what later happened, I think Reid sensed even on first meeting Charlie that he could easily be manipulated.

Lillian was ecstatic over Charlie's new position. In Alaska, still a territory with minimal government, circuit court judges were powerful. The local people called them "czars." And Reid intended to clean up Alaska's Third Circuit by getting rid of the prostitutes and the saloons. Charlie's part in this crusade would surely refurbish his reputation. But Lillian overlooked the graft common in the Alaska courts, for which judges and court officials were frequently indicted.

In January, 1908 Charlie went to Fairbanks with Reid. Lillian didn't go along, which was just as well. Fairbanks, a new town, had so many dance halls that a woman couldn't walk down the streets without being accosted as a prostitute. As Reid's secretary, Charlie joined the elite Tanana Men's Club, and he hobnobbed with lawyers and bankers. I have no doubt he also frequented Fairbank's saloons and dance halls. Gambling, drinking, being with dance hall women—such behavior was too much a part of his nature for him to stay away, as long as Lillian wasn't there.

Alaska statesman James Wickersham lived in Fairbanks at the time. In his diary he commented on the Reid judgeship. Soon after Reid's arrival, Wickersham noted with amazement that Reid issued a bench order closing the dance halls and summoned a grand jury to issue indictments against the prostitutes and the "tough element." "What a hoot!" he exclaimed. But six months later, Wickersham suspected that Reid's officials were extorting bribes from defendants. He now called them the "Oklahoma gang."

In September Lillian and Melba joined Charlie in Fairbanks. By December the situation blew up. The newspapers charged that Reid had improperly appointed his brother-in-law a court official, violating nepotism rules. A federal investigator was sent, and this official uncovered other irregularities. Reid had had Charlie forge inflated bills for meals for government repayment; Charlie and other court officials had extorted kickbacks from defendants. Desperate, my grandfather confessed to the charges, contending that he had gone along with the Oklahomans because they threatened to kill him. Placing all the blame on Charlie, Reid fired him.

Lillian must have been devastated. Her worst fears had materialized. The Justice Department file, containing documents and depositions collected by the federal investigator, includes affidavits from prominent Valdez citizens denouncing Charlie: "He has a terrible reputation"; "he is a dangerous man." On the outside of the envelope containing the affidavits someone wrote: "Parkes is a crook." In November 1909 a grand jury investigation was held, with my grandfather the main witness, but the jury issued no indictments. The case must have been political dynamite, involving influential men. Charlie was lucky, for he could have wound up in jail. As for Reid and his entourage, they were dismissed.

During the scandal Lillian must have met the man with whom she fell in love. Given the small numbers of women in frontier Alaska and the large numbers of young, unmarried men (including those on Reid's staff), it would have been easy. I don't doubt that Charlie forced himself on her and that he didn't use birth control, hoping that pregnancy would keep her with him. His life was in shambles; he needed her strength. It's possible that Eddie was the son of the man she loved, although I doubt it. Both in looks and personality, Eddie bore a striking resemblance to Charlie.

My grandmother's scrapbooks contain snapshots of friends in Fairbanks, including Reid and his court officials. But she kept no record of the scandal, even though the local newspapers covered it for months. Leaving Alaska, Charlie and Lillian returned to Spokane, back to Lena's home. He found low-level clerical employment, and Lillian took over the family leadership, formulating the official family line that celebrated Charlie and overlooked his misdeeds. Sometimes I speculate that by living in obscurity in his mother-in-law's home, Charlie was hiding from the "Oklahoma gang," feaful that they might seek revenge.

Lillian's Lutheranism, with its harsh creed that suffering was a sign of God's favor, solaced her. But it couldn't erase the emotional upheaval Charlie had caused in her life. Nor was the power she gained over him because of his immorality enough compensation, for he often eluded her. She turned toward ambition: through public renown her children could restore her pride and counter her husband's unwanted fame as a crook.

Thus Lillian nurtured her children's musical talent. Melba played the piano, Eddie the trumpet. Lillian found teachers for them; they soloed at church benefits and with school orchestras. Eventually she moved her family to Los Angeles, a national music center, so that her children might have more opportunity to achieve the fame she sought through them. But she could never stamp out her husband's enthusiasm for masculine pursuits nor prevent him from passing his taste for horseracing and gambling on to their children. He captivated her into marrying him, and he captivated them, too.

Yet she came to love the son her husband had forced on her, for Eddie inherited her husband's good looks and his winning ways, as well as a musical talent equal to his sister's. In her scrapbooks Lillian kept the mash notes girls sent him in high school and the later newspaper reports of his car crashes and his divorces. His troubled life caused her pain, but on some level she admired his independence. He had the nerve to leave failed relationships, but she never had that nerve, and her life had been seriously compromised as a result. She wound up disliking Charlie, suspicious of men, and deeply ambivalent about sex.

To her daughter, my mother, Lillian passed on the notion of family leadership by women, with the chain of powerful women in my family passing from Lena to Lillian to Melba. In the house on Hillcrest Melba reconstituted that grouping, based on mother-daughter bonding, even as she drew strength from the community of women in her church, her school, and her city. In her own way Melba dealt with the family ambition. She persuaded my elders to buy the house on Hillcrest, and then she neither decorated nor used it in the elegant manner for which it had been intended. And as Lillian's daughter, she contemplated her own children's talents and decided what she should do.

CHAPTER TWO

Melba

My grandmother Lillian wore a small antique ring of diamond chips set in silver filigree, which I now possess and wear. But I didn't know that Melba gave the ring to her one Mother's Day in the 1920s until I found, in Lillian's scrapbooks, the note Melba enclosed with it. In the note my mother asks Lillian to wear the ring always, like a wedding ring, as a symbol of their love. The ring expressed the deep bond between them, but both of them also knew that Charlie had never given Lillian such a fine ring, only a small gold band at their hurried wedding in Seattle.

Did my mother also know what had happened in Alaska? Had her father's indiscretions and her mother's infidelity been so traumatic that, although only three at the time, she had some memory of them? Did Lillian confess the truth to her in later years, as she confessed parts of it to me? Did Melba intend the ring as retribution for Charlie's misdeeds? I don't know the answers, for my mother never spoke about Alaska with me. When she died, I was only thirteen.

Lillian managed our household, but Melba provided its emotional center. Lena's depressions, Eddie's willfulness, Charlie and Lillian's frayed marriage—my mother moderated disputes among the adults, calmed them, and soothed their hurts. Even though she grew up with parents at odds, she seemed to emerge unscathed as an adult; her personality combined Lillian's firmness with Charlie's sweetness. She controlled our household, but her authority was subtle. She rarely raised her voice or showed anger. Her diary reveals a more intense emotional makeup—the fears and angers, anxieties and depressions concealed by her calm, smiling surface—until death intruded and she couldn't always maintain her composure.

Her devotion to her religion and to the racetrack expressed differing sides of her character, as did her love for her family and for her career. She told me that she had always wanted both, although after graduating from college she put off marriage while she attempted to become a concert pianist. To enter this field, in which few make it to the top, may seem foolish, but she had talent: perfect pitch, a great facility at sightreading, and a technical skill praised in newspaper reviews of her performances.

In Spokane she studied piano with a Justine MacCall, who had studied in Vienna with Theodor Leschetizsky. The most eminent piano teacher of the nineteenth century, he had trained Ignace Paderewski as well as most of the major U.S. women concert artists of the era, such as Fanny Bloomfield-Zeisler and Julia Rivé-King. Unknown today, they were more famous than their male counterparts in that age when piano playing was associated with women. Melba felt connected to those women through her Spokane teacher, who had known them as students in Vienna. When Lillian moved her family to Los Angeles, MacCall helped Melba win a scholarship to the University of Southern California music school, among the best music schools on the West Coast.

So determined was my mother to succeed as a concert artist that she hired an agent and changed her middle name Magdalena (after my great-grandmother) to the more exotic and stageworthy Madeleine. But her impulse toward the theater didn't last long. Perhaps she lost her nerve; perhaps she decided she wasn't talented enough to make it—or that she didn't want fame, that it was Lillian's dream, not hers. Lillian told me my mother gave up the concert stage when her agent tried to seduce her. Even if Lillian, suspicious of male sexuality, exaggerated, any such action could have offended Melba's piety and propelled her toward my moral father. Marriage itself raised the issue of how she could have a family and still concertize—with its long hours of practicing and much travel. She told me she chose high school teaching because, with a work day ending in the afternoon and summers off, she could spend more time with her children. That was her explanation to me, but I think she also didn't want to repeat her mother's disastrous marriage. She would compromise for her family—although her compromises always allowed her a good deal of independence: before she died, in addition to teaching, caring for her family, and serving as the church organist, she was working part-time for a Ph.D. in Music Education at USC.

My mother liked domesticity. On the weekends she helped with housework, and she often cooked for company. Like Lena she did handicrafts: it was she who taught me how to knit. She took great pleasure in us children. She supervised us after school; she took us to operas and concerts; she taught each of us piano. She organized a community children's chorus, which she accompanied and in which we sang.

She also took her maternal nature into the high school and the church, treating each as another family. People came to her with their problems, for she was a good listener; and she knew how to give useful advice and make others feel special. She mothered students and colleagues so successfully that for many years she chaired the high school's music department. When she died, the music building at the high school was renamed after her; a fund for a new organ at the church was established in her name.

Her renown in the community especially came from the recital her high school piano students gave each spring; the local newspaper always covered it. The concert, beginning with solos and duets, reached its peak when all her students played together, sharing by twos the pianos loaned her by a local piano company. On each piano one student played the base line of the same score and the other the treble, thus simplifying complex pieces for students without much ability and providing a stirring finale. The event was typical of my mother. High musicianship wasn't her goal in these concerts. She wanted these students to have a moment in the limelight and to feel important, no matter their talent.

Daughters whose mothers die young often idealize those mothers, and I must admit that, before my mother became seriously ill, I have few negative memories of her. Nor do I blame her for not intervening to stop the serious sibling rivalry that existed between my sister, my older brother, and me. Perhaps I am wrong to exonerate her. Dutiful as a child, I performed well in school, exhibited Christian piety, and helped with the housework when asked. But I was also shy and given to tantrums. When I go back to my recollections of my earliest years, the years before the deaths, the frustration and anger that produced those tantrums is directed not against the adults in my family but rather against my older sister and brother, who often excluded me.

Their rejection wasn't simple. We formed a band when we climbed trees, rode our bikes, and thought up mischief to annoy the adults—like buzzing the buzzer system for servants when we first moved in. Sometimes gender conventions separated my sister and me from our brother. When he did chemistry experiments and carpentry, we acted out fairy stories or played "dressup" with our mother's clothes. My younger brother wasn't part of our trio bound together by love and jealousy. Six years younger than me, he seemed like a baby. Sometimes we played with him, but mostly he wasn't with us.

My sister was independent, a mother's helper who identified with the adults. A typical eldest child, she was fearless—climbing trees, leading us in playing active games like cops and robbers or kick the can. Like my older brother, I inherited Charlie's athletic ability, and in high school I became an athlete. But as a child I was less physical than my sister. I liked domesticity: dressing dolls and playing house were my favorite games. With her tomboy ways, Lila wooed my older brother to her side, and they scorned my domesticity. They often went off together, while they teased me and drove me into tantrums.

The third position in birth order can be difficult. My experience of exclusion by two older siblings isn't unusual. But our rivalry was intensified because my family had adopted my sister, while the rest of us were our mother's natural children. I'm sure my elders felt guilt toward Lila and feared that she would especially resent being adopted. Thus they told her that she was special because they chose her, while the rest of us had simply been sent. It was an admirable strategy, but it didn't work. Being adopted didn't trouble my sister, but she was jealous of me—of my ability at performing and at schoolwork. "I sometimes tormented you," she told me. "You were the child that people praised to our mother. I felt inferior; I had to get back at you." What she didn't know was that I was jealous of her because I hadn't been adopted. I felt inferior because I hadn't been chosen but only sent.

Perhaps Melba—or Charlie or Lillian—should have tried to stop our rivalry. They knew we quarreled, but they didn't pay much attention. In my mother's daily diary she refers to the tension between us only once. When I came sobbing to my elders and demanded that they make my sister and brother play "house" with me, they talked about Christian forbearance and persuaded me to do something else. But much of our dissension went on away from them, since in the warm Los Angeles climate we played out of

34

doors year round; and my sister and brother called me a "cry baby" and a "tattler" to stop my compaints. Ignorant of formal psychology, my elders too easily dismissed our rivalry as childish squabbling. I was their emotional child, echoing Eddie in my acting-out behavior, and they didn't like it any more in me than they did in him. As families easily do, they called me "high strung" and hoped that I would outgrow my outbursts. For wanting to please and often shy, I could be quiet and restrained.

Where did my brother stand in our rivalry? He contends today that he wasn't aware of it. "I did what I did because I wanted to," he told me. "Anyway, I was a boy and I didn't think that girls were beings boys competed with. You loved singing and performing, but it didn't excite me. I liked my chemistry set and my science courses. You were emotional, but I kept my emotions to myself." In fact, his self-control, as well as his high marks in school, angered me and increased my insecurity.

My rivalry with my sister and older brother damaged me, but in retrospect I realize that it also toughened me. I always lost in my clashes with them, but I kept coming back, kept devising schemes to force them to include me. I never gave up because until I grew up there wasn't any way out. (My older brother, with a Ph.D. in physics and a career as an inventor and entrepreneur, is today a retired multimillionaire, while my younger brother has had a successful career in advertising and management. My sister has primarily been a mother and a homemaker; despite the differences in our adult lives, we are very close.)

My mother, as was her way, dealt with my shyness and emotionality obliquely. Given my singing talent and my histrionics, she decided to single me out by putting me on the stage. The decision wasn't easy for this religious woman, who had named me after an obscure Old Testament figure rather than an opera singer and who once wrote in her diary that she wanted her sons to be ministers and her daughters Lutheran schoolteachers. My older sister and brother and I all sang in her childrens' chorus and took lessons from Bunola Kay, but I was the one who did solos and lead roles, and I loved being on the stage. The local newspaper praised me in reviews. When I was eight, those reviews prompted Bunola Kay to advise my mother that I was "ready for the movies right away." No matter that Kay was only a neighbor with a sometime theatrical career and our newspaper only a local daily.

My mother decided to advance my career to Hollywood. She enrolled me in the Screen Children's Guild. This agency, for a fee, entered a child's photo in a catalogue sent to modeling, radio, and movie companies casting children in their productions. I auditioned for the "Abbott and Costello" and the "Blondie and Dagwood" shows, and for a movie role at the Samuel Goldwyn studio. I reached the finals of a "Little Miss Hollywood" contest; I modeled clothing in fashion shows. But eighteen months later, when my uncle died and my mother became seriously ill, her energy for promoting me waned. After my mother's death, my grandmother, dealing with her own severe depression, also opted out. If I wanted a career as a performer, I had to do it on my own.

As a child I identified with my mother. I wanted to be like her when I grew up. I didn't resent her working; I was proud of her musical ability and her career. Moreover, she wasn't the only working woman in my family. With their lower middle-class backgrounds and having experienced the Depression, my elders were accustomed to husbands losing jobs and wives taking over family support. Even my grandmother Lillian had sometimes made money—as a stenographer, or a seamstress, or by selling her paintings. My uncle's four wives also all worked: as waitresses, salespeople, and nurses. Their jobs weren't high in status or well paid, but Eddie always married beautiful women who could mimic, in dress and appearance, women much wealthier than they. To me they seemed glamorous and independent, and I identified those qualities with their working.

Eddie's third wife, our Aunt Blanche, remained close to my family even after she and Eddie divorced. To support herself, she sold cosmetics at Schwab's Drugstore in Beverly Hills, a place frequented by film people, where legend has it that stars were discovered. Blanche had a genius for friendship, and her customers confided in her. She told us fascinating stories about the movie stars she knew and the prominent men she dated. She took pride in my siblings and me, for we were the children she never had. She encouraged me to have a career; she told me never to depend on a man.

Those women in my family served as positive examples to me, as did the women in our congregation who edited the church newsletter and organized its social activities and who seemed to me as assertive and accomplished as their husbands. So did the women copywriters my father knew in advertising, whom my family often praised. With the exception of the church women, few of these working women had children. But my mother did, and that influenced my response to the rest of these working women. In later life I rarely questioned having both a career and a family. When I had my own children, I felt no guilt leaving them with sitters and at daycare centers. I never felt abandoned by my mother; I liked having my grandparents as my caretakers. When I was alone with my mother, I had her complete attention; when she was with us children, she focused on us. I never tired of her, nor she of me. When feminists in the 1970s wrote about "quality time" as the key to successful parenting, I understood immediately what they meant.

My mother wasn't a feminist. Even if a strong women's rights movement had existed in the domesticated 1950s, I doubt she would have joined it. There wasn't any activism in her background. Lillian and Lena had neither marched in suffrage parades nor worked for women's rights. Melba paid no attention to discrimination against women, even when she encountered it. She wasn't concerned that the principal at her high school was always a man, even though most of the teachers were women. She didn't seem to notice that the Missouri Synod wouldn't allow women to be ministers, serve on vestries, or even pass the collection plates in the service.

Yet my mother participated, along with Lillian, in a sphere of women's activities separate from men. That sphere was descended from the nineteenth-century variation, with its quilting bees and its women's rituals at weddings and funerals. From Lena, to Lillian, to Melba—through the generations the women in my family participated in it. By the 1950s the consumerism of America's modern age had reshaped its activities, which now included shopping, going to bridal and baby showers, and to luncheons, visiting the beauty parlor, and playing the game of bridge. Together with women, Melba and Lillian talked about subjects that didn't interest the men in their lives. They exchanged cooking recipes, and they discussed clothing styles, their children, pregnancy and childbirth, menstruation and menopause. That separate women's world of theirs had nothing to do with careers or with women's rights, but it validated the importance of their lives as women.

I often experienced that world with them. As a child, I stood at its boundaries and reflected their enjoyment, while I absorbed its definitions of womanhood. To go shopping with them at their favorite department stores was exciting: satins and sequins shined and glittered; perfume scented the air; stylish saleswomen deferred to us. An afternoon spent shopping was a sure antidote for depression. We mostly shopped for clothes, and we created an adventure in making selections from the counters and racks and trying on our choices in dressing rooms, where floor-to-ceiling mirrors reflected our bodies displayed in new styles that promised a new self. Shopping was also challenging. Given their frugality and the ups and downs in family income, Melba and Lillian usually only purchased clothes they found at bargain prices. I loved the way they made a game of it. Sometimes they scouted the stores for desired items and then waited to buy them until they were marked down in price.

They also went to women's luncheons, frequent events in Inglewood. There were many women's organizations in the city, and many of them were auxiliaries of men's clubs, such as the Opti-Mrs. for the Optimists and the Lion-Ls for the Lions. The woman's page of the Inglewood newspaper featured descriptions of those luncheons—the food served, the fashions worn, the decorations and the entertainment. Only much later, after I left Los Angeles, did I realize that those clubs existed for socializing not for social change. In that anticommunist era, they avoided controversy. The speakers at their luncheons lectured on topics such as fashion and gardening. Often a local chorus sang—sometimes our children's chorus. Or, after finishing their meal the women played bridge.

To me their women's world held out the promise of adulthood and of the mysteries of marriage and motherhood. Bridal and baby showers did so directly, and they were frequent in this era, when the average age of first marriage was lower than it had been for nearly a century and birthrates were at a twentieth-century high. I liked the talk about weddings and babies at those showers, and I liked the gifts. The shiny new pots and pans at bridal showers signified to me the creativity of domesticity, of decorating and managing one's own home. The negligées hinted at the sexuality forbidden until marriage. I liked the handmade gifts some women gave—crocheted booties at baby showers or decorated fileboxes at bridal showers, filled with cards containing favorite recipes.

Another location in Lillian and Melba's women's world was the beauty parlor. They went there to have their hair permed or set whenever they could afford it. I loved the beauty salon's mirrors and imitation gilt, the smells of its lotions and powders, and its pile of women's magazines to read. I first went there as a client at the age of eleven to have my long hair cut short and permed on the occasion of my confirmation ceremony at our church. At that event I was publicly examined in Lutheran doctrine along with my parochial school classmates before being formally accepted into church membership. The visit to the salon, in combination with the religious ceremony, seems to me now like a rite of passage from childhood to adolescence. Now I could begin taking communion at church, and I could also begin the nightly ritual of twisting my short hair into spirals that I fixed to my head with bobby pins, to set into curls as I slept.

As a child I delighted in Melba's and Lillian's women's world. It provided them a release from their regular lives, affording them the sensuality of taste, touch, and smell and the childhood pleasure of playing games. But I didn't realize its dangers. It wasn't connected to male public space, and it masked discriminations against women in that male arena. Any benefits it conferred were tainted by its link with the fashion and beauty industries which defined and enforced the era's confining "feminine mystique."

Reading the Inglewood newspaper from the 1950s, I came across a Woman's Page article on a speech on "charm" and "personality" given by Bunola Kay at a women's luncheon, in her function as a beauty consultant. Her speech counsels women to dress well and to do their make-up and hair in line with the current ideals of beauty. Read the fashion magazines, she recommends, to find out the most up-to-date styles. Perfect grooming, she asserts, always produces confidence in oneself and success with others. For whether at home or work the woman who looks right suffers none of the inferiority feelings of women inattentive to good grooming. Promoting herself, she advised her audience to employ her as a consultant.

The speech perplexed me when I found it. I hadn't identified Kay, my singing teacher, with the Inglewood women's world or with 1950s gender conservatism. To me she was a working woman who enouraged me to have a career in music. Yet in her speech she objectifies women by holding up a single standard of appearance, while she draws from the age-old contention that women's true power lies in using their bodies to get ahead, now under the guise of "good grooming." Her message commodifies appearance by recommending the products advertised in the fashion magazines. Her talk, presumably about "personality" and "charm," was really about how a woman should standardize her appearance. But personality, a favorite 1950s concept, implied the manipulation of self to please others, while charm, another slogan of the era, implied a dependent femininity.

When I was growing up, I saw nothing wrong with the 1950s celebration of femininity; nor did Lillian and Melba. To them their women's activities were fun, and wearing makeup and going to the beauty parlor were necessary if they were to look right. They passed these attitudes on to me, and they have always influenced me. To my dismay, most of the feminist women I met in the 1970s also seemed influenced by this same point of view.

In my memory the pleasures of Melba's and Lillian's world of women are symbolized by the game of bridge, which they often played at showers and luncheons. They liked the game so much that they belonged to two women's bridge clubs, each of which met monthly at our large house. I vividly remember those bridge evenings, for at them the devotion of my mother and grandmother to each other shone. The ritual was always the same. To prepare for the evening, we cleaned our house until it glistened, polished silverplate bought in some period of affluence, and set up folding tables and chairs stored in a closet. Melba and Lillian spruced up their best clothes; if they could afford it, they had their hair done at the beauty parlor. As night approached, they shooed the men of the family out of the house and us children off to bed.

After the guests arrived, we children tiptoed from our second-floor bedrooms to hide in the dark at the top of the stairs. We smelled the delicious scents of the women's perfumes mingled with the aroma of brewing coffee. We listened to the sounds of the game: the shuffling of cards, the slap as they hit the table. We heard the murmuring voices, low but excited, until our mother or grandmother, laughing, came up the stairs to send us back to bed. They always knew we were there; they indulged us in our own game.

The next day they discussed the evening's gossip: who was taking vacations or having babies. But they rarely spoke of adultery or divorce. This was the conservative 1950s, and these were church women devoted to Lutheran values. Besides, the details of the evening absorbed them. They liked to reminisce about their bridge hands and the reactions of their guests to the desserts they served, along with coffee, at the end of the games.

I never learned how to play bridge. As a child I played simpler games such as hearts or gin rummy. After my mother died, Lillian didn't play bridge any more; and she didn't teach the game to me. Nor did I want to learn it. When I was in college and there was a nightly game in the sorority house where I lived, I always refused when invited to join in. But by then the deaths had occurred, and I had endured high school. I no longer regarded my family through the romanticism of childhood eyes.

The Inglewood of my childhood had a small town flavor, enclosed and familiar. Although the city had no town square, its boundaries formed a rectangle. To the north lay my Hillcrest house, the Woman's Club, the Freeman mansion, and the Episcopal church. To the south was our Lutheran church. To the west was the high school and beyond it Fran's house and the airport. To the east, nor far from the racetrack, was Inglewood Park Cemetery, one of the largest cemeteries in Southern California.

Many of my family members are buried there. In 1949, when I was ten, they began to die. First Eddie; then Charlie the next year; then my mother two years later, just as I entered high school. Lena died four years after that. When I left Los Angeles for New York City in 1960, Lillian and Harry were my only elders left in the Hillcrest house.

Most of my relatives died from cancer, and my memory of each of their deaths has a similar ritual quality to it: the first horror at the diagnosis; the initial operation; the surgeon's hopeful statement that all the malignancy has been removed; the initial convalescence; the return to work. Then the months of waiting to see if the cancer will come back; the cheery insistence on keeping up a normal life; the recurrences; the hospitalizations. Then the hopes for remission, and the clutching at anything positive the doctor says. Finally comes the realization that the suffering is so intense that the victim wants to die and that everyone else wants that release.

I remember that pattern distinctly, but in each case my family kept its details from us children, shielding us from the horrors of terminal illness. In her diary my mother recorded those details. Because they played a role in shaping me, my narrative of the deaths draws from her diary as well as from my own recollections.

My mother began her diary on New Year's Day 1945, soon after we moved into the Hillcrest house. The war was ending, and its traumas were fading—especially the fear of Japanese invasion, strong on the West Coast. Harry and Charlie had been too old to go to war, and the army had rejected Eddie because he had a shortened arm due to a bout of childhood polio. But men they knew had served; some had been students of my mother. Some had died; some were coming back. Rationing was ending, and they could buy products, such as cars, that had been largely unavailable during the war. The local race track, used as a marine base during the war, would soon open again: they were excited about that.

They had come through the war unscathed, and now the family fortunes seemed assured. The Pritchard advertising campaign was underway; they were living in a large, sumptuous house. To keep a chronicle of family activities and of Melba's own life seemed appropriate. Indeed, my mother wrote a paragraph in her diary every day for nearly six years, until she abruptly stopped in September 1950. But the diary is more than a skeletal narrative. Despite her external control and her desire to maintain a myth of family perfection, she couldn't resist using her diary as a confidante. In it she records my father's employment problems, Lena's depressions, arguments between Lillian and Charlie.

She also translates public anxieties into private fears. A fundamentalist Christian, she was especially susceptible to the postwar hysteria over internal communist subversion. She feared communism's militant atheism, not just Soviet aggression. Throughout her diary Cold War anxieties surface; her respite from World War II fears was brief. On December 7, 1947, she notes the anniversary of Pearl Harbor and comments: "and now we face the communists." On February 9, 1948, she writes of the possibility of war with Russia and concludes: "Permanent peace seems an impossible dream."

In early 1947 normal family tensions escalated when the difficulties with my uncle became severe. His drinking suddenly increased; he wrote bad checks and wrecked his car; his fourth wife left him. He had always binged and repented—a standard pattern for alcoholics—but this time his behavior was outrageous. His gambling debts were so large and he was so far behind in alimony payments that two of his ex-wives joined together and took him to court, winning a judgment against him. For the first time my family refused him the room above the garage. In July my mother wrote in her diary that she was nervous. "This business with Eddie is more than I can bear." But the problems with my uncle inaugurated a series of family disasters; she had much more to bear.

October 1947: another serious crisis. A friend of Eddie's telephones in the middle of the night to tell us he has found Eddie in his home lying in a pool of blood, unconscious, a rifle beside him. My uncle has been shot in what looks like a suicide attempt. They call the police; an ambulance takes him to the hospital. Raving incoherently, he's admitted to the psychiatric ward. Regaining consciousness the next day, he confesses to the police that, despondent over marital problems, he attempted suicide after a bout of heavy drinking.

My elders were frantic. What could they do? In fact, they didn't have to do anything. This time the closeness of death shocked Eddie into deep repentance, and he turned toward the religion he had rejected long before. My mother recorded in her diary Eddie's statement that "a curtain seemed to lift in his mind." The next Sunday he attended services at a local Baptist church. When the minister issued a call for conversion, inviting the penitent to the altar, Eddie joined those who went forward.

Eddie's attending the Baptist church wasn't accidental. Its minister happened to live next door to him, and they became friends. Learning of Eddie's instability, he tried to rekindle my uncle's faith. The shock of being near death made Eddie listen to him. I suspect my uncle finally admitted his anger against his family—against his forced conception, against his mother's manipulation of his talent and his older sister's emotional control, how she could handle any situation. Like Melba, he had been hailed as a musical prodigy as a child. By the age of eighteen he played in dance bands, and music magazines called him a rising star. Even then his drinking was heavy; he probably used drugs, readily available in Hollywood. He started a number of bands, but they fell apart because of his instability. He was lucky to land in a movie studio orchestra.

My elders were pleased that Eddie found a church; because of his divorces the Missouri Synod didn't want him back. He was the "black sheep" who had come home; and like the father in the Bible story, they forgave him his sins and rejoiced in his return. Eddie stuck to his new life. He persuaded his wife to reconcile with him; he stopped drinking and gambling. Months of sober behavior followed. "He is a changed person," my mother wrote in her diary.

But the crises didn't let up. In December 1947, several months after Eddie's conversion, Melba and Lillian indulged in a day of shopping. Lillian became tired, and she went to rest in the women's lounge of a store. She found a magazine, and she happened to read an article on cancer in it. The article recommended that women examine their breasts for lumps. Standard today, this procedure was new in the 1940s. That evening Lillian examined her breasts. She felt a lump in one. Within a month she underwent a mastectomy. But she was lucky; she lived another twelve years.

That spring my mother enrolled me in the Screen Children's Guild and took me to auditions: she was determined to maintain a normal life. Yet that was also the spring my father's business failed, and he became moody and difficult. The financial problems didn't let up. In November 1948, toward the end of the year that began with Lillian's surgery, a repeated buzzing of the doorbell awakened the adults at six in the morning. A sheriff's deputy had a court writ secured by creditors to attach my father's salary. The action failed, however: in her diary my mother gloated that "Harry won out."

April 1949: a phone call again announces disaster. Eddie is seriously ill, with chills and a high fever. Near death, he's rushed to the hospital. The doctors order blood transfusions: the diagnosis is leukemia. Over the next months he rallies and relapses; rallies and relapses. One week my mother writes that he looks like a concentration camp victim; the next, miraculously, he's regained color and weight.

By the middle of August, he was near death. My mother spent an afternoon with him in the hospital. He was incoherent. "It is so terrible to see him—bloated, all blood-spotted, gasping for breath—out of his head." But that wasn't the end. The next day Melba and Lillian remained at his bedside, keeping vigil. My mother recorded in her diary that Eddie was "very wild." They didn't know what to do. Then my grandmother found a solution.

Over and over in a gentle voice she repeated to him the prayer we all knew, the prayer that generations of children in Lutheran families said each night before they went to sleep.

> Now I lay me down to sleep
> I pray the Lord my soul to keep
> If I should die before I wake
> I pray the Lord my soul to take. Amen.

The prayer confronts childish fears of the dark and gives reassurance that even though the night might be menacing, God will care for us. Yet like so much of my childhood religion, it's a morbid reminder of the ever-present threats of God's displeasure and of death.

Over and over Lillian said that prayer to Eddie. Finally the words soothed him. "Like a little boy he haltingly said the first line with her and then went on and said the whole prayer." They recited it together, over and over, a chant of love and peace. Lillian was once again his beloved mother, the woman who never rejected him. He was her darling boy, the brilliant trumpet player to be, the child forced upon her whom she came to adore. In the end it was just like bedtime during any night in the safety of childhood. He wasn't dying; his mother was putting him to bed. And so he went to sleep. He died several hours later.

To deal with her grief, my mother focused in her diary on Eddie's funeral, held at his Baptist church. Nearly two hundred people attended. Floral displays flanked his casket; a horn ensemble of fellow musicians played "Rock of Ages" and "Abide with Me." It was, in my mother's words, "a true victory service." For Eddie had conquered his demons and reconciled with God.

They didn't grieve in front of us children. They mourned in private, and they soothed us with Christian pieties. They buoyed themselves up by praising the mortician's art and by admiring the skill with which makeup was applied to mask the ravages of disease. The dolled-up body repelled me, but I kept my reaction to myself. Once the funeral was over, we quickly returned to our normal lives. "We will never forget Eddie," my mother wrote in her diary. "We are sure he is with God, and his memory will help us to stay close to God." Her diary contains one more entry about Eddie, recorded just before Christmas that year. "All the holidays are dulled for me because Eddie is gone," she wrote. And continued: "I wonder how much longer the rest of us have?"

My mother was a stoic who had to keep going because she was the emotional center for our family and she knew it. But throughout her diary, as the problems continued, she recorded bouts of anxiety and depression. Photos of her show an increasingly aging woman. She looks more and more worn out. Her body sags; her smile has no spirit. When she died at forty-six, she looked ten years older.

Throughout Lillian's and Eddie's illnesses, my mother had her own medical problems. After the birth of my younger brother, her doctor found so much internal damage from the delivery that he recommended she quit working. She recorded his advice in her diary, but she didn't follow it; she didn't easily give in. Several years later she was diagnosed with uterine fibroid tumors, and she underwent a hysterectomy during the same month of August that Eddie lay dying. The removal of ovaries plunged her into a premature menopause, a common result of this surgery. A year after her surgery and Eddie's death she abruptly ended writing in her diary. I suspect that she couldn't continue this record of her life because she had discovered a lump in her own breast and feared that she, too, was going to die.

The winter of 1950 wasn't easy. My mother had her first operation for cancer. Once she came home from the hospital, she recuperated in a hospital bed in the dining room, in its first use as a sickroom. I was also ill that winter with recurring bronchitis. I spent weeks in bed, listening to the bells of the Episcopal church across the alley tolling the hours. I wondered whose knell was next, if I might be the next to die.

One morning that winter I awoke to find that Charlie had died in his sleep of a heart attack. The adults seemed curiously happy. "He experienced no pain," they kept saying. "He was so lucky." "God gave him a special blessing." "Rejoice that now he is with God in heaven." Taking my cue from them, I felt no sorrow. So completely did I accept the Lutheran belief that life is a vale of tears and heaven the reward of the faithful that I didn't mourn the death of this beloved man, who had been a father to me. For the same reason I hadn't mourned the death of my uncle—nor would I that of my mother.

Even then, with her own life threatened, Melba kept the family in order. She agreed to my sister's marriage to her high school boyfriend, even though Lila was only seventeen. She continued the rehearsals of the chorus in which we children sang and resumed teaching whenever she could. For my grade school graduation she directed me and my classmates in what seemed to me an extravaganza, as she had for my sister and older brother when they had graduated from grade school. She died four months later.

My mother's slow and painful death was unbearable to me. When she was finally hospitalized, I refused to visit her. With tubes dripping liquid into her veins and others draining her body, she frightened me. My father told me that she became addicted to morphine and that the nuns in the Catholic hospital where she was a patient converted her to Catholicism. I didn't believe him. She wasn't the sort of person to allow a drug to take her over or to violate the Lutheran prohibition against professing other faiths.

The death of a parent is hard on a child, who naturally represses grief and anger at being abandoned. Yet had I grieved openly, my elders would have stopped me. They believed that Melba, like Eddie and Charlie, had gone to heaven. My father told me early one morning that she had died during the night, and I remember his words: "Your mother now rests in peace. The Lord has taken her to heaven. Rejoice in her release from her suffering and from this earthly vale of tears." He didn't cry, and neither did I. Like the other members of my family, I visualized how happy she must be in heaven and how I would join her there some day.

The house on Hillcrest now turned into a house of sorrows. Among the adults, only Harry, Lillian, and Lena were left. Several years later, Lena became seriously ill, lost most of her body functions, and turned into what was called a "vegetable." My grandmother nursed her at home, again turning the dining room into a sickroom. I remember Lillian washing Lena's emaciated body, spoonfeeding her like a baby, and putting diapers on her and changing them. I spelled Lillian occasionally, but the tasks repelled me. In our interviews Noura described to me her impression of my house in the period after the deaths, after she and I became close friends and she was there with me. "Your house smelled like death," she told me. "It reeked of depression and the decay of old age. It was dark, unkempt, musty." Noura's description corresponds to my memory. Once a mansion, my house now seemed a mausoleum.

After my mother died, there were no more bridge evenings and no more excursions to the race track. We stopped eating together as a family. Lillian still cooked a roast or goulash every day, but we each ate when we were hungry. My sister, married and with her own home, no longer envied me; my older brother took a paternal interest in me by helping me with homework and teaching me to play tennis. My father became even more preoccupied with his work, for the loss of my mother's salary plunged us into the financial difficulties my elders had always feared. When asked about my childhood, then and for many years after, I responded that I grew up in poverty and that my parents were failures.

Lillian now tried to enforce rigid rules on me. When I began to date, she told me about her marital problems and how men couldn't be trusted. She canceled my membership in the Screen Children's Guild; she looked for Lutheran boys for me to marry. Yet I doubt I could have expected anything better from this depressed widow whose children had died and who faced the possible recurrence of her own cancer. She had lived her life through Melba and Eddie, and she had expected them to achieve in ways that could wipe out the shame of Alaska. To do it all over again by placing her hopes on her grandchildren was too much. She only wanted to be certain we were safe.

She turned to her Lutheranism for comfort, and she decided that she was marked for martyrdom. "Whom the Lord loveth he chasteneth, and scourgeth every son whom he receiveth." Continually reciting that verse, she tried to convince us that our family tragedy was a sign of God's favor. She developed a fear of crime; she read aloud newspaper accounts of rapes and child murders. I thought she was losing her sanity.

Yet I've discovered that influences unrelated to the deaths in my family motivated those fears. Historians have recently unearthed a public "sex crime panic" that broke out in the late 1930s and again in the late 1940s. Sensationalized stories of child murders committed by male "sexual psychopaths" ran in the nationwide media. Inglewood was a center of the hysteria. In 1939 a child was killed in the city, and a mob bent on lynching a suspect in custody stormed the city jail. In 1949 protest marchers in Los Angeles demanded harsher penalties for violent crimes against children. Historians conclude that the incidence of sex crimes didn't increase in this period and that the hysteria erupted in response to familiar villains: the Cold War, homosexuality, women leaving the home for work. Nonetheless, my grandmother believed what she read. In cautioning us against sex criminals, Lillian wasn't crazy. Public hysteria fueled her private demons; history was partly the culprit in causing us trauma.

In therapy sessions in later life, I obsessed over those deaths; they caused me to suffer from anxiety and depression and a fear of abandonment and imminent catastrophe. At the time they occurred I may have repressed my grief, but it returned to haunt me throughout my adult life. The sense of guilt I felt over those deaths fed into the guilt I'd internalized from my Lutheran religion: a sinner, I was somehow responsible for my family dying. The shock of those deaths increased my shyness and my sense of inferiority and caused me to act out adult versions of my childhood tantrums. More than death was involved: in the end all the adults in the Hillcrest house abandoned me; for Lillian and Harry seemed unable to recover from depression over those deaths. Yet the deaths toughened me. A compulsion to achieve what I considered my mother's ambition for me bolstered the success drive my family had already instilled in me. As in the earlier rivalry with my brother and sister, I had to be self-reliant to survive.

As I matured, two people seemed to exist inside of me. One was shy and frightened, inarticulate except on the stage or in front of a class. That person could seem cold and arrogant to others when masking the shyness. The second was tough and determined, talkative and smart; she was driven to compensate for the deaths by realizing the family ambition. Over time, especially with the coming of feminism, the second personality became dominant; but the first has never disappeared.

Perhaps I would have been less shy and more willing to commit myself to the social activism of the sixties I so admired had I not experienced such an ordeal as a child. In a letter Fran wrote me after college, she contended that I withdrew in difficult situations. "When things are ugly and there isn't love enough to change them, you simply cut them out. So you were able to live in your family's house after those deaths." Perhaps Fran was right. Perhaps I did withdraw and cut off my feelings, although I suspect Fran was describing my mask of coldness, not my own interior state. I spent many years in therapy coming to terms with the deaths; during many years of my adult life I had little to do with my sister and older brother. When I was forty-eight, my emotionality peaked and I, like my mother, broke down. But I didn't die. Instead, I realized that my breakdown occurred when I reached the age at which she had died. Once I had lived longer than she had, I understood that I had always feared dying when she did. But through the breakdown I had symbolically died, and her death lessened its hold on me.

My mother left me many legacies: ambition, a strong will, the knowledge of how to manage a career and a family. And she taught me more—about pride in being a woman and about the value of women's friendships and loving ties between mothers and daughters. Like scenes lifted out of a montage, two recollections of her predominate in my memory: neither probably occurred exactly as I remember it. Over the years each has helped me cope with my fear of abandonment; in each memory I've cast my mother's legacy to me as one of love and hope.

The first memory is set in the summer of 1950, a year after Eddie's death and my mother's hysterectomy. That summer I spent two weeks at a Girl Scout Camp in the mountains near Los Angeles, in my first experience of living away from home. Not surprisingly, I came down with a case of intermittent sobbing in what was called homesickness. I was afraid that disaster might strike again if I left home. The camp nurse tried to shock me out of my distress with a typical 1950s warning: "If you can't leave your family even for two weeks at this camp, how will you be able to leave them to marry?"

My mother must have learned about my breakdown as well as the nurse's comment. When I returned from the camp, tired and dirty, she bathed me in the bathtub as though I was a small child. I remember her soaping and rinsing my naked body. Then she remarked on my developing breasts and pubic hair. "Soon you will be a woman," she said, "and then you will marry and have your own family and be as happy as I have been." Her musings about my body were prophetic, for I experienced menarche shortly after. But did she actually express such sentiments? The bath occurred; she mentions it in her diary. Yet her words may be my embell-ishment, a memory constructed to soothe my anguish over her death and to envision her life as happy and to pass that happiness on to me. The phys-icality of the memory is important, for it expresses in the most intimate manner my sense of our love and her understanding that, just as she might leave me, I would have to leave her to make my own life.

The second predominating memory of my mother includes Lillian. In a department store dressing room Melba, Lillian, and I are trying on clothes. I see their naked bodies, each with a scar where a breast should have been, each having endured a mastectomy. But they aren't disturbed by those scars, and neither am I. For the scars are signs of their womanhood, signs that they have lived and survived. They don't hide the suffering they've experienced and the strength of character they've gained.

In later life I feared dying, but I never feared cancer or losing a breast. That memory connected to the excitement of being in a mirrored dressing room with Melba and Lillian, creating a new self through clothes, has sus-tained me. Significantly, in that memory I've cast them as heroic characters unbound by social conventions about women's appearance. And that mir-ror which dominates the memory has resonances for me. When I look at myself in a mirror, I resemble my father, not my mother. I have the same color eyes and hair as he and similar facial features. Like him, I seem to have the tough body that my mother didn't possess. As an adult I've rarely been ill and despite my fear of dying when my mother did, I've always believed paradoxically that, like my father, I would live a long, healthy life.

I'm now nearly sixty, with a lifetime gone by and with a strong urge to forgive my family and to celebrate them. I now look on my life as having had a Janus-faced quality, with the goddess Fortuna showing me her fair and foul sides alternately and sometimes both at the same time. As the years have gone by and my memories of the past have filtered through the immediacy of the present, I'm not certain what experiences have been pos-itive in my life and what negative. Thus those deaths brought me Fran and her mother. Without Fran, I doubt I could have withstood our high school culture and its unrelenting pressure to conform. Through Fran I came to know her mother, Lydia. Lydia completed my early education for life.

II

FRAN AND ME
1952–1956

CHAPTER THREE

High School

I've never been able to recall precisely when and where Fran and I first met, although I always assumed that meeting occurred early in our freshman year in high school. We were both enrolled in what passed as a college preparatory track; perhaps we sat next to each other in a class. We both played tennis and participated in school athletics; perhaps we met on a tennis court or in the after-school sports program for girls. Fran was a serious art student and I sang; perhaps she painted a backdrop for a performance I was in. My mother's death soon after the start of freshman year blocks my memory of other events that fall, even my meeting Fran.

In Alexandria, Egypt, Noura described to me our first meeting. "Don't you remember?" she asked me, as we sat in the living room of her apartment, high above the Mediterranean Sea. "I remember that meeting precisely, as though it happened yesterday. It didn't occur in high school; we actually met earlier, in the summer after sixth grade, and our meeting was connected to that Girl Scout camp where you became so homesick. Don't you recall that I was at that camp and that we spent time together there? We first met while waiting at a bus depot in Inglewood to board a bus for the camp. Our mothers had brought us to the depot, and they happened to stand next to each other and to begin talking. They hadn't met before, but they knew of each other through Inglewood musical circles. Realizing that both of us were apprehensive about leaving home, they brought us together and made certain we sat together on the bus."

"As we pulled away," Noura concluded, "I looked out the window. I saw them talking, animated. It's a final tableau etched in my memory. I never saw your mother again."

Noura connects our first meeting to our mothers, and that link helped to define our friendship. Fran was as close to her mother as I was to mine. Melba's death troubled her, for it reminded her of her own mother's mortality. Fran must have been curious about my mother; she couldn't have missed the high school ceremony dedicating the music building to her. Sensitive to others, Fran must have sensed my pain, no matter how I tried to conceal it. I think she brought me to Lydia partly as compensation for having lost my own mother.

Fran remembers our first meeting so clearly because that summer camp had a strong impact on her, and thus she has vivid memories of everything connected to it. She discovered there that she liked mountains and forests, the smell of pine trees and the crunch of their fallen needles underfoot, the black sky at night dotted with stars invisible in the city. She liked living outdoors, sleeping in tents, and eating food cooked over campfires. She missed her family, but she didn't mind being away from home. Fran never forgot that camp; after it ended, she dreamt of marrying a forest ranger and living in the woods. Later in her life, the memory of that camp would influence her when she decided to move to a community on a mountain in New Mexico.

My reaction to the camp was ambivalent. I enjoyed going on hikes, doing crafts, swimming in a lake. If asked today I could even sing our camp songs, "Marching to Pretoria" and "There Once Was A Little Ship." But in contrast to Fran, I wasn't taken with the primitive lifestyle. I didn't like the latrines, or the mosquitos, or the sun that burned my light skin if I didn't wear a hat and slather my exposed body with lotion. Most of all, I didn't want to leave my family. My most vivid memory of the camp is my homesickness. I don't remember the parting from my mother because I didn't want to say good-bye to her, even for two weeks. And I recollect the girls at the camp only vaguely because of my embarrassment at acting like a baby and winding up in the infirmary when I was almost an adolescent.

Whatever association Fran and I had at the camp ended once we returned home. We didn't attend the same school; we didn't have the same friends. We didn't phone each other; we didn't arrange to meet. Nor did our mothers meet again. They may have meant to contact each other and never got around to it. Lydia could easily have dropped in at our Hillcrest house some Sunday; she attended services at the Episcopal church in back of my house every week. But our mothers both led busy lives, and my mother was struggling with serious illness. As with many life encounters, they met, connected, and then passed each other by.

No matter where Fran and I met, our friendship at that high school was inevitable. For the similarity between us was striking—as was our mutual difference from our classmates. Besides our enthusiasm for tennis and art, we were both determined to achieve high grades and to go to college. As a result, our classmates often ostracized us; they had little respect for academic success, especially in girls. Most of them came from Inglewood's working-class population, and many were the children of the dust bowl migrants who lived in the small houses near the airport. A majority at the high school, they dominated its social order.

They seemed molded by 1950s gender conservatism; their families had no connection to the worker radicalism that might have tempered their conformism. They had no interest in attending college and were suspicious of those who did. Even I was surprised to learn at my graduation that, of the five hundred students in my class, no more than fifty aspired to college, even two-year junior colleges. Out of the remaining students, the boys found employment in working in factories, repairing autos, or selling cars, while the girls married. Like my sister Lila, they married soon after graduation.

When I complained to Lillian that I didn't fit in at the school she expressed sympathy, but she didn't intervene. "When your mother first taught there," she told me, "the curriculum was rigorous, and students studied hard. The immigration during World War II changed the school." She continued: "If only we lived several blocks to the north, you could go to the newer high school, with students whose families have more money. That high school would be better for you." The students there, drawn from the tract of split-level homes built in the late 1940s, were college bound; and they valued academic work. But the boundaries of its sending district stopped short of Hillcrest Boulevard, and Lillian didn't have the energy to try to have me transferred.

My sister and older brother had gone to Inglewood High without difficulty, and I suspect that, despite my emotionality, Lillian decided I could also cope. But my sister, with no interest in a career, married the first boy she dated, while my brother, quiet and controlled, managed in most situations. Before her death my mother spoke of sending me to a private school, one in Brentwood or Bel Aire; but the loss of her salary made paying the tuition at those schools out of the question.

Private school tuition was also prohibitive for Fran's family, who also struggled to make ends meet. Fran's older brothers and sister, like my siblings, had gone to the high school without incident. But it had undergone major changes since Fran's sister, closest to her in age, had graduated five years previously. That was before the building of the newer high school siphoned off most of the city's academically motivated youth. Besides, Fran's oldest brother, nine years her elder, had been captain of the football team and president of the student body. His success encouraged the family to accept the school and overlook its faults.

The physical appearance of Inglewood High School embodied its social climate. An earthquake had severely damaged the original buildings, tall and red brick and dating from 1905; they had been torn down in the 1940s and replaced by nondescript concrete block structures, separated by blacktop pavement and a few scraggly trees. Even today no decorative elements adorn these buildings to catch the eye; no sweeping lines provide drama. Their design reflects no educational purpose: they could be manufacturing plants or prison barracks.

Our student culture was a Southern California and working-class variation of the standard 1950s high school culture. You can read about that culture in studies by historians and sociologists and in such novels as Lisa Alther's *Kinflicks*. You can see it dramatized in movies such as *Peggy Sue Got Married*. My experience, as unique as it seemed to me at the time, was a variation on a standard theme. We had jocks and hoods, prom queens and cheerleaders, brains and geeks. All interacted under the aegis of a cult of popularity, which decreed that what mattered was to be liked by one's peers. This cult of popularity promised security through admiration from others, but it actually delivered self-doubt. It operated according to a complex hierarchy that awarded real popularity only to the few at its summit.

Devising strategies to become popular took a lot of energy. Our system was as demanding and capricious as the religion of my childhood, and it was much more diffuse. Its rules weren't written down; there wasn't any guidebook or catechism to lead one through its mazes. For instance, despite its hidden elitism, it held out hope to all: the standard line was that anyone could be popular if only they had a good personality and that everyone had an attractive side that they only had to show to gain access to the hallowed ranks. But just what side of ourselves was attractive enough to constitute a good personality baffled Fran and me. The standard solution— "Just Be Yourself!"— made no sense to us. Displaying the qualities we admired in ourselves—like intelligence and athleticism—didn't get us very far.

For girls, the right personality required obeying a code of femininity by hiding good grades, exhibiting a sugary demeanor, and showing interest only in matters of appearance and social life. Then one might attract a boyfriend and "go steady" with him, and that relationship was the ultimate goal of popularity for girls. But the code of femininity prohibited girls from initiating romantic contacts, even making phone calls. Hiding behind a smokescreen of passivity and waiting to be chosen, we could only give off hints and think up subtle ploys to snare the boy we wanted.

Fran and I tried to follow this code, but it also made us angry. Thus we consistently violated it, sometimes without realizing our sins. We thought we understood the rules about male and female behavior, but we didn't grasp the full extent of the code's gender inequities, especially its privileging of boys. They could become popular through a reputation for wit or cleverness or because they had the ability to sell themselves. Such talents, which hinted at independence, were suspect in girls. Being a class or the student body president insured a boy's popularity, but those offices were forbidden to girls, who never aspired to any office beyond that of class secretary anyway. Excelling in sports gained a boy high esteem, but outstanding girl athletes held an ambiguous status. Their success implied a lack of femininity.

At the apex of our popularity system stood the football players. Their large chunky bodies and displays of masculinity in a violent sport underscored the gender divisions of our system, while their size and solidity provided an aura of security not only to us but also to the outside community, caught up in Cold War fears. Symbolic warriors, they could keep us safe. Our Friday night football games attracted crowds of ten thousand, drawn from the city population as well as from the high school student body. In October 1950, the city newspaper describes our high school team as "champions" with "blood in their eyes." Even though none of the players was more than eighteen, they were expected to "rip" the rival Redondo Beach High School line "to shreds" and to trample it "into the turf."

At the high school our football players usually dated only the popular girls, although sometimes one of them would choose an unknown girl from the lower grades. This arrogance only increased the renegade's status and encouraged fantasies among the rest of us that other football players might do the same—and choose us.

A brawny masculinity defined our ideal boy, and the ideal girl was his opposite. She should be petite and winsome, with large breasts and a tiny waist. Central to her personality should be "poise" and "charm." "Poise" meant balance, maintaining the cool self-control essential in this era of a sexual "double standard" which encouraged necking but prohibited intercourse for girls until marriage. "Charm" implied femininity. It connoted something small and dainty, like the small talismen, the "charms"—hearts, whistles, arrows—that hung from the charm bracelets we wore. Charm schools for girls that taught etiquette and "good grooming" advertised in the day's newspapers; Bunola Kay, promoting herself through her lectures on "charm" and "personality," offered the same curriculum to private clients.

For a girl, achieving a reputation for beauty guaranteed popularity. In our Southern California of beaches and bathing beauties, the site of the movie industry, appearance held a special importance. There were constant beauty contests in those years—from the Little Miss Hollywood competition I almost won as a child to the contests for queens of the Pasadena New Year's Day Rose Parade and of local cities. Local colleges had homecoming queens and the Inglewood racetrack a "Goose Girl." Carrying a crook, she walked around the large pond in the center of the track during the racing season, presumably tending its geese, while probably hoping that a photographer would snap her and she would be discovered for the movies.

Hollywood saturated our lives. Films were shot on our streets; our relatives worked in the movie industry. The mythology was that talent scouts lurked everywhere, looking for beautiful girls. Our high school continually held beauty contests, and we especially associated beauty queens with the movies because Jeanne Crain, an Inglewood High beauty queen who graduated several years before Fran and me, had become a major film star. Her success fueled the hope that such favor might descend on any of our queens.

At the center of our beauty competitions were five song girls, selected by a committee of faculty and students. They pranced and waved pompoms at football and basketball games, wearing short skirts that skimmed their buttocks. Another group of five (usually the runners-up to the song girls) copied their dress and routines and performed at the girls' intramural sports competitions. A squad of some fifty girls (the so-called "pep team") performed marches and waved pompoms at half time during football games. Three drum majorettes, twirling batons and wearing the obligatory short skirts, led our band.

Whenever a sports event or a dance provided an excuse, queens were elected by ballot or chosen by committee. We had basketball and baseball queens and queens for our junior and senior proms. We even had a queen for the yearly "backward dance," when gender codes were briefly suspended and girls could ask boys to escort them for an evening. We had a Spring Sports Queen and a so-called "Mystery" Queen for our Beachcombers' Ball. (Her name wasn't announced until the ball began.) The most important of our queens was the Homecoming Queen, attended by four princesses, each princess from one of the four high school years. Indicating their exalted status, the football team chose them.

At the end of our junior year the mania for queens grew to such proportions that a competition was held for a Campus Queen, presumably to reign over the rest. Yet this position in the end didn't carry much prestige, probably because a minor movie actress, a friend of one of the teachers, chose the winner, and the girl she chose wasn't one of the popular people. The Campus Queen wasn't even nominated to compete in the contest held our senior year to elect the most popular boy and girl in our student body. Predictably, the winners were the captain of the football team, who was also student body president, and the Homecoming Queen, his girlfriend. They married soon after graduation.

Popularity didn't descend on the Campus Queen, and our drum majorettes were also deemed second rate, probably because they were identified with the male band members, who were classified as unmasculine geeks. The girls on the large pompom squad occupied an even lower status, for belonging to that group conferred no popularity at all. The problem was that anyone who applied was admitted: popularity bore no relationship to democracy. The several girls who participated on our cheerleading squad (along with several boys) did somewhat better. They were well-liked, although far from the top of the popularity pyramid. Stocky, with thick legs, their bodies had an unsettling masculine quality.

Neither Fran nor I had bodies like theirs, but our success as athletes made our femininity suspect. So did our high grades, which we didn't try to conceal. We were "bookworms" and "brains," and those kinds of girls, everyone knew, simply weren't beautiful.

As I've said, I couldn't have survived that high school without Fran. I was too sensitive to slights and too fearful of rejection after the deaths in my family to deal with the rigidities of the popularity system on my own. And the high school was filled with land mines for me. My brother, two years ahead of me, soared in popularity when he won tennis tournaments and, acting totally out of character, ran for student body president. He didn't win, but suddenly everyone seemed to admire him. His successes fed into my sense of rivalry with him, although he still made an effort to father me. My mother's symbolic presence hovered over the school, but the teachers who were her friends never spoke about her to me. Shocked by her death and fearful of their own mortality, they seemed to me mostly to want to forget her. If my mother had lived, she might have used her influence to help me get elected a song girl or a queen. She was herself too conformist to have challenged the system, but at least her presence would have buffered its cruelties for me. Caught in a dilemma with few solutions, I found Fran.

Aside from my Uncle Eddie, Fran was the most magnetic person I'd ever known. Tall, big-boned, and rangy, she had naturally wavy hair I envied and a skin that tanned in the sun and didn't burn the way mine did. She moved gracefully, like an athlete; she walked forcefully, as though she knew where she was going. I found her beautiful, even if my classmates didn't. Adventurous and inventive, she liked to challenge the rules. She would go off on her own with a mischievous grin, beckoning me to follow her up stairs marked private and through doors marked no admittance. Fearful of authority, I would try to stop her. But admiring her courage and not wanting to risk her displeasure, my attempts were usually halfhearted: I would follow after.

Dramatic, she liked to be in the spotlight, at the center of activities. Intense about everything—books, games, boys—her intensity drew me to her like metal to a magnet. Invariably upbeat, she made fun of our popularity system in ways I couldn't; for in the immediate years after the deaths I was serious, without much sense of humor. Fran was assertive: she challenged the authority of teachers; she phoned boys. (She recently told me she was terrified of making those calls. But she made them and that is important in understanding her.) She was thoughtful: when some enterprising students set up a valentine delivery service one Valentine's Day, she sent me a card signed "anonymous" so that everyone would think I had an admirer. She had boundless energy; following her, I overcame my shyness to participate in the extracurricular activities needed for college admission. I patterned myself after her; I depended on her emotional strength. She was the leader in our friendship and in our assaults against the popularity system.

Our attraction was partly one of opposites: I was light in complexion and hair color, she was dark; I was shy, she was assertive; I was overly sensitive, she was more practical. She thought fast on her feet and was a skilled debater. During our senior year, she reached the finals in the annual speech tournament of the California State Forensic League in the category of impromptu speech. I entered the prepared speech category, but I didn't have the nerve to attempt impromptu speech, which involved the daunting task of delivering a ten-minute oration on a topic assigned only a few minutes before. In our debate partnership I gave the prepared opening statement and the final summation, and she did the rebuttal arguments in the middle. In these contests her rational mind and her skill at creating an argument both logical and compelling were in full force.

"Why were you friends with me in high school?" I asked Noura during our interviews. "All my childhood," she responded, "I wanted a soulmate—someone who loved books as I did, who had an artistic disposition, and who was offbeat like me. In the neighborhood where I lived, in my elementary and junior high schools, I'd never met anyone like you. You were intelligent and ambitious, with a passionate nature which matched mine, but you were also responsive and emotionally fragile, and I was drawn to your sweetness and your shyness. Sometimes you were so childlike that I thought you might shatter, but underneath that you were tough and you always came back. I liked leading you, but you were also a confederate. You may have been quiet in public, but you talked all the time with me. When I met you the attraction was immediate, for you were the person I wanted. Whatever you felt about me, I felt about you."

Powerfully drawn to each other, confederates in our misery and our scheming, Fran and I tried to scorn our high school culture. We had some understanding that intellectuals liked to appear offbeat, and our families had given us some pride in being unique. But the drive toward popularity was so powerful that we often followed its rules. Daily under its influence, we directed our energies to mastering it by both rising above it and finding a niche within it.

We avoided the students outside of respectability. The male "hoods" smoked cigarettes and drove motorcycles; their girlfriends wore heavy makeup and had a reputation for being sexually fast. (In our school some of these students were Mexican American but never Black, because of the municipal codes forbidding African Americans to remain in the city after sundown.) One recent historian of 1950s high school culture contends that white girls like Fran and me, with some independence, foreshadowed the youth rebellion of the 1960s by being attracted to our "hoods." On the contrary, they seemed to us to exist in another world. They violated our standards of dress and behavior, especially the prohibitions on female sexuality we carefully observed. We were intent on achievement; they got poor grades and took different classes from us. We had no interest in them.

We also kept aloof from the male students devoted to science. They displayed small slide rules in their upper shirt pockets and played chess every day during lunch hour, openly flaunting their contempt for the anti-intellectualism of the popularity system. We didn't have their nerve, and we feared that identification with them might typecast us more firmly as "book worms" and "brains."

We took a different path from the science boys by participating in extracurricular activities. With a student body of two thousand, our school had music ensembles, many clubs, and a student government. Those activities offered the participation needed for college admission; they also provided companionship and some sense of accomplishment. Fran and I launched a debate team. I sang in the school chorus. Fran designed posters and invitations for school dances. We decorated the school gymnasium for those dances with tinsel, crepe paper, and murals she drew, turning this place smelling of wax and sweat into a fantasyland even if neither of us had a date for the dance and couldn't attend. Above all, we tried to maintain a reputation for not caring if we were snubbed. Being good-natured was a respected attribute of the popular people.

Participating in the after-school sports program for girls gave us some distinction. Our gym teachers were tough women who had been WACs during World War II. Wise to the popularity system, they admitted some popular girls to the program to insure its success, while they provided the athletes among us with long hours of training and team competition in a number of sports. Unmarried and clannish, they probably were lesbians. That designation may have carried over to Fran and me as well as to the other female athletes. But we were naive in the 1950s; such a possibility didn't enter our minds.

Our activities kept our names in the student newspaper; at least we were well-known. But we never were able to translate that notoriety into real popularity. Our classmates appreciated our extracurricular efforts but not our intensity in doing them—or our attempts at innovation. They regarded our debate club as bizarre since they had never heard of debating—and we were just about its only participants. When Fran and I won lettermen sweaters for our tennis-playing, rather than wearing the sweaters of boyfriends as an emblem of going steady, we went too far. The sweaters were a key symbol of masculinity.

Still Fran and I tried to fit in. We hid our envy of the girls chosen as songleaders and queens. We even scrounged flowers from florist shops and gardens and decorated the cars in which the Homecoming Queen and her princesses rode around the football field at halftime during the fall homecoming game. We went to the football games and cheered for our team. We went to the Friday night dances after the football games, hoping that by force of some magic we might be asked to dance. But that rarely happened.

During our sophomore year, I snagged a second-string cross-country runner with whom I went steady. I wore his letterman sweater, and we held hands on campus. We had regular dates on Friday nights at school sports events and on Saturday nights at the movies. The popular people approached me as a possible recruit. But that relationship of mine didn't last long. I knew going to college meant resisting the pressure to marry, and I wasn't daring enough to violate our sexual code. Anyway, I preferred being with Fran, even though the popular people dropped me once my boyfriend and I "broke up."

After he went to college, my brother Paul sometimes persuaded his friends to date me. Older, mysterious strangers, they briefly brought me the envy of my classmates. For several weeks my brother dated Fran, although she was too exuberant for him and he too quiet for her and their involvement soon ended. Yet Fran and I both expected that some day "Mr. Right" would fall "head over heels" in love with us and sweep us "off our feet" into a blissful marriage. How we would combine this marriage with a career was hazy in our minds. But thinking about our futures in practical terms didn't seem pressing as we studied, played tennis, and painted and sang. From the beginning, our friends were drawn from the girl athletes, and they were a spirited bunch. None were song leaders or queens, and none dated much. Because we associated with them, the popular people shunned us even more.

We were vulnerable to dismissal on many counts. No matter what we wore, we never felt up to the fashion standard of the popular girls. They worked part-time after school to afford the latest fads, such as expensive cashmere sweaters. Involved in schoolwork and extracurricular activities, Fran and I didn't have time for paying jobs. Yet I yearned to be chosen to exhibit my favorite outfit of clothes in a display case in the school's front hall as winner of the monthly competition for the "best groomed girl-of-the-month." But "brains" like Fran and me could never win such titles.

I look today at the pictures in our high school yearbook and discern no difference between our clothes and those worn by the popular girls. All of us appear dated in fifties dress. Our skirts are either very tight or very full, and small scarves are knotted around our necks. Our breasts, molded by bras, come to points under tight sweaters to produce the sexy figure of the fifties female ideal. But covered up to our necks by our sweaters, sometimes with rounded "Peter Pan" collars attached to them, we signal our containment of our sexuality. To my eyes today, Fran and I seem dressed like the others, but at the time I was painfully aware of differences.

My blonde hair and Nordic features matched the day's beauty ideal, yet my high school peers would never have selected me a song girl or a queen. To them my brains canceled out whatever beauty I possessed. During our senior year an external panel chose me beauty queen for the city of Inglewood, and I rode as Cinderella on the city float in the Pasadena Rose Parade on New Year's Day. My classmates were stunned. The song girls, the Homecoming Queen, and the other reigning beauties at the high school had entered that contest; no one could understand why I had won it. I felt some vindication, yet I also was baffled. There was no apparent reason why I should succeed in this realm from which Fran and I had been excluded and from which, as Noura described it in our interviews, we felt separated by a vast gulf.

Despite occasional success, popularity always eluded us. In later years I came to suspect that our striving had been doomed from the start because we lived in big houses unusual among our classmates; thus they considered our families to be wealthy. By definition we couldn't fit in with the popular students, who came from working-class families. We had to be "snooty" and "stuck up." Those words from fifties slang were drawn from a vocabulary of class difference that we used as a means of scorn. I'm certain those words were applied to Fran and me. In 1991, at my thirty-fifth high school reunion, a classmate confirmed my suspicions. "We did treat you badly," she confessed. "But we thought you were different from us because you lived in that big house on Hillcrest and had all that money."

I replied that my family had little money and that the house was just a large place where a lot of people lived. She appeared confused by what I said, as though I had challenged a comfortable memory; I didn't pursue the matter further. Yet I wonder if I criticize my classmates too harshly. Did I, in fact, perplex and frighten them, with my connection to a high school teacher who had died and with my shyness that could seem like coldness? Do I distort the power of the popularity system and fail to realize that my preoccupation with it allowed me to avoid facing my growing dislike of my family's Lutheran religion and my despair over the deaths in my family? Was I the problem and not my classmates?

Even if I inflate its power, the popularity system existed, and its ranking order was damaging to the psyches of insecure adolescents. If that was the case, why did our teachers tolerate it? Why did they, in fact, encourage it? They participated on the selection committees for the song girls and the queens, and they thought up the good grooming award. Even though none of those teachers appeared to me to have any style, they probably thought we would profit by following Bunola Kay's counsel that attention to appearance would produce self-confidence. Perhaps they thought we all could be beautiful if we worked at it. After all, a number of them participated in that separate culture of Inglewood's women so important to my mother and grandmother. They went to the bridal and baby showers I attended; they belonged to Melba's and Lillian's bridge clubs. The high school fixation with beauty was an extension of the values of that culture, which centered around appearance. Our contests over beauty functioned as a powerful initiation into mores meant to domesticate us and to turn us into good consumers.

Perhaps I am too harsh on those teachers. Like my mother with her piano recitals, perhaps they wanted to award a moment of glory to students with limited futures and to provide them with a treasured memory for life. And promoting beauty wasn't our teachers' only interest. They initiated the clubs and choruses; they suggested that Fran and I found the debate team. Influencing everything they did was their worry that our adolescent energy might lead us all, not just the hoods, toward the dreaded state of juvenile delinquency, an American phobia in the Cold War era. Thus we had continual pep rallies to foster school spirit. Our school newspaper is filled with diatribes against student messiness. One of our teachers explains in this sheet that we had queens to teach discipline to unruly adolescents. "Many high schools," she claimed, "do not have the privilege of crowning a grid queen for the simple reason that most students can't behave and pay the tribute that is expected for such a dignified event." On some level I realized the inanity of this statement, for I find myself quoted in the student newspaper as responding that I wished our teachers "would treat us like adults."

Fran and I were in the college preparatory track in the high school, but we didn't learn much in it. We endlessly memorized rules of grammar and historical dates, and we recited from textbooks in our classes. We never wrote papers, and we read only condensed books. Perhaps student indifference prevented our teachers from accomplishing much more, but their methods hardly fostered independent thinking or critical skills. We made few complaints, for getting the good grades needed for college admission depended on those teachers. Many of them praised our abilities, and they awarded us academic honors. At graduation they named us joint valedictorians.

In our junior year our male physics teacher took Fran and me aside and advised us to become engineers. His advice mystified us. Like most girls, we didn't view science as a profession for women. We thought science and engineering belonged to the brainy chess-playing boys. But neither we nor our teacher knew that, even if we aspired to such careers, we would encounter discrimination because of our gender. We hadn't heard of feminism; we had no way of understanding the gendered nature of our world.

Fran's response to our high school culture wasn't exactly the same as mine. At five feet ten inches tall, nearly four inches taller than me, she was too large to be a song girl or a queen. All those campus beauties were petite and small-boned, as is evident in the photos in our yearbooks. She couldn't covet these positions as I could, for her body disqualified her.

Moreover, she took greater pride than I in our intellectualism and our athletic ability. She didn't have to contend with the death of her mother; she had a functioning family, and they supported her efforts. Her parents had many friends outside Inglewood, and eventually she dated their sons. She found a mentor in one of the art teachers, and he encouraged her independence. A sophisticated Jew from Chicago, he lampooned our cult of popularity, praised Fran's talent, and fostered her pride in being different.

He intimidated me. I couldn't handle his biting wit, and I mostly avoided him. Fran never forgot him. In our correspondence after college she wrote me that "in no private art school in the country could I have found better art instruction and general mental stimulation than from Dan Cohen."

In that same letter Fran also took a different perspective from me on the high school. Where I attacked it for its rigidity and its anti-intellectualism, she contended those qualities had toughened us. "If anything," she asserted, "that school made our will to learn stronger rather than lessening it. We were used to fighting for every available scrap of learning, to using every available second of time, and we knew the value of being educated because we knew at first hand from living in Inglewood what it means not to be." Perhaps Fran was right. Perhaps that high school strengthened us, as my rivalry with my sister and brother and the deaths in my family strengthened me. At the time I refused to accept her position, for what I saw as the wounds inflicted on me by that high school culture were too fresh for me to see it in any positive light.

During those high school years Fran seemed my double, my twin in tennis, in intellect, in "boy-crazy" behavior. Yet in one way we differed, a way that seemed so minor then that I paid little attention to it. Fran often pointed out objects that pleased her. She would take a flower in her hands, bring it to her face, and smell it with her eyes closed as though she was a temple priestess and it a sacred relic, before she passed it on to me, implying that I should do the same. At times the ocean, the sky, and the landscape seemed alive to her. She seemed to want to touch something beyond the world, while reaffirming a connection with humanity by touching your arm, with a knowing, dreamy smile on her face.

She did the pointing and touching in Alexandria, even though we were then in our fifties and she was a Muslim. When we were young, I found this behavior silly and even pretentious. I failed to realize that it might be connected to spirituality. I thought it was a pose to prove that she really was an artist and not just a teenager fixated on boys. I had begun to deny my religion, disliking my family's insistence that I go to church and exhibit piety. Thus I forgot my own experiences of spiritual ecstasy when as a child I had considered becoming a Lutheran deaconess and when, even during high school, I looked at a sunset and fantasized that I saw God and his angels coming down from heaven to swoop me up.

I also respected Fran's artistic talent, and I kept my criticism of her aestheticism to myself. I cherished our sense of togetherness; I wanted our friendship to be perfect. We were united in striving for achievement, in reading books and studying together, in struggling with our high school culture. In the heterosexist 1950s I had little understanding of the homo-erotic nature of our friendship—a typical feature of the "best friend" rela-tionship of female adolescence. She was like a sister to me; there was no overt eroticism between us. During those years it seemed that our friend-ship could never end.

Yet the intensity of our striving may have sparked competition between us. We defined ourselves as with different skills, but I was jealous when Fran beat me at tennis or received a higher mark on a paper. I secretly thought her talents superior to mine, and I sometimes felt resentment over this. Toward the end of high school, when she won major scholarships and competitions and I didn't, my resentment increased. Before then I mostly accepted her accomplishments, and I felt pride in my friend. I was aware that, although I had a resonant singing voice, I hadn't inherited my mother's musical gifts. My father was tone deaf, and I often sang off key. I didn't like to practice the piano or vocal scales, which I found boring. Fran was dif-ferent. She could capture perfect likenesses on paper. She had an unerring sense of color and design, and she drew and painted all the time.

The national mood was particularly conservative in the early 1950s, shaped by the Korean War and the rampage of McCarthyism. By mid-decade that conservatism began to wane. McCarthy was dethroned by Senatorial cen-sure in 1954, and that same year the Supreme Court issued its pathbreak-ing decision ending racial segregation in *Brown v. Board of Education*. In 1955 rock and roll burst into mainstream popularity, and *Rebel Without a Cause*, the bellwether film for a new adolescent realism in movies, was released. In 1956 Elvis Presley first hit the charts.

But Fran and I didn't experience this new music and film. The movies we saw were mostly romances, women's films, and Christian epics. Holly-wood, under attack by anticommunists, produced these sorts of films in the early 1950s to demonstrate the industry's adherence to mainstream values: Christianity, marriage, the nuclear family. We listened to songs of romantic love and longing, the ballads glorifying heterosexual desire sung by heartthrobs and crooners like Frank Sinatra and Dinah Shore. When I occasionally soloed in high school assemblies and before community groups, I sang the soprano love songs from musical comedies such as *South Pacific*, *Brigadoon*, and *Guys and Dolls*. Throughout our high school and even our college years, we danced the foxtrot and the two-step and occasionally swing. The new dances sweeping the nation were from Latin America: the tango, rhumba, and mambo. Not until much later did I learn the defiant dances of the 1960s such as the twist.

Fran and I often thought of ourselves as rebellious, but our rebellion didn't go much beyond matters of style. Part of a subgenerational group that has been overlooked in the large body of writings on the generations of recent decades, we straddled the conservative 1950s and the radical 1960s. Born in the late 1930s, we were too young to be part of the Depression generation. But we were too old to belong to the Baby Boom generation, born during the war and its aftermath. (Analysts identify this cohort as the base for both the radicalism of the 1960s and the narcissism of the 1970s.) Our adolescence coincided with the height of the "feminine mystique" based on femininity and domesticity. We experienced it fullblown in our formative years, and its effects have reverberated throughout the rest of our lives. Focusing on the rebellious 1960s, historians have underestimated the continuing influence of the traditionalist 1950s throughout the lives of women such as Fran and me.

Yet the message of the 1950s ultimately influenced each of us in a different way. In fact, even at the time there were differences in our experiences of the decade. Those differences become clear in our reaction to Fran's mother, Lydia. Lydia provided both of us with a space to withstand our high school culture. When a teenager, I thought Fran and I occupied it together. But from our first interviews in Alexandria I learned the extent to which our responses to Fran's mother hadn't been the same. I was wrong to remember Fran as a replica of me. I didn't understand that what then seemed like nuances between us could later turn into a glacial divide.

CHAPTER FOUR

Lydia

Why Fran's parents lived in Inglewood was a mystery to me, although I never asked them the reason. An adolescent absorbed by my peer culture, I was both intrigued by and uninterested in their adult world. Yet I couldn't miss the differences between Fran's parents and mine, and Lydia was so striking a personality that she left an indelible impression on me.

In their late forties when I met them, Lydia and Al still looked slim and fit. Their bodies weren't overweight and sagging, like those of most of the other middle-aged people I knew. They both were tall, with regal bearing; when they entered a room all heads turned. Fran's father, Al, had well-defined features: an aquiline nose, a strong jaw, a cleanshaven face. His whitening hair, thick and wavy, showed no hint of baldness. He kept his athletic body trim by playing tennis; he resembled the Arrow shirt man grown older. Fran's mother, Lydia, had high cheekbones, a skin that tanned easily, and a shock of straight, prematurely white hair, cut shoulder length, without the perm and tight curls I expected on women her age.

I had seen this look and the patrician behavior that often accompanies it in Grace Freeman Howland, the daughter of Daniel Freeman, whom I'd encountered briefly. Like Mrs. Howland, Lydia had a to-the-manner-born air. She had the casual grace of assured social standing and the ability to put others at ease that often seems the birthright of individuals with a privileged upbringing. Like Fran, she stood straight, strode confidently, and moved gracefully. Yet she hadn't become a grande dame. She hadn't taken on the air of dowager authority that aging women of her sort sometimes assume, even if they don't have money. Although she often wore gloves and a hat in keeping with the dictates of fashion, the 1950s code of femininity didn't always constrain her. She wasn't above walking around her house barefoot or flopping down on the floor.

She shopped for clothes at I. Magnin's and Saks Fifth Avenue, upscale Beverly Hills department stores my mother and grandmother never entered, for they would have felt out of place in them. Yet Fran's mother didn't have money; she had savoir faire. She had learned what Lillian and Melba didn't know: that an occasional purchase of expensive clothing can be a longterm investment, while cheap clothes can easily lose their shape and style. In the 1920s she studied for several years at Miss Traphangen's School of Design in New York City, where she learned how to make clothes as well as how to sketch and design them. Lydia often made both Fran's clothing and her own. Often she found designer clothing in second-hand shops, and she refitted and reshaped it in line with the mode and her own sense of style. She had an eye for fabric and cut, and she could spot a well-turned seam.

I thought Lydia and Al should have lived in Pasadena, Beverly Hills, or Hancock Park, the elite residential areas of Los Angeles. In fact, most of their friends lived in these areas. They had made those friends during their undergraduate years at Stanford University. Both had been stars at Stanford: Al a cheerleader and a member of the tennis team; Lydia the daughter of a Stanford professor of classics and a member of an elite sorority, one that guaranteed access to upper-class Los Angeles. Both were exuberant and outgoing; everyone knew them and loved them. As a teenager I wasn't aware, but I later found out, that the sort of Los Angeles families Lydia and Al knew sent their children to Stanford and that its alums had great loyalty to the school and to each other.

Her Los Angeles friends were important to the gregarious Lydia, since in moving to Los Angeles with Al she had left her childhood family and friends behind in Palo Alto, where she had been raised. Occasionally she took me along with Fran to her wealthy friends' homes. I remember those houses as large, with waxed and shining antique furniture—silent witnesses to the maids who cleaned them. Sometimes the interiors were all white, with abstract paintings in the style of Picasso and Miro on the walls and with an ambiance that I later came to associate with a "decorator" look.

(In our interviews Noura told me that those paintings actually were originals by Picasso and Miro.) Compared to my family's house, with its lackadaisical housekeeping, floral rugs, and antimacassars, those houses seemed like museums—or stage settings for luxurious living. I couldn't imagine actual people with real problems living in them.

Lydia fit well in those houses. She could be a cool sophisticate, accomplished at the small talk expected at her wealthy friends' receptions and their cocktail and dinner parties. She could speak like them; she could affect their mannerisms. She always looked understated. She wore simple, classic styles, with beiges and grays—or light blue and lavender—her basic colors, and her only adornment a strand of pearls or a small piece of antique jewelry inherited from her family. She knew that loud clothing and lots of jewelry were unerring signs of being nouveau-riche in her Los Angeles circles. It was the dignity of old wealth that her Stanford friends admired.

In addition to the right clothes and manners, Lydia had an impeccable background, one that was meaningful to her wealthy friends. Through her mother she was a descendant of Pilgrims who sailed on the Mayflower. Through her father, whose last name was Murray, she was descended from the Scottish nobility. The original Murray had been a Moreton who fought for Henry of Normandy in his 1066 conquest of England. When Henry gave Murray a title and land in Scotland, he moved there. In the early eighteenth century a descendant migrated to New York City, and his son, Robert Murray, became a leading New York merchant. Murray Hill, located on Robert's estate in what was then rural Manhattan, was named after him.

Contemporary histories of the American Revolution celebrate Robert's wife, Mary Lindley Murray, for having saved General Putnam's army from British attack when his forces retreated from New York City in the summer of 1776. The British general in pursuit of Putnam passed by Mary's house, and she persuaded him to stop and visit. She knew him well, for her husband was a prominent Loyalist and she had often entertained the general. She plied him with wine and cookies, and she convinced him that the rebel forces had left the vicinity, although she knew they were nearby. But she secretly supported the rebels, and her husband was out of town.

Noura tells the story of Mary Murray with a flourish. It seems to symbolize a family pride in strong and clever women, able to make do in difficult circumstances and with the social grace and persuasive power that men like the British general can't resist. No one in Noura's family seems to know how Mary Murray hid her rebellious sentiments, but it really doesn't matter to family hagiography. What matters is her character: quick witted and independent, she was skilled at getting her way.

Mary's son Robert, like her husband, became a prominent New York City merchant. A philanthropist, he helped found the New York City Hospital, the New York Historical Society, and the Free School System of New York City. Mary's son Lindley became the early nation's greatest grammarian. His book on English usage, the standard source for teachers across two continents throughout the nineteenth century, was published in over two hundred editions. Mary's grandson, Augustus, was Robert's son and Lydia's father. An eminent classicist, trained at the University of Leipzig and at Johns Hopkins, he founded the classics department at Stanford University when the school was little more than a few buildings on Leland Stanford's farm. In his day classics was mainly philology, and it focused on the language and grammar of Greek and Roman texts. Augustus Murray spent his career translating ancient literature, and he was good at it. His translations of Homer, as well as other authors, can be found on library shelves today. For many years they set a standard for work in the field.

As a classical scholar, Murray took sabbaticals in Greece, and one year Lydia and her best friend went with him. They traveled around Europe, visiting churches and museums, monuments and castles. Lydia learned about history and literature, art and architecture at first hand, acquiring the sophistication that travel can produce. No one in Noura's childhood family has forgotten Lydia's story about spending an evening with her father at the home of Henrich Schliemann, the famed archeologist who discovered the ancient city of Troy. During the course of the evening, Schliemann recounted the legends of the Trojan War. He described how Paris of Troy abducted Helen of Sparta, the world's most beautiful woman, enraging her husband Menelaus, and provoking the outbreak of the war. At one point, so Lydia's story went, Schliemann pulled a jeweled necklace out of a chest and had Lydia put it on. It had belonged to Helen of Troy, he told her.

The story is probably apocryphal. Schliemann died before Lydia was born; she couldn't have spent an evening with him. But the tale places Lydia in legend, and it extends the mystique of the Murrays. For now Lydia, the descendant of conquering Normans and pious Mayflower Pilgrims, is identified with a fabled enchantress. To her family Lydia was enchanting, as she was to me. She was beautiful in face and form, with an intense manner that could sweep you up in her enthusiasms. And her daughter, my friend, could do the same.

Lydia's childhood family wasn't wealthy, but the family had enough money for servants and private schooling for Lydia and her five siblings. Lydia's upbringing included art and music lessons, cultivated family conversation, trips to San Francisco for concerts and museums, and dinner parties with other professors and their families and friends from the community. Often the company included Stanford students, for Lydia's father held classes at his home and invited his students to dinner.

Despite her upbringing, Lydia was not a snob. She relished the upperclass social circles to which she had entrée, but she equally liked walking on the beach, reading books, playing the piano, growing flowers, and sketching them. Raised in a university milieu, she had absorbed an academic taste for nonconformity, and she had a bohemian air appropriate to the several years she had studied in New York City.

She was also influenced by turn-of-the-century ideas about art. She believed that art can shape lives as well as feelings and that an ideal beauty exists beyond cultural conventions and critical stances. This conception of art paralleled the vision of the classical world her father's generation of scholars created. Their classical world was a platonic one of serenity and rationality, with white temples and statues representing the purity of truth and beauty fashioned in line with Victorian ideals. Lydia regarded art as an antidote to modern ugliness, while she felt an esthete's drive to produce beauty. Her interest in art wasn't motivated by personal ambition; rather, she relished experience. She applied in her own life the turn-of-the-century aesthetic prescription that the greatest personal fulfillment lies not through any focus on past or future preferment but rather through concentrating on each moment as a sacred experience. The process of sketching a fashion design or mastering a difficult sonata satisfied her more than showing off her accomplishments to an audience.

Fran remembers that Lydia played the piano at home for hours, by herself, with no listeners. Fran's return from school was supposed to be the signal for her to stop her playing and to begin her domestic tasks. But sometimes Fran crept quietly into the house and hid under the piano so that Lydia, absorbed in her playing, wouldn't notice her and so that Fran could lose herself in her mother's music. The sound of the piano gave her a sense of contentment and joy. Lydia never gave a public performance during the years I knew her nor expressed any desire to do so. Despite her considerable ability at Beethoven's sonatas and Chopin's preludes, she always took lessons from a master teacher; and she always tried to improve her technique and to expand her repertoire. But she studied and practiced primarily for her own satisfaction, not for any professional goal. She didn't possess the career ambition that motivated my mother's piano playing and her high school teaching.

Lydia had an intellectual side, and she kept up with the latest knowledge in many cultural areas. She could talk about art and plays, opera and lieder singers, what the symphony was performing. The family subscribed to *Life* magazine and the *Readers' Digest* for Al, who didn't read much, but Lydia took the *New Yorker* for herself. She treasured the magazine, for it kept her in touch with the culture of the city she had come to love as a student there. Matched sets of Shakespeare and Scott, Thackeray and Austen, Dickens and Eliot filled the bookshelves in her living room, along with travel guides and art books—histories, catalogues from museum collections, and large volumes on the work of one artist. She especially collected children's books illustrated by Arthur Rackham, the early twentieth-century artist whose style ranged from lyrical delicacy to burlesque caricature to Art Nouveau sinuosity and who was perhaps best known for his Gothic drawings of gnomes, dwarfs, and fairies.

Lydia also appreciated sports, for there were outstanding athletes in her family. Her father had been a star tennis player as well as the quarterback of the football team as an undergraduate at Haverford College. Her brother Lindley, a tennis player, twice won the U.S. Open at Forest Hills. Another brother, Francis, captained the Stanford track team, and a third brother, Frederick (Feg), won the hurdles in the Olympic games. Al also played tennis and loved sports, and Lydia respected him for it. They went with their friends to football games when Stanford played USC or UCLA in Los Angeles, and they encouraged Fran in her tennis playing.

As soon as I describe one of Lydia's characteristics, I remember another. Absent-minded, she talked all the time, and her sentences trailed behind her as she moved out of earshot. Exuberant, she could be led by her enthusiasms to approach anyone, anywhere. She had a passion for irises, which she both grew and sketched. Whenever she saw a new variety in a garden, she would ask the owner for a piece of root so that she could grow it herself. Always busy, Lydia never seemed downcast. But perhaps she hid depression from me. Well-brought-up women of her class and generation were supposed to exercise such self-control. They were expected to exhibit a cheerful demeanor and a kindly manner, to be Pollyannas to others no matter how despondent they might be.

One evening when I was at Fran's, we rolled back the rugs in her living room so that we could practice dance steps. We had the foolish hope that we might attract partners at one of the Friday night dances after the football games if we improved our technique. But we soon lamented that such improvement wouldn't make any difference. Lydia must have overheard us, for she came into the room, a twinkle in her eye. "Let me show you what we did at your age," she said. She pulled a record from a shelf, put it on the phonograph, and began doing a rousing Charleston, the signature dance of the 1920s. The years fell away, and I saw her as a 1920s flapper, an icon of female emancipation, with her long legs and arms swinging in syncopation. She danced and helped us with steps and rhythms for a while, and then we all fell down on the floor, laughing. We lay there while she told us about dances she had gone to in the 1920s and about men she had dated. She talked about bootleg gin, bobbed hair, speakeasies, and beaver coats.

Her stories were hilarious, and she kept us laughing. We forgot our misery listening to her caricatures of the gawky young men of her youth, for they seemed replicas of the boys we longed for; and that's precisely what she intended. For a moment she gave us freedom from our high school through leading us into the world of imagination that was her kingdom. She taught us how to do the Charleston to perfection. In college I always attracted a crowd around me on a dance floor when I did the antique movements. Although everyone had heard of the dance, few knew how to do it. And when I did the Charleston, I always thought about Lydia and felt grateful for having known her.

Lydia had a conventional side. After she married she gave up any thoughts of a full-time career to devote herself to her husband and family. She liked being a mother. She and Al had four children, two boys and two girls, with Fran by far the youngest. Meeting their needs required a lot of work, and Lydia and Al couldn't afford servants. Nor did Lydia have any adult relatives in Los Angeles who might have helped out. Al's mother, LaVaughn, had lived with them for a time when Fran was a child, and she had taken over some of the chores. But her death when Fran was still young left Lydia with sole responsibility for the household.

Nonetheless, Lydia pampered her family. She cooked and cleaned, helped the children with their homework, and ran errands for them. She even brought breakfast in bed not only to her husband but also to her children—sometimes even to me when I slept over with Fran. In Lydia's later years Fran's sister, Betty, chided her for doing too much for her family. "Mother," she said, "you never were a feminist."

Yet I had a different perception of Lydia. She catered to her family, but she wasn't much of a housekeeper; like my grandmother Lillian she saved time by overlooking dust. I often saw her playing her piano, but I rarely saw her cleaning her house. She grew beautiful flowers and had a proverbial "green thumb," but the corners of her rooms often contained cobwebs and the shelves a layer of dust. When she expected company, she cleaned the house quickly, dusting with whirlwind speed and vacuuming with an old electrolux while listening to a Beethoven symphony or a Mozart concerto on the phonograph. I suppose she appeared disorganized as she moved from one activity to another, leaving projects scattered around the house. But that didn't matter to me. I saw that, like my mother and grandmother, she could do many things at once without missing a beat.

To my young eyes she seemed akin to the other working women I knew. Like my grandmother, she usually earned income. In the 1930s she did fashion drawings for the *Los Angeles Times*: those I've seen are chic renditions of the long-waisted, elegant fashions of that decade, and the models who wear them look like Lydia. When I knew her, she taught piano students in her home, mostly local children; after my mother's death I took lessons from her for a time.

Yet I don't think that she and my mother would have become friends, even if Lydia had dropped in at the Hillcrest house some Sunday after church. Although they were the same age, with the same number of children and with a similar devotion to music, they were too different in style and experience. My mother hadn't been to Europe; she hadn't traveled beyond the West Coast. Before entering USC, she had attended public schools, and she had lived with her family until she married. She was comfortable with the homey women in her bridge club; Lydia would have intimidated her. Lydia and Al were liberal republicans; my mother and father were McCarthyite conservatives.

I suspect Melba had never heard of the *New Yorker*; she read women's magazines such as the *Ladies' Home Journal*. She knew her music, but I doubt she could have identified a Picasso or a Miro. Lydia's many women friends lived mostly outside of Inglewood; she didn't go to the women's luncheons in the city or to the women's group at her church; and she rarely played bridge. Her friends hosted cocktail parties rather than showers. She didn't retreat to a world of women away from men. My mother, quiet and restrained, didn't easily make small talk. Lydia was dramatic; she kept up a continual chatter.

During the time I spent with Lydia and Fran, I remember Lydia speaking of my mother only once, and her comments were critical. She spoke slightingly of my mother's annual piano recital, when Melba would put her students on the stage with a lot of pianos and have them play in unison. "It was tacky," Lydia said, "a travesty of a real musical performance." I knew she was right, for by then I had picked up some of her critical acumen. My mother's piano recitals lacked style and musicianship, but those qualities weren't what those concerts were about. I explained to Lydia my mother's intention that students from impoverished backgrounds would have a chance to dress up, to be in the limelight, and to feel important.

Lydia was chagrined. I had aroused her sympathy for the less privileged families among whom she lived, and she realized that in criticizing my mother she might have hurt me. She apologized profusely, but I wasn't upset. I understood why she didn't like the recitals. No matter how much I mixed up Melba and Lydia, I knew that they lived in different worlds. My mother was part of the Lutheran church and the high school, the familiar places of an Inglewood that gave me security and yet constrained me. Lydia pointed to a magical world outside that city, one of style and sophistication. When I met Grace Howland, I had glimpsed that world. Now I was encountering it head on.

It was an exciting vista for a girl whose family had fallen to pieces and who was struggling with a difficult high school experience. I had come to dislike the Hillcrest house, filled with tragic memories and depressed aging people, but I always felt at peace at Lydia's; I found sanctuary there. By the time I met Fran, her older brothers and sister had left home. It was almost as though I was a member of the family—Fran's sister, Lydia's daughter.

In our interviews, Noura told me the reason why Lydia and Al lived in Inglewood, and it wasn't mysterious at all. They settled there because of Al's job. With a B.A. in history, an outgoing personality, and a handsome face, Al became a stockbroker in Los Angeles after graduating from college. He had grown up in Los Angeles and gone to high school there; he had friends and contacts in the city. Like my father, he was also drawn to the city's booming economy in the 1920s and to the career opportunities opening up for young, ambitious men.

Al's background wasn't as distinguished as Lydia's; he was descended mostly from German peasants. But there were adventurers among his ancestors. His father, like my grandfather Charlie, had gone on the Alaska Gold Rush in 1898, before he became a mining engineer in Montana and New Mexico and then moved to Los Angeles. Al's mother when a young woman left her home in Maine to teach in frontier Montana, joining the pioneering women who brought education to the West. She met Al's father there; once they married, she gave up teaching.

At first Al was successful as a stockbroker. Tall and solid, his gracious, old-fashioned manners inspired confidence in his clients. He was passionate about sports, and like many fervent sports fans, he knew football and baseball statistics—invaluable information for dealing with men in business. A cheerleader at Stanford, he never lost his cheerleading exuberance. That trait was also attractive to clients, although at times he approached problems as issues he could resolve by sheer enthusiasm and that tactic wasn't always wise.

In 1929 the stock market crash wiped out his clients' investments. A man of honor, convinced that he could regain his business success, he determined to repay them himself, even though he wasn't required by law to do so. Paying those debts burdened his family's finances for years. Noura contends today that he was too moral a man for the business world. My family often drew the same conclusion with regard to my pious father's career in advertising.

Because public suspicion of the stock market after the crash made selling shares difficult, Al looked for employment in other areas of sales. Eventually he found a job as a broker in an Inglewood real estate agency. Noura doesn't know why that position was offered to him; it's probable that he found it through Stanford connections. He sold real estate in Inglewood during the remainder of the Depression and throughout World War II, when new home construction in Inglewood opened up sales opportunities. When the war ended, he was in his forties. Even if he had wanted to move closer to the areas in Los Angeles where his and Lydia's friends lived, he faced age discrimination and stayed put.

Al wasn't especially successful as a real estate broker. Like my father he achieved major career success, then lost it, and was never able to regain it. Like my father he was always at work, cultivating clients, making sales, staying late at the office to make phone calls and catch up with paperwork. Yet no matter the difficulties, his enthusiasm carried him along. He never gave up. When I was at Fran's house, he usually wasn't there. We ate in the kitchen without him, and Lydia would often put a plate of food aside to warm up for him when he came home. Noura told me that he sometimes worked seven days a week but that he was so moral and so sympathetic to clients without much money yearning to own their own homes that he reduced his commissions for those with hard luck stories; he sometimes took in-kind payments that never equalled the percentage he was due. Occasionally he came home with produce or poultry, once with an old car.

For her part Lydia coped. Careful to economize, she stretched his income and the small sums she earned to maintain a lifestyle that resembled that of their well-to-do friends. But sometimes she faltered; sometimes their finances were so overburdened that she borrowed from her children's savings to pay overdue bills. Noura remembers one occasion when her mother raided her piggy bank for money to pay the utilities bill so that the electricity wouldn't be turned off. Lydia and Al were proud. I doubt their relatives and friends knew their exact situation.

As much as their financial problems and Al's obsession with work troubled Lydia, she was happy with him. She respected his enthusiasm and kindness and his loyalty and sense of obligation. Their Stanford experience, their mutual friends, and their admiration for each other and their children drew them together. Their marriage was one of opposites, but their union of opposites worked. Soon after Fran married, she wrote to Lydia that her marriage was a model for her. "I keep remembering being young at home in Inglewood, eating in the kitchen, and Daddy coming in, and you throwing your arms about him as if all the work in the day were worth it." That image helped to sustain Fran's own marriage for some time.

After Al's failure as a stockbroker, he and Lydia couldn't afford to live in the elite areas of Los Angeles, near their Stanford friends. But they loved the ocean, and houses in the beach cities were inexpensive to rent. When Al found employment in Inglewood, they settled in Hermosa Beach, twenty minutes from Inglewood by car, and Al commuted to work. Showing properties to clients required considerable driving, and that became difficult with gas rationing during World War II. They moved to Inglewood to reduce his gas consumption.

There they found a large house for their large family. Located to the west of the high school and near the airport, the property had been part of Daniel Freeman's original rancho, in a section of Inglewood sold off as small farm plots. Fran's house was the farmhouse for one of them. By the time Fran's family bought it, developers had acquired its fields and built small houses for dustbowl migrants.

Fran's house still stands in Inglewood today, still in the midst of small stucco houses. When Fran lived there, the area looked working-class tidy, with unoccupied fields all around and a few larger houses here and there. Today it's dilapidated, overtaken by poverty. The San Diego Freeway, built in the late 1950s, is nearby. Its traffic creates a constant hum in the air. Jets from the expanded LAX roar overhead, for the house is now directly under the flight approach path to the airport's runways.

The house has two stories, with wood shingles on its sides still painted barn red and with white trim on the windows and roof edges, just as when Fran lived there. But it doesn't stand out from the small houses around it. Square and boxlike, it seems built for utility not aesthetics. It's a house for a working farm, not a gentleman's estate. It's not a grand house, nothing on the order of the Freeman mansion or my Hillcrest house. But it accommodated Lydia's large family and gave her good-sized rooms for entertaining. With his real estate connections, Al acquired the house at a good price.

No matter its simple design, Fran remembers her childhood house as vividly as I do my own. It was primarily Lydia's space, and her creativity, her ability to turn anything into an adventure, brought it alive. She could weave webs of enchantment, inspiring visions of magical kingdoms and far-off lands. Often left alone as a child, Fran followed her mother's inspiration to create her own world in the large garden in the backyard of the house. Her brothers and sister, much older, led separate lives. Her mother wasn't especially friendly with the parents of the other children on the block, and Fran didn't often play with them. The garden was her special territory. She came to know its flowers, plants, and creatures: birds, spiders, bugs. She gave them names, regarded them as friends, and included them as characters in her fantasy games. In this world of play, long before she went to the Girl Scout camp where we met, she acquired a reverence for nature that never left her.

Lydia encouraged Fran in her fantasies, for Lydia understood the connection between imagination and creativity. Like Fran, Lydia was a youngest child, and she also was much younger than her siblings. Left to play alone, like her daughter she had also become involved with the natural world and had also come to regard it as alive and nurturing. She was influenced by the late Victorian vogue for gardens with children and fanciful creatures in them—as in *Alice in Wonderland* or *The Secret Garden*; it's no wonder she later admired Arthur Rackham's work. When young she played under a large pepper tree in front of her house in Palo Alto. She told Fran that she once sat under the tree and drew page after page of fairies in a sketch pad. But the fairies, she explained, weren't imaginary; she really saw them. So strong was her conviction that Noura believes her to this day.

Next to the matched sets of nineteenth-century English novels on Lydia's bookshelves were volumes of fairy stories and fanciful tales, many illustrated by Rackham. The shelves also contained an edition of the stories compiled by the Grimm brothers, as well as one of the *Tales of the Arabian Nights*, the ancient Middle Eastern folk stories, written down in the eighth century c.e. Scheherazade told these stories to the king of Persia, and they include Alladin and the lamp and Ali Baba and the forty thieves, as well as other tales of genies with fantastic powers imprisoned in bottles and magic carpets that could provide incredible adventures. Muslims relate those stories to spiritual themes and objects within Islam, such as lamps that light the way to Allah and carpets on which the faithful pray.

Fran and I often read those volumes of fairy tales together, and we poured over Lydia's original edition of the *Wizard of Oz*. Both of us dreamt of being Dorothy, swept away from her home in Kansas by a tornado to land in a mysterious, magical kingdom and to experience an exoticism both glamorous and comforting. We loved and feared the witches and the thundering wizard of the Emerald City of Oz, who was only a sleight-of-hand man from a country carnival.

When Noura described her conversion to Islam to me in our interviews many years later, she often cast it in terms of the fairy tales of her childhood, as though the Muslim religion represented a final land of enchantment for her. She mused about her wonderment over places far from familiar childhood spaces, over worlds bearing little similarity to the one of her upbringing, over masjids and minarets, Makkah and the Ka'abah. With all her encouragement of fantasy and fairy stories, Lydia may have sown more seeds of creative imagination in Fran than she bargained for. And Fran's conversion to Islam may have had roots in the turn-of-the-century aestheticism that had so strongly influenced Lydia and had produced its own contemporary converts to the ritual splendor of Catholicism, High Church Anglicanism, and even Islam. I think of T. E. Lawrence, Richard Burton, and Isabella Eberhardt. Those adventurers, all fascinated by Islam, were explorers of the geography of the soul as well as of the earth.

Lydia, the garden, the books—beyond these influences there was still more in Fran's childhood to stimulate her imagination. Al's mother, LaVaughn, who had left her home in Maine to teach school in Montana and who had lived with Fran's family, told my friend stories of her adventuring. Like Lillian telling her stories to me, Fran's grandmother described the thrill of leaving her home to live in a new, uncharted land. Like me, Fran never forgot the stories her grandmother told her.

Lydia furnished her house with antiques inherited from her Murray ancestors: original oil portraits of Lindley Murray and other forebears hung on the walls. Lydia's piano in the living room was a Steinway from the 1880s; it had been a gift from her parents when she was in college. But the upholstery on the living room sofa and chairs was faded, and the oriental rugs on the floors were frayed. If I had been older and more experienced, I might have realized that Lydia's decorating was characterized by the seedy elegance typical of the interior design of descendants of old wealth who haven't inherited family money. In any event, the look of the interior of Fran's childhood house differed greatly from that of mine.

Even the food at Fran's house was different. Like my grandmother, Lydia cooked quickly and efficiently, but her meals were light—rice, salads, broiled chicken or fish. Her results, in contrast to Lillian's, tasted delicious to me. Lydia used a wooden bowl for salads made with lettuce, and that was novel to me, as was her trick of rubbing that bowl with a clove of garlic to flavor those salads. (Lillian didn't make lettuce salads or use garlic.) Lydia made salad dressing by mixing olive oil and wine vinegar, avoiding the bottled variety that ever since then has tasted synthetic to me. She used spices and herbs—oregano, basil, tarragon—that I had never before tasted, for my grandmother flavored her cooking only with salt. Lydia made white sauces with white wine and red sauces with red wine, achieving flavors new and fascinating to me. When I follow her recipe for a casserole of beans, tomato sauce, and sausage, even today it tastes rich and exotic to me. She made this dish for large parties, and I suspect she did so because it was simple and inexpensive and it resembled a French cassoulet, a peasant dish translated into high cuisine. I believe that if I had investigated the source of Lydia's cooking, so novel to me, I might have traced much of it to the French, whose sophisticated cuisine upper-class Americans had adopted a century before.

Lydia influenced me on many levels: intellectually and socially, even in matters of food and taste. She introduced me to a world different from that of my family. She offered me an alternative to working-class Inglewood and the confusions of a family that lived in a mansion, yet killed chickens and used chamberpots, and that death had destroyed. Even though my father worked in advertising and my uncle had been in the film industry, I was a provincial. When Lydia suggested to me in my senior year in high school that I apply to Radcliffe College, I didn't know how to respond. I hadn't heard of Radcliffe, and I certainly didn't know that Harvard University had a women's college attached to it.

Lydia regarded me as Fran's special friend with talent and as a mother-less child who touched her maternal nature. She took me along with Fran to concerts and museums, and I once went on a vacation with the two of them to Carmel, the seaside resort in Northern California. At her parties Lydia occasionally asked me to sing. With an undaunted spirit, she often indulged in hyperbole. Young and impressionable, I was buoyed up by her sympathy and optimism. I believed her when she told me she expected that I would be the star vocal pupil at the Juilliard School of Music in New York City some day and that she would attend my debut in Carnegie Hall when, dressed in cloth of gold, I would conquer the musical world.

She described her years as a student in New York City to Fran and me. She told us that she and a friend shared an apartment in a chaperoned build-ing. She studied fashion design at Miss Traphangen's and piano with a pri-vate teacher, while her friend studied music at Juilliard. She described how they explored the city, went to museums and plays, walked in Central Park, and shopped at the Fifth Avenue stores. She created an enchanted city, just like the one I saw in movies that glamorized New York City—whether those movies featured socialites, aspiring actresses, women exec-utives in fashion or publishing, or Deborah Kerr in *An Affair to Remember* los-ing Cary Grant at the top of the Empire State Building and finding him again. Like other young women of my generation, I dreamt about Green-wich Village, Broadway theaters, and skating in Rockefeller Center. "How am I going to get you two out of Inglewood?" Lydia often ruefully asked Fran and me that question, as she worried about our unhappiness with the high school and feared we might be trapped—by our high school, by Ingle-wood, by provincial conformities we somehow might not be able to escape.

As a wedding present when I married, Lydia gave me a wooden salad bowl and a file box containing cards with recipes for the simple and fast dishes she made. The box looked like any of those boxes containing favorite recipes that were standard Inglewood bridal shower gifts. But there was a difference. In the front of the box Lydia included a card in her own handwriting. "Someone who sings as gloriously as you," she wrote, "should not have to cook meals." I assumed she meant the words to encourage me toward a singing career and to absolve me from being domestic in my later life.

Noura interprets those words differently. She thinks that, as much as Lydia meant them to honor me, they were also an ironic comment on her own situation, "slaving for her family, washing clothes with an old wringer washer in the garage, doing all the cleaning and the driving herself since my father was always at work." In fact, Fran didn't romanticize her mother as I did. Her reaction to Lydia was much more ambivalent than mine.

CHAPTER FIVE

Differences

I always assumed that Fran learned the same lessons from Lydia I learned, lessons about personal fulfillment through music and art, cooking and gardening, marriage and family, and especially through a career. In my interviews with Noura, however, I discovered that my assumptions weren't entirely correct. In those interviews, Noura told me that Lydia emphasized marriage and motherhood to her above any thoughts of a career. "My mother programmed many messages in my head," Noura said, "and one of them was that there never was any question about marrying. She expected that my life would wind up like hers, with my main interest in taking care of my husband and children. My mother assumed that in this marriage my husband would support the family and I wouldn't work."

According to Noura, even if her mother had wanted her to become a professional artist, Lydia didn't have a clear notion of how artists trained for their careers or even how they lived their lives, especially if they were women. "Her message about the possibility of my entering the art world," Noura asserted, "was deeply conflicted and never so clear as the message about domesticity." Mostly, Noura said, Lydia thought of female artists as working in fashion or commercial design, fields she knew about through her own experience in them. Lydia's brother Feg, who won the hurdles in the Olympics, was an accomplished cartoonist whose drawings appeared for decades as the weekly syndicated strip "Seein' Stars." But the professionals in Lydia's family were mostly businessmen and scholars; the occasional female relative who took up art was never more than an amateur. Indeed, Fran's three older siblings, including her sister, all entered careers in business.

Noura remembered that when Lydia talked about eminent painters, her examples were famous males: Michelangelo, da Vinci, Picasso. Fran admired them, but their obsessive devotion to their art and their freedom from housework and childcare didn't provide much guidance to a girl expecting to marry and assume responsibility for a home and family as an adult. As I recall, Lydia's collection of art books didn't contain any volumes on women artists such as Georgia O'Keeffe, whose paintings had taken New York City by storm in the 1920s, when Lydia was living there.

Lydia's dramatic narrative about her years in Manhattan focused on Miss Traphangen's School of Design, not on any art school. She included Juilliard, the renowned music school, because her roommate attended it. Was her life in New York City in fact distant from the world of professional art? Did she know painters, go to art galleries and openings, frequent their studios and their summer communities? Or was that world foreign to her? After all, she came back from her glamorous New York days to marry Al and take up domesticity.

In our interviews, Noura contrasted her youthful attitude toward career women with mine. Noura: "Your mother had a career. You observed a career woman on a daily basis—dressing for work, leaving home for a job, talking about it after hours. I had no idea what a 'career' for a woman meant. My mother played the piano for her own enjoyment; she didn't perform in public. Most of her woman friends didn't have real careers, with the exception of one who was a successful portrait painter, and she did her work at home. And her life, embroiled in a messy, drawn-out divorce and not very happy, was no inspiration to me. The rest of my mother's women friends stayed at home, supported by their husbands. They oversaw their children's lives and managed their households, even when they had servants. If they did any work, it was volunteer and for a philanthropy—the symphony, a favorite hospital, a school. None of them talked about feminism or women's rights—nor did my mother.

"When I dreamt of a future close to nature after the Girl Scout summer camp, I decided to become the *wife* of a forest ranger, not a ranger myself, and the distinction is important. Women weren't employed in that occupation then, and I had no idea that they might ever enter it on their own. My response was to decide on marriage, not to consider taking on the forest service or forging some new career in ecology. When our high school science teacher suggested that we become engineers, I was baffled. I had never met a woman scientist; I didn't connect our high school science courses to any future employment. I was aware that the women who taught us had careers, but I didn't want to be like them, for most seemed unimaginative and conventional. By the time I knew you well, your mother, with her career, wasn't there any more.

"Your frame of reference began with a working mother, and you extended it outward to include adult working women you admired. My frame began with a mother who had mastered domesticity, who took care of her house with what seemed minimum effort, but who was the exclusive caregiver for her children. You saw my mother's working as a variation on your mother's professionalism; I viewed it as a supplement to her real work of caring for a home and children." After Al's mother died when Fran was young, Lydia was home alone with Fran; no other adult woman in the house moderated Lydia's influence or provided a different example. Fran didn't encounter families in which individuals other than mothers raised children. Even Lydia's wealthy friends with servants oversaw their children's lives. There weren't any daycare centers in Inglewood, and when Fran met my caretakers—Lillian and Lena—they were old and embittered and hardly positive models.

I have come to realize that variations in class and family attitudes shaped Fran and me differently, making what was obvious to me about women and work obscure to Fran. Yet it has been difficult for me to accept the truth of Noura's memory that Lydia stressed domesticity as inevitable for women. For that emphasis doesn't fit with my memories of Lydia as the replacement for my own mother and as a working woman connected to a privileged upper-class world. I remember only one occasion when, in my presence, Lydia referred to homemaking as a female priority. One evening, after we had finished eating dinner, Fran began to wash the dishes, taking over a task that Lydia usually did. Coming into the kitchen, Lydia saw what Fran was doing, and she gently took the plate her daughter was holding out of her hands. She told us to go into the living room and do our homework; she would clean up. Then she said to Fran, her voice still ringing in my ears: "Once you are married you will have years of washing dishes. It is time to enjoy your childhood freedom while you can." Perhaps she expressed such sentiments many times in my presence, for Fran remembers them as her mother's main conviction. But I remember her stating such an opinion only once. It wasn't the message I chose to hear from her—or to remember.

According to Noura, Lydia felt guilty that she couldn't provide her children with the same privileged upbringing she'd had, with servants to take care of everyday needs, trips abroad, and a private school education. No matter how hard it was on her, Lydia tried to give them a similar upbringing, serving herself as both their servant and their mentor. Her reproving Fran for doing the dishes may not have indicated any affection for domesticity on her part but rather a resigned acceptance of her own fate: living with a man she loved who wasn't a financial success; reconciling herself to putting the best face on genteel poverty. Like the note she enclosed with her wedding gift to me, the reproof may have been an ironic comment on her own life as well as a subtle teaching for Fran, a teaching as much about social class as about gender. Lydia hoped Fran would marry a man of means. But she might not, and she needed to be prepared for the possibility that she, like Lydia, might have to take on many household tasks in later life.

Lydia didn't teach Fran how to cook or clean, and she didn't expect Fran to help her with household chores. After Lydia married she taught herself how to manage a home, and she expected her daughter to do the same. Lillian hadn't taught Melba domestic skills; my mother taught them to herself after she married. And that would be the case for me, as for Fran. We play "house" when we are children, fascinated by maternal authority, trying it on in miniature. But adolescent girls from indulgent families often don't pay much attention to housekeeping until they marry and establish their own homes, which they control.

Yet I remain perplexed by Noura's recollections of her mother's expectations for her. I assumed that Lydia regarded Fran as the most talented of her four children, as a daughter whose genius shouldn't be consumed by marriage. Lydia encouraged me in fantasies about a debut in Carnegie Hall, and I had similar fantasies about Fran. I envisioned openings of shows of her work in New York City and marriage to a wealthy husband who would adore her and humor her every whim. I thought Lydia had similar fantasies. Sometimes I worried that my dreams of career success for myself were foolish, that my shyness made success impossible for me. But Fran was outgoing and articulate, daunted by no one. In my estimation, she couldn't be constrained by normal conventions. When I thought about the matter, I concluded that women who stayed home and raised children were nothing like Fran: they were even more shy and retiring than me. Women of courage and conviction like Fran had careers.

Yet those fantasies about Fran's future may have been solely mine and not Lydia's. She may have been proud of her daughter's achievements simply for their own sake and not as a prelude to a career. Perhaps I projected my family's driving ambition onto Lydia and assumed that she had dreams for Fran's future when she didn't. Perhaps Lydia felt freer to indulge my fantasies because she wasn't my real mother and because, pitying me, she wanted to help me overcome my shyness and find some consolation for the deaths in my family. Perhaps she realized that all that existed for me from that family were those dreams. Perhaps on some level she responded to my need for her to be Melba, and thus she gave me advice she thought my mother would have given. Or did I simply take portions of who she was and construct her in my memory as the woman I wanted her to be?

Whatever Lydia's intentions, Fran's letters to her during college reveal the complexities in their relationship. In a letter from Paris, when Fran was on a semester abroad program, she displayed the range of her responses to her mother. She appealed to Lydia's aesthetic sensibility and love of adventure, while showing her own emotionality, by describing the shapes and colors of flowers she had seen. "Paris is color, color, color," she wrote. "Geraniums, red and orange, like the color of flourescent paint, the color that cannot be seen in definite outlines but jumps and skips before your eyes and begs, challenges to be transformed into a picture. It is all boiling in me so much that I think I'll explode with colors and ideas." In the same letter she linked herself to the practical side of her mother, a woman who had raised four children almost single-handedly; she told Lydia that she was visiting arts schools in Paris to see if she might want to study at one of them after college. On her way home from Europe, she stopped in New York City, and she wrote her mother that she intended to visit Columbia University to find out about its graduate program in art.

The letters contain many passages describing Fran's tours of monuments and art museums and her experiences of meeting people, particularly men. Fran doesn't mention marriage in these letters. I presume that both she and Lydia took that eventuality so much for granted that Fran didn't need to refer to it.

I wasn't always with Lydia and Fran. On weekday evenings I was mostly at home. In fact, Fran and I carried on much of our friendship over the telephone. Like most adolescents, then as now, we phoned each other regularly when apart, talking for hours at a stretch. Our houses were on opposite sides of Inglewood, nearly ten miles distant. Bus service was spotty, and we never used it anyway. Until senior year in high school, when we were old enough to obtain driver's licenses, we couldn't borrow our families' cars and go where we wanted. In addition, Lillian posed an obstacle to our friendship. She was jealous of my closeness to Fran and my admiration for Lydia, and she feared, with some justification, that Lydia's sophistication would lure me away from my family and from Inglewood, drive me away from Lutheranism and, her imagination overheating into realms of the ridiculous, propel me toward some feared sexual misdeed. She didn't like Fran's sense of adventure or the way I followed her wherever she led. My grandmother didn't attempt to end our friendship, but she tried to keep me at home.

Disliking Lillian's control and unhappy in the Hillcrest house, I idealized Fran's family. I pictured them as out of a storybook romance, in a reverse mirror image of my devastated family. I envied Fran for having Lydia as a mother; I thought Fran had a perfect life. I discerned none of her own unhappiness. For her part, schooled in her family's tradition of optimism and self-control and with a typical adolescent drive to maintain the fiction of personal perfection, she hid her discontents from me. In our interviews, she finally shared those dissatisfactions with me when I reappeared in her life some forty years later, offering the solace and stimulus of a confessional.

Sometimes she resented her brothers and sister, Noura told me. For their older ages allowed them adult privileges which she wanted and was too young to have. With different interests, they were often unwilling to play with her. But her envy, in contrast to mine, wasn't intense. Like my younger brother, she was the fourth child in birth order and the baby of the family. Her older siblings indulged her as much as they overlooked her.

A sensitive child who wanted to please, Fran felt responsibility for her family's financial difficulties; thus she vividly remembers Lydia borrowing money from her piggybank. She translated those feelings of obligation into a drive to achieve—in art, tennis, grades in school. Her parents heightened this drive with their expectation that she would attend Stanford. That university, central to Lydia's childhood in Palo Alto, where her father had been a professor and she and Al had met and made lifelong friends, was a paradise to them. No matter the difficulties of their life in Inglewood and no matter their financial problems, as long as the children went to Stanford their futures would be assured—and Lydia's and Al's lives would be justified. "My mother and father were obsessed with Stanford," Noura told me. "From my earliest days I felt compelled to attend that university; there simply wasn't any other choice. And because my family had little money, I also knew I had to win full scholarship support." The pressure on Fran to succeed increased when her older sister and the younger of her two brothers didn't adjust to Stanford and left after their freshman year. More than ever Fran felt she had to uphold the family honor.

For professional art training, Stanford probably wasn't the best school for Fran. She could study drawing and painting there, but its art professors preferred the realist style of the 1930s over the abstract expressionism in vogue. The innovative art teachers in California, the ones who might have challenged Fran toward new directions, taught at art schools: Cal Arts in Los Angeles and the California School of Fine Arts in San Francisco. Yet Lydia had attended Stanford and then design school, and Fran could do the same. Fran had internalized her family's goals: she felt only pride in going to Stanford.

Her disaffections lay elsewhere: the vague rivalry with her siblings and her distress over family finances. Moreover, she was ambivalent about Lydia's wealthy friends. That confession of Noura's in our interviews startled me, for when we were teenagers she often spoke with enthusiasm to me about those elite people; she didn't hint that they might have been a problem for her. I assumed that she basked in their attention and felt part of their society. But my assumption was only partly correct. While Lydia's friends accepted Fran, their children weren't certain about her. Sometimes they were friendly and confiding, sometimes haughty and teasing. Fran attended neither their private schools nor their after school dancing classes, which were key institutions for them. She couldn't gossip about school cliques with them; she wasn't acquainted with the intricacies of their friendships. They looked down on her for living in Inglewood and attending a public school. As adolescents, they weren't as charitable as their parents. Loyal to Lydia and Al, those parents invited Fran to their daughters' debutante parties. But Fran wasn't a debutante, and she felt excluded. She couldn't hide the reality that her parents didn't have the money to pay for the dresses and parties required to be a debutante. In our interviews Noura told me bluntly: "I was from the wrong side of the tracks."

Perhaps I should have guessed Fran's problem. For I met the son of one of Lydia's friends at a party she gave, and he showed an interest in me. Later that night we walked on the beach; he promised to call me and never did. Eventually Lydia told me sadly that he had dropped me because I came from Inglewood. Our city, with its working-class population, was simply too far removed from his world; he would have been embarrassed to tell his family and friends he was dating me. (His rejection was a blow to my self-pride that I later countered in marrying an Easterner with Ivy League credentials.) Fran, on the other hand, became seriously involved with the son of another one of Lydia's wealthy friends during the summer before our senior year. That serious romance seemed proof to me that Lydia's set fully accepted my friend. Her parents' background, I assumed, absolved her from the stigma of living in Inglewood.

During the school year Fran's boyfriend attended the elite Lawrenceville Academy near Princeton, New Jersey. I met him once or twice; he had a worldly air absent in Inglewood boys. He wrote Fran letters and sent her his school pin. What more could a girl from Inglewood want? The relationship, however, was flawed; for he couldn't sustain intimacy. He wooed Fran to the point of serious commitment and then pulled away, confusing and hurting her. He repeated the cycle several times more during their first years at Stanford, which they both attended, until she managed to break with him.

Lydia's wealthy friends both attracted and repelled Fran. She both liked being with them and then retreating from them into our high school world, where she could take pride in achievements which bolstered her sense of self-worth. Seeming to follow Lydia's wishes, she even married the son of Stanford alums on the periphery of her parents' wealthy circle. (Noura insists that he was as alienated from that world as she and that alienation was part of his attraction to her.) Then, midway through her Stanford years she began to develop, as she puts it, her own obsession: to live her own life, to shape her own destiny.

Much of that obsession resulted from her attitude toward her mother. On one level she adored Lydia, loving her for the same compelling qualities that I loved her for. Yet sometimes, Noura confessed in our interviews, she found Lydia overpowering; sometimes she felt that her mother prevented her from having a life of her own. Although Fran liked learning about art and literature from Lydia and appreciated the clothes Lydia made, the problem was that her mother seemed to do everything for her. By acting as Fran's servant, by doing too much for her, Lydia may have

erased too many boundaries between herself and Fran and in effect controlled her. Fran's identification with Lydia went beyond matters of domesticity. It extended into family relationships and values I was only vaguely
aware of at the time.

Noura: "When I fell in love with my first husband in college, I couldn't
betray my parents' values by only having an affair with him; I had to marry
him. Once we were married, I wanted children; my mother and father had
their first child soon after they married. Once I had children, I felt guilty
if I didn't stay home to raise them, as my mother had. The pattern was there
for me to follow, and I followed it. I lived my mother's life until I was
thirty; then I wanted to live my own life." To assert independence in her
life was one of her motivations for moving to Lama. The New Mexico community, without pretensions to wealth or status, was the opposite of Lydia's
social world.

Fran speaks about her mother today with a mixture of love and sadness.
Together we laugh about our mutual dream as adolescents to escape Inglewood and about how intensely we both felt the longing to leave. Lydia
placed at least that idea firmly in both of our heads. But Fran's longing to
depart included not only the desire to flee the city's provincialism; it also
included the desire to leave her mother.

In 1985, on Lydia's eightieth birthday, Noura wrote her mother an elo-
quent letter celebrating their relationship. In the letter Noura describes the
tree in Palo Alto where Lydia saw and sketched fairies. She remembers hiding under the piano so that her mother wouldn't stop playing. She details
colors and scents that remind her of Lydia. "Here I am nearing fifty," Noura
writes, "and at the smell of an iris or fresh-cut grass, at the sight of certain
shades of blue and lavender, I am five or six or seven again and you are there
inside me." "You are there inside me:" that is the telling phrase, for it indicates that Noura couldn't eliminate her sense of being an extension of her
mother. She asks for forgiveness from Lydia for "so many absences and so
much silence."

Despite the affection in the letter, Noura didn't travel to Los Angeles
for her mother's milestone birthday; she addressed the letter from a hotel
room in Washington, D.C., where she was staying on a stopover during one
of her journeys in the 1980s to the Middle East on behalf of Dar-al Islam.
Noura's absence from an important family gathering wasn't unusual: after
Fran left Inglewood for Stanford, she rarely returned. During her years
away, Fran wrote her mother so infrequently that Lydia sometimes sent her

stamped, self-addressed postcards on which to write messages. Fran had to absent herself that completely to be her own person; correspondence was futile, since she didn't know what to write. As she put it in the 1985 birthday letter: "It may sound foolish to say I forget to remember the one closest inside to my own soul."

In fact, forgetting, both necessary and impossible, grew out of her need for a separation she couldn't achieve. No matter how hard she tried, she couldn't distance herself completely from her mother. To this day, Noura tells me, she hasn't found a style of dress she considers completely her own. Despite several rebellions against her mother's subdued taste, Lydia hovers over her. Lydia had such style, such expertise in fashion, that Fran sought out her judgment and deferred to it. Fran felt merged with her mother to the point that she had to reject that merger to be her own person, but she couldn't help but feel guilt over her rejection of the woman she loved.

To posit that Fran's taking up Islam resulted from her need for distance from her mother takes this analysis too far. I have suggested already that Fran's radical change in belief was partly an outgrowth of her mother's attitude toward life. For her part, Lydia had difficulty understanding Fran's move to Lama and her profession of Islam. Lydia often wrote Fran, but she rarely visited her at either Lama or Abiquiu. Yet during the major crises in Fran's life, during her divorce and her remarriage, when many of her friends and family turned against her, Lydia supported her. Noura remembers with gratitude and relief Lydia's ability to put her love for her above any personal expectations: "I'm glad you've finally found what you were looking for." Noura remembers that statement as her mother's final judgment on her life.

Lydia was part of Fran—the aestheticism, the sophistication, and the domesticity—my friend couldn't escape what she had internalized. Nor did she really want to. My romanticization of Fran's family isn't inaccurate. Her mother did create a magical childhood world out of books, nature, and imagination. Fran respected her for it. No matter how far she has traveled and how much she has changed, Fran speaks of her mother with great love and admiration.

Fran may have felt the stigma of being from the wrong side of the tracks, of coming from Inglewood, but she was proud of her patrician heritage. Her Murray background gave her the courage to make her radical break and to move to a commune in New Mexico. Unlike me, she didn't feel she had to work to attain high status. It was hers by birthright. Akin to those reformers in the American past whose social standing freed them to lead unconventional lives, Fran was in the tradition of Elizabeth Cady Stanton rejecting her Livingston forebears to become a woman's rights agitator; or Eleanor Roosevelt turning her back on the Roosevelt tradition of dutiful wives to take up political causes; or Mabel Dodge Luhan spurning the Buffalo, New York, bourgeoisie to support artists and radicals and to move to Taos, New Mexico. Fran could reject a regular path to achievement because her personal lexicon, her family history, already included it.

The descendant of farmers and workers still attached to their ethnicity, I had to marry a man of elite background and become a successful professional to fulfill my family's overreaching ambition. The drive for achievement was my birthright, handed to me by a family whose members for several generations had fallen short of the mark. Fran's motivations could be more disinterested. She could renounce status for worthier goals when her search for the American Dream through conventional channels failed to bring her contentment. For a long time, I couldn't give up that dream. I couldn't release it until, like Fran, I had achieved it. Then I might consider a different path.

Although I remember the complexities of Lydia, I paid little attention to one of her central traits. For she was deeply pious, and she expressed that piety in the Episcopal church across the alley from my Hillcrest house.

I knew Fran's family attended that church, but neither Fran nor Lydia talked about it much around me. Immersed in our high school culture, Fran and I didn't discuss the subject of religion. Realizing how devout my family was and probably sensing that Lillian resented my friendship with Fran, Lydia was reluctant to say anything that might undermine my Lutheranism or cause Lillian to intervene in my friendship with her daughter. Yet even if she had seriously discussed the subject of religion with me, I would have paid little attention. I still went to Sunday services at our Lutheran church to please my family, but deep inside I was angry with my family for their belief in this religion, with its God who had destroyed my childhood with no reason. I might still imagine visitations of God and his heavenly hosts, but my rational self wasn't interested in religion. I thought Fran felt the same.

Besides, Lydia and Al appeared secular to me. They didn't quote from the Bible in their conversation, as my father and grandmother continually did. Their living room didn't contain devotional tracts or a portrait of Jesus. When I spent the night at Fran's house, they didn't hold family devotions, and we didn't pray before going to bed. Fran went to a public grammar school, not a parochial one. Fran's family appeared non-religious to me since what I considered the objects and practices of true piety were absent from their household.

Lydia told me that she had been raised a Quaker and that the Murrays, her ancestors, had long professed that faith. Lydia's forbear Mary Murray had even converted her husband, Robert, to Quakerism. Mary's sons, Robert and Lindley, were both well-known Quakers in New York City. Augustus Murray was a leader in the Society of Friends in Palo Alto; he held Quaker meetings in his house. Herbert Hoover, a devout Quaker, was a student of Murray's at Stanford and a lifelong friend. When Hoover was elected President, he persuaded Murray to move to Washington, D.C., to become the leader of his Quaker church.

Before dinner at Lydia's house, we often observed a few minutes of silence. This was the Quaker form of prayer, Lydia told me. She sometimes talked to me about the religion of her childhood. I found her descriptions strange, for the faith she depicted bore little resemblance to my Lutheranism. She described church services with neither a minister nor a sermon, only a leader who called the meeting together and oversaw it. There were no hymns, no liturgy, no Lord's Prayer, and no Communion. The meetings consisted only of silent meditation until individuals were moved to speak about their spiritual experiences.

To me the Quaker service sounded even more tiresome than our Lutheran one. At least we sang hymns and listened to a choir, thus alleviating the boredom of our minister droning on about sin and damnation. When I admitted my negative reaction to Lydia, she defended the Quaker service she so enjoyed. "You don't get bored in those meetings, even though nothing is happening," she contended. "You feel great elation in being alone with your thoughts, together with like-minded people, in a spiritual setting." She spoke of the Quaker belief that everyone possesses an "inner light" which reflects the sanctity of God. Within the devout, she told me, the "inner light" burns brightly, prompting them to live Christian lives, to do good works, and to rise from among the silent group on Sundays to speak when moved by the spirit of God within them. She described the Quaker meeting with such enthusiasm that I asked her why her family went to an Episcopal church rather than a Quaker meeting house. The main reason, she explained, was that there wasn't a meeting house in Inglewood—or anywhere nearby. Besides, Al had been raised an Episcopalian, and she didn't mind attending his church. Unlike Mary Murray, she didn't try to convert her husband to the Society of Friends.

Sometimes a quiet mood would come over her, when her normal flow of conversation would stop. She would stare into space, with a haunting smile on her face. I didn't connect that mood with religion, just as I discounted Fran's similar dreamy silences when she pointed to flowers or clouds as though they had special meaning. Since Lydia's descriptions of Quakerism were often set in a distant past, I didn't connect them to her present. I didn't realize that she was still deeply religious.

Lydia and Fran didn't discuss their Episcopal faith with me. I assumed that the Inglewood church was Al's church and that they went there to please him and to meet the social elites that I imagined attended that church. In our interviews, however, Noura explained that their involvement wasn't a social gesture. Al brought them there because, no less than Lydia, he was deeply religious. Raised an Episcopalian, he remained devoted to that faith throughout his life.

Noura's descriptions of her father in our interviews in Alexandria perplexed me. I never discerned that she was close to him. I had no relationship with him; I rarely spoke to him. When I was with Lydia and Fran, he was almost never present. Identifying with Fran, I assumed that her father, like mine, didn't play much of a role in her life. But I was wrong. Al was a pillar of that Episcopal church. He ushered in Sunday services and served on the vestry. But his real acclaim came from reading the lesson in those Sunday services, for he was a superb reader. Fran has never forgotten the passion in his face when he read the Sunday Bible passages, and she relates that passion to his piety. In later letters to him, she wrote of her respect for his Christlike life and his indifference to material possessions. That's what really matters to her, she wrote him, not that he didn't win high professional status or make a lot of money.

Out of all that Noura has told me about herself and her family, out of all those feelings and relationships which I either didn't perceive at the time or don't remember, her recollections of her family religion have puzzled me the most. I didn't know that as a child Fran had been as religious as I. She studied the Bible and the Episcopal *Book of Common Prayer*; at the age of twelve she was publicly confirmed in a rite similar to mine.

To better understand this information, I visited that Episcopal church in Inglewood. Perhaps there, I thought, I might find some visual clue to help me figure out more fully the childhood influences on my friend. As I entered the nave of the church, I realized with a shock that I had never before been inside the church. During all the years I lived in the house on Hillcrest, during all the times I climbed the tree in the church's courtyard with my sister and brother, I had never entered the building. Now approaching its central space, I was overwhelmed by its unexpected grandeur. The exterior of the church is simple, but the interior is flamboyant. Gothic in design, with a lofty, wood-beamed ceiling, its lines lift one's eyes upward. An arched motif extends throughout the church—in the shape of the stained glass windows and the decoration of the pulpit, even in the spires of gold above the heads of a sculpted Christ and his archangels who dominate a huge screen on the wall behind the far altar. I knew that Grace Freeman Howland had provided the funds to build this church, but I didn't know that she had donated enough money to build a small Gothic masterpiece.

Christ is everywhere in the church—in the nave intersected by the narthex, representing the cross on which Christ was crucified, and in large sculpted scenes on the walls, between the stained glass windows. The scenes depict the twelve "stations of the cross." Sculpted in alabaster and painted in light pastels—pinks and blues mostly—they glow with warmth. A mosaic of tiny gold tiles stands behind each scene, sanctifying it. The stations move from Christ taking the cross on his shoulders, through his dropping it several times, with the mythic Veronica and others helping him pick it up, to his crucifixion. The scenes point to the altar screen, which depicts Christ's resurrection. Had I been in Fran's place, I would have spent Sunday after Sunday looking at those scenes, wondering about them, making up fantasies about them. And, Noura told me, that's precisely what she did.

Then there's the Episcopal service, filled with pageantry. Garbed in sumptuous robes, carrying a gold cross and other religious objects, the priests and their assistants march down the aisle at the beginning and end of the service. Also robed, the members of the choir follow them, to sit in pews behind the pulpit. They increase the size of the procession, giving it even more a dramatic, medieval look. Such elaborate ceremony in the Episcopal service dated from the mid-nineteenth century, when a "high church" faction moved Anglicanism closer to its Catholic roots. Thus the Gothic architecture, the processions, the sumptuous costumes.

What was Lydia's reaction to this church? How did she reconcile

Quaker simplicity with Anglican ornamentation? I don't think she actually had difficulty blending the two. Her love of European architecture with its medieval castles and Gothic churches helped, as did her admiration for the art nouveau illustrations of Arthur Rackham, with their sinuosity and the medieval cast of his figures. As the daughter of a Quaker leader, Lydia knew about periodic divisions in Quakerism between groups who wanted less decoration and ritual and others who wanted more.

In fact, Augustus Murray's faith was ecumenical and mystical. His last publication, which appeared in 1934 soon after he became the leader of Herbert Hoover's church in Washington, D.C., was an edition of the poetry of John Greenleaf Whittier, the nineteenth-century Quaker poet and abolitionist. In his introduction to the volume, Murray acknowledges that Whittier's talent was minor. The "spiritual quality" of Whittier's work drew him to the Quaker poet, Murray explains, as well as the poet's presentation of his ideas "in terms of the heart rather than in terms of the intellect." Murray asserts that Whittier's writing is cast "in a vein of pure mystical religion."

Anglicanism is infused with spirituality. Its Sunday service seems to me to stop just short of open mysticism. It verges on issuing an invitation to translate piety into close communion with the divine. Lydia's "inner light" could burn brightly in that resplendent Episcopal church; she could honor her family's Quakerism there. In their turn, the sumptuous service and elaborate ornamentation of that exotic church profoundly influenced Fran.

Episcopalianism has similarities to Lutheranism, for both were originating Reformation theologies. Both stress sin and salvation; both emphasize the Lord's Prayer. Both have two sacraments, Baptism and Communion, rather than seven, as in Catholicism. But where my Lutheranism focused on God the father and his awful decrees, Fran's Episcopalianism focused on the grace of Christ. My church celebrated Communion once a month. Episcopalians celebrate the rite every Sunday, as the service enacts through Christ's suffering, death, and resurrection the expected passage of his penitent believers from worldly involvement to heavenly grace.

My church building was spare and stark white, with hard wooden pews on a concrete floor and no decoration on the walls. The bareness of that church symbolized the austerity of Missouri Synod Lutheranism, no seedbed for mysticism. When my final apostasy happened in college, fierce and conclusive, it matched the unyielding fundamentalism of my early faith. Fran's falling away from Christianity was less dramatic. It was more like an interlude than a divorce, with her spirituality and her belief in the existence of the divinity left largely intact.

Shortly before she left for Lama, she wrote her father about her attitude toward Christianity. "I have never lost faith in God," she wrote Al, "and I believe very much in the truth of Christ's life and work. I simply don't agree with some of the man-made structures and dogmas that have gone into formalized Christianity." On Noura's desk, close at hand, lie a copy of the Qur'an and a string of prayer beads. Muslims use prayer beads as Catholics use the rosary. As they finger each bead, they recite the name of Allah, while Catholics recite phrases centering around the name of the Virgin Mary. Catholicism borrowed the beads and the practice from Islam. The shelf above Fran's desk contains the copy of the Episcopal *Book of Common Prayer* she used in her childhood.

When I left Los Angeles for New York City in 1960, I drifted away from Lydia, as I would from Fran. Much later, when I lived in Washington, D.C., in the late 1970s, teaching in one of the temporary academic appointments that occupied so many years of my professional life, I wrote Lydia a letter. I wanted her to know what had become of me and how much she had influenced me. I wanted to thank her for that influence. I told her of my successes and of the books I'd written; I explained how I hoped eventually to secure a permanent academic position, as her father had. I told her that she had drawn out of my system the venom produced by the deaths in my family and that she had helped me to become much stronger. But the letter was returned, marked address unknown. I grieved for having lost her. I felt guilty for not having written her sooner, for simply having let time and a new life far from Los Angeles intervene. I learned later that she was still alive when I wrote that letter but that she was a victim of mental deterioration, with little memory. Even if my letter had reached her, my gesture would have been futile.

But Lydia wasn't my mother; I never rebelled against her. I've learned many lessons from Lydia and Fran. One is about how we all construct differing childhood memories, shaping them as scenes in our heads validating the person we think we are, while we mold others in those memories to conform to our needs. Another lesson is about the complexities of adult relationships between mothers and daughters. If my mother had lived, would my life have become a study in rebellion, as was Fran's? Or as much as I conformed to my mother's expectations, did I reject them in my own way?

Lydia inspired me to look beyond Inglewood and to break through the boundaries of the space which defined my childhood world. Her house pointed to the airport: that place of travel was only ten miles from the cemetery and the high school, but to my child's eyes it had seemed a continent away. I always loved that airport. On high school and college dates, when I was older, a favorite destination of mine was its observation deck. There I could watch the planes taking off and landing; I could fantasize about where I might fly some day, far away from my home city.

Not far from Fran's house, in a dirt strip along the highway, one could park a car to watch the silvery chariots as they taxied down the runway and slowly gathered speed, lifting into the air at the edge of the highway and roaring overhead. I loved to watch those liftoffs. It thrilled me to hear the roar of the engines and to see a plane's nose pointed upward and its wings spread back, like a huge bird taking flight, a cleansed consciousness being born and flying away. I've always loved flying, for I feel liberated in the air. My only phobia is that I may miss the plane; before any flight, I always get to the airport hours early.

Fran's feeling about that airport, I recently discovered, was similar to mine. "I used to go to the airport with the family to see off the friends going to Hawaii or South America or New York," Noura told me. "Of course, given our financial situation, we never went until later years when my brothers began to fly here and there. To me the airport was a place for dreaming. After I got my driver's license I used to go out there alone and imagine possibilities. The sky was the limit at that point. I thought anything could happen in the future, and the truth is that it did."

III

PASSAGES
1956–1982

CHAPTER SIX

Alma Mater
1956–1960

High school friendships, formed at the height of adolescent intensity and insecurity, are often fragile. Viewed from the vantage of college maturity and its new relationships, they can seem outdated relics of the past. I hesitate to suggest that Fran and I didn't remain close during the four years we spent at universities in different parts of California—she at Stanford and I at UCLA—but we lost the intensity of togetherness. That had already started to happen toward the end of high school, when I began to resent her successes and she began to focus on Stanford. It continued as she left Los Angeles and I stayed behind, part of a past she was abandoning. It increased as we found other intellectual and artistic women as friends in college, dated men the other didn't know, and underwent our socializations to college life, no less powerful than that of high school.

Perhaps if Fran had come back to Inglewood more often for visits, we might have continued on as if nothing had changed. But she often spent holidays with friends or stayed in Palo Alto, and she spent one summer in Europe. Then Lydia and Al sold their house in Inglewood and moved to one of the beach cities, and I didn't see them much. With Fran gone, Lydia didn't invite me over. I felt an occasional pang of regret, but my relationship with her was always carried on through Fran. I would have felt awkward alone with her. Anyway, she was just as powerful a presence in my imagination as in real life. Nor did I visit Fran at Stanford. I went there once and, not knowing Fran's friends or understanding their conversation, I was uncomfortable. I suppose I might have tried to attend Stanford, but Lillian and Harry insisted that I remain at home and go to UCLA, which was tuition-free. I wasn't yet independent enough to defy them and, to be perfectly honest, I wanted some space from Fran.

Friendships, like marriages, are rarely simple. Beneath my desire for independence from Fran and my juvenile resentment of her lay an image of her as perfect. Over the years other women would fascinate me with sensitivity, intelligence, and offbeat ways enough to replace her in my affections; but none could quite match her particular combination of qualities. I could go for years without thinking of her and then a grin, or someone's stride, or a turn of phrase, would bring memories of her flooding back. I would fleetingly grasp how profoundly she had influenced me in the immediate years after my family disasters. I would realize for a moment how she lived in my unconscious mind as the person I wanted to be.

Fran also had lingering memories of me, as well as a deep and sometimes hidden affection for a friendship, so intertwined with her mother, which had once seemed without limits. When we occasionally met during our college years, we could easily re-create the old intensity. (We still can, today.) We continued to fantasize about living together in New York City after graduation. In one of our many conversations over the past several years, Noura told me that if she hadn't married she probably would have gone off with me to Manhattan. Perhaps she would have: she did write her mother when on a stopover in New York City returning from her college semester abroad program that she was planning to visit Columbia University to find out about its art program. Yet I suspect men would have come between us no matter what we did. At the very least, our fantasies of glamorous independence together in New York City sustained our friendship for some time.

In the 1950s UCLA was large and bureaucratic, and most of its students lived at home and commuted to the campus. I knew that was the situation before I enrolled, but the prospect of entering an environment that promised real learning as well as a new social life dampened my doubts. My father bought me an old used car for my transportation; I was proud of that car for it conferred a new adult status on me. But I didn't realize how alienating living away from college would be. Nor did I anticipate how isolated I would feel even at school, as I confronted large impersonal classes and remote professors, pressured toward publication by a university intent on boosting its national reputation. I wasn't pleased that most of my courses were lecture classes and that graduate assistants provided most of the attention I received, but I won good grades and words of praise written on exams and essays. Those achievements quieted my discontent. I sometimes worried because I never spoke in my classes, but no one seemed to mind. When I applied to graduate school my senior year, I managed to find professors willing to write me letters of recommendation.

After the intellectual wasteland of my high school, the erudition of my professors and the breadth of reading they assigned amazed me. Before I entered UCLA, I had never heard of Plato, Augustine, Rousseau, or Marx. I had little knowledge of political ideologies, the history of music and art, or theories of human development. It seemed as though I was learning a powerful language to enter a new world, with the professors its gatekeepers and the good grades I received my ticket of admission.

The curriculum I studied at UCLA was mostly conservative. The sense of national superiority generated by World War II in addition to the anticommunism of those years dampened radical criticism in general and influenced my professors toward centrism and cynicism. I entered UCLA soon after the loyalty oath controversy had occurred. Spurred on by McCarthyite repression, the California state legislature suddenly demanded that the professors in the University of California system sign an oath pledging loyalty to the U.S. government and disavowing any connection to communism. Although the professors who were fired for refusing to sign were eventually reinstated, this incursion on civil liberties in the name of national security polarized the university and left professors fearful about their jobs. Its effects lingered on after I arrived: in order to work part-time in a university office, I had to sign a loyalty oath.

Whether they supported or opposed anticommunism, my professors approached radical ideologies and movements gingerly and critically, if at all. They couldn't avoid teaching Marx, because of his profound historical impact, but they weren't sympathetic to his ideas about class conflict and inevitable revolution; and they stayed away from most other ideologies of the left. Aside from *The Communist Manifesto*, the most leftward book I was assigned in any class was Jack Kerouac's *On the Road*, and that book is about alienation and the search for self, not about politics.

My philosophy professors seemed captivated by existentialism (then at the height of its postwar popularity), especially by its emphasis on the alienation of the individual and the monotony of daily life. "New Criticism" dominated my English courses, with its focus on the formal elements of literary works divorced from historical and cultural contexts. In sociology functionalism ruled, with its analysis of institutions in terms of static operations, not from any historical or leftist perspective.

I majored in history, and I remember reading in my history classes books such as Arthur Koestler's *The God That Failed*, a collection of confessions of prominent ex-communist writers about their disillusionment with communism. I also read Crane Brinton's *Anatomy of Revolution*, which argues that revolutions invariably result in dictatorships, and Jacques Barzun's *Darwin, Marx, and Wagner*, which proposes that his three subjects were less innovative than representative of their times. My U.S. history professors liked the writings of Richard Hofstadter, especially his pessimism and irony. My senior essay on historical methodology reflects the mode of analysis I was taught. It draws from Hofstadter's irony and Barzun's historicism. "The Greeks saw a spiral progression in history," I wrote. "Christianity added a teleology and made the spiral linear; 19th-century empiricists threw out the plan-in-history, while Communism revived the teleology." I could connect systems of thought, but I didn't have any ideological standpoint from which to evaluate them. After years of an education that had consisted of little more than memorizing in high school and listening to lectures in college, I believed what my professors told me and applied their ideas in what I wrote.

Both UCLA's educational system as well as the prevailing temper of the times discouraged the development of a questioning intellect, especially in the case of an insecure young woman like me. My intellectual naïveté also extended to matters of gender. I didn't notice that all my professors were men. Nor did I realize that they assigned books only authored by males and that they rarely discussed women in class. Gender simply wasn't an issue— and that was probably just as well, given the sexism they could have visited on me. On the other hand, their neutrality may have resulted from their not paying much attention to me at all.

I studied ancient Athens and its philosophers but not its homosexuality or misogyny. I read Rousseau's *Social Contract* but not his other works that depreciate women. I learned nothing about Sappho, Christine de Pisan, Mary Wollstonecraft, or Virginia Woolf—important figures for the feminist rewriting of history. I knew that queens named Elizabeth had ruled England and that Madame Curie, Eleanor Roosevelt, and Indira Gandhi were "great women"; but I had no conception of women as historical actors nor any inkling of women's oppression throughout history.

Yet the conservative curriculum I studied had a radicalizing impact on me. Its emphasis on secularism and rationality destroyed whatever religious beliefs I still held. I can date my final apostasy precisely; it occurred during an introductory course in Western philosophy my freshman year as I listened to the professor's lectures on Western rational thought and the history of secular humanism. Ever since the deaths in my family, I had questioned Lutheranism. Even in high school I realized that if I followed its precepts I couldn't act freely. "I think, therefore I am." Descartes' argument that free will proceeds from the rational mind dealt the final blow to my Lutheran beliefs.

Away from my family, I called myself an atheist. I found Kirkegaard's "leap into faith" absurd. I agreed with Nietszche that "God is dead" and with Marx that "religion is the opiate of the masses." I liked Freud's contention that the mystic's "oceanic feeling" is an illusion relating more to childhood needs and desires than to any true spirituality. The world of learning made me feel emancipated and fulfilled. I was finished with Lutheran rigidity; I was suddenly free of its authoritarian God and its guilt-laden doctrines. In retrospect that revolution in my worldview seems not unlike a religious conversion, but my conversion was to the life of the mind. Descartes found his truth pondering the nature of things in his study before a flaming fire. I found mine in a lecture hall listening to an impassioned professor, as I once had listened on Sundays to my Lutheran minister.

That philosophy class ended at twelve o'clock, precisely when the bells of the university carillon rang out to announce the mid-day break. The ringing at high noon lasted a full five minutes, displaying the carillon's range. I felt cleansed by those bells; their pealing at the end of the philosophy lecture seemed to applaud my professor's stand for rationality. And they staunched the pain caused by those earlier bells at the Episcopal Church in back of my childhood home. Their ringing had been the call of a vengeful god who capriciously punished humans and who had, for no reason, cut down my mother and uncle in the prime of life. Rejuvenated by the campus bells summoning me to the life of the mind, I could be independent of the past—or so I thought.

Giving up the fervor of religious conviction made it difficult for me ever to adopt any other belief system. The decision to leave Christianity was mine, but it also felt like the God who had destroyed my family had set me up to betray me and that it wasn't my independence but his manipulations that had cut me off from his grace. I felt liberated, but I also felt hurt and angry. I didn't want to experience another rejection by adopting another ideology with an overweening worldview. Thus I applied theoretical relativity in my senior essay and interpreted even Marxism in terms of my waning Christianity. For many decades feminism would be the only ideology that attracted me. I couldn't resist a belief system so relevant to my life.

Intimidated by the size and impersonality of UCLA, I didn't join clubs or try out for the tennis team or the debate squad. Without Fran to inspire me, my high school energy flagged. I did some singing and acting and won some minor roles in Opera Workshop productions. But my deficiencies as a singer caught up with me. Considering myself an intellectual, I wanted to sing opera, but my music professors realized my limitations and advised me to stay with musical comedy. The problem was that I didn't want to play the ingenue roles that went along with those songs, for I found them insipid. Devoting myself to my schoolwork, I mostly gave up performing.

To gain some sense of belonging, I joined a sorority just before freshman year began. Participating in what was called "rush week," I displayed myself at each sorority house in turn. At lunches and teas I engaged in polite conversation with members who were privately judging me. After several days, most houses dropped me. The rejections hurt, and I blamed them on my shyness. Then I remembered my Inglewood background and found out that the elite sororities rarely pledged girls from my city. I wasn't astute enough to figure out that a recommendation from Lydia might have countered the Inglewood stigma and landed me in the UCLA chapter of the sorority she had belonged to at Stanford, a top one at UCLA.

I soon discovered that such discrimination was central to the sorority system, under which each house was informally ranked and each member rated according to the ranking of her house. Given my miserable experience with a ranking system in high school, I considered resigning, but my house actually provided what I wanted: female friends and an active social life, one revolving around meeting men at get-acquainted "mixers" with fraternities. Besides, my sorority sisters functioned as allies against the Greek hierarchy, while they actually respected scholastic achievement and esteemed me for my good grades.

In this environment my high school yearning to date a football player turned into a yearning for a Fiji or a Sigma Chi. My high school desire for a male athlete's letterman sweater turned into a desire for a fraternity man's membership pin. I fantasized that some evening this boyfriend's fraternity brothers would serenade me from below my sorority house balcony. Through this time-honored ritual, they would acclaim me a lucky girl who had landed a fraternity steady and was "pinned," with his symbol of membership worn next to my sorority pin over my heart.

Yet my sorority didn't control me. For I was older, and away from the intense pressures of high school I managed to be less conformist. Given my love of learning, I soon realized that I didn't have anything in common with most fraternity men, who drank a lot, avoided studying, affected a tough masculinity, and planned on careers in business. In this regard—and in other ways—I differed from my sorority sisters. Most of them happily dated fraternity men and majored in elementary education so that they would have some means of support if disaster struck during the marriage they anticipated. I, on the other hand, was serious about my studies and about having a career. I hadn't forgotten the lessons about achievement I had learned from my family and from Lydia.

During my last two years at UCLA, I spent time with the bohemian, "beat" crowd, after I met one of its members in a class and began to date him. I liked his intellectualism and his stance against conformity. Our relationship became serious, and we spoke of marriage. Romantic and moody, the son of a middle-class Jewish family from the Midwest, he was different from the boys from Inglewood—and from Pasadena. I went with him to poetry readings and coffee houses in Venice, where Lawrence Lipton and his Holy Barbarians were contesting the beat leadership of Allen Ginsberg in San Francisco. But I never went to Venice on my own nor tried to join its culture. As much as those men in blue jeans and beards intrigued me, they frightened my conventional side. After too much exposure to nonconformity, I retreated from my boyfriend to sorority life.

My boyfriend introduced me to the Zen Buddhism that was then in vogue at colleges. He talked about meditation and koans, puzzles in the form of paradoxes that have no real answer, such as, "What is the sound of one hand clapping." They are intended, he told me, to force the mind beyond the rational mode of thought into the realm of intuition. Together we read popular Zen interpreters such as D. T. Suzuki and Alan Watts. I feigned interest to please him, but in actuality I was indifferent. I had no interest in religion, even one as nondoctrinaire as Zen.

The beat community at UCLA was tiny, with no institutional structure, and its rebellious voice was drowned out by the student body's devotion to

football and by the power of the fraternities and sororities, which dominated campus life. After all, UCLA was located in upper-class Westwood.
With its manicured lawns and huge brick buildings in a Spanish revival,
neo-Renaissance style, the university even then seemed to me to resemble
an exclusive country club. Its location and look should have reminded me
that behind my lust for education lay the drive to improve my social status,
even though that drive was hidden from my external self, which was
focused on studying, getting good grades, and having a good time.

Political radicalism didn't exist on college campuses in this era, and that
absence was as true of UCLA as elsewhere. We didn't have demonstrations
or marches, sit-ins or teach-ins. We did, however, on one occasion have a
halfhearted "panty raid" on sorority row, staged as a joke by fraternity men.
During my college years I didn't meet any "red diaper babies"—the children of 1940s communists whom historians now identify as prime instiga-
tors of the campus radicalism of the 1960s. Nor were my parents liberals
against whom I might react by turning to the far left—another pattern typical of the radical youth of the sixties. To follow my boyfriend and scorn the
McCarthyite conservatism of my parents by supporting Adlai Stevenson
and the left wing of the Democratic Party—this was as much political
rebellion as I could muster.

Unhappy in high school, I was content in college. At UCLA I wasn't cat-
egorized as a "brain" and then automatically judged unpopular. In fact,
everyone now seemed to consider me attractive. Yet this new rating was as
puzzling as its opposite had been in high school. Beauty was a mixed blessing; it could be a liability as much as an asset. When I applied for scholarships, the men who judged me invariably eliminated me because they
thought I was "too pretty" to be sincere about a career. "You are so pretty
you will only get married," they told me at interviews, "and then our
investment will be wasted." Not only strangers made such judgments. At
the end of my senior year, with my Phi Beta Kappa key in hand, I rushed to
the campus office where I worked to tell my coworkers of my success. In
the midst of their congratulations, as they shook my hand and hugged me,
I heard one of them whisper: "I thought she was a dumb blonde."

Such evaluations upset me, although I didn't know what to make of
them. Now that I was "pretty" I attracted men; yet my looks were an obstacle elsewhere. Characteristically, I assumed that the problem lay within me
and that I was to blame. For the most part, however, I avoided the issue and
hoped it would go away. At the time I didn't realize that male interviewers

judged many women the same way they judged me and that many other women were being rejected for scholarships and jobs because they were "too pretty"—or simply because they were female. My women friends and I didn't share such episodes with each other, for they were failures we found embarrassing. Nor did we connect those rejections to the "wolf whistles" and the male comments on our appearance we encountered on the streets. As in high school I faced the gender discrimination of the 1950s, but I still had no way of dealing with it because I still wasn't conscious of its existence.

Although we hid our failures from one another, my female friends and I were close. Most of those friends came from my sorority. Indeed, that organization constituted another female world, one similar to that of Melba's and Lillian's experience. With a name and a set of rituals, my sorority had a more precise structure than their world of women in Inglewood, held together by affection and shared activities. Yet female bonding was central to both, and both were at the same time liberating and repressive. I participated in sorority activities such as mixers and dances designed to promote heterosexual dating and marriage, but I also formed special friendships with several sorority sisters intent on careers, and those friendships were empowering to me. One of my sorority friends was an artist and another an aspiring doctor. A third hoped for a position in government; a fourth wanted to be a journalist. None came from a privileged background; the top sororities had mostly rejected them. But their backgrounds and that rejection fueled their ambition and linked us together.

The encouragement of these women gave me the nerve to make a final break with my grandmother and my father and to leave the Hillcrest house. During my junior year I found a job to support myself, and I moved into the sorority house. All my sorority friends came from Los Angeles, and most expected to leave the city after they graduated. Still under Lydia's spell, I expected to do the same. Supported by their friendships, I no longer needed Fran. For a time they replaced her in my affections.

Associating with women intent on achievement and freed from my family, by my senior year I had no sense of limits. Unaware of discrimination against women in college teaching and able to identify with my male professors, I resolved to become an academic. I looked forward to lecturing to students, an activity which seemed to me similar to performing on a stage. In retrospect I'm amazed at my nerve, but the audacity of youth, my soaring ambition, and my ignorance about graduate training made me bold. I applied to Columbia University because I wanted to be in New York City and because, through my college reading, I had at least heard of Richard Hofstadter and Jacques Barzun, both on the history faculty at Columbia. I didn't have the courage to apply anywhere else or to ask my UCLA professors for advice. The act of filling out an application was anonymous, as the letter announcing my fate would be. If Columbia turned me down, no one would know.

To my surprise, I received a letter of acceptance. With my future in New York City suddenly assured, I decided not to marry my beatnik boyfriend, whom I identified with the Los Angeles I was leaving behind. Then I had to deal with my family's fears that someone as shy as me couldn't manage alone in a strange city. But with my father remarried and Lillian suddenly senile and living in an old people's home, they no longer had any control over me. "Why would you leave the sunshine of Los Angeles for the cold of the East?" my older brother and sister asked me. Their question was mostly rhetorical, for they knew I was different from them. More conventional than me, they saw no reason to leave Los Angeles.

I wanted a life in a cosmopolitan city, and Los Angeles wasn't that. With no art museums, few good restaurants, and not many theaters, its culture seemed especially materialist and anti-intellectual to me. Lydia's New York was the place for me. I may have been shy, but like Charlie I was adventurous. I needed to explore the world on my own, far away from the scene of those deaths. I hoped Fran would join me, but if she didn't I would realize Lydia's dreams on my own.

What was happening to Fran during the four years I was at UCLA? On the face of it, Stanford seemed different from UCLA. A private institution dependent on tuition, it had a much smaller student body. Stanford offered its undergraduates what my university lacked: small classes, personalized instruction, and the comaraderie generated when students and professors live on campus or nearby. Fran took many seminars and easily found mentors. But Stanford was even more isolated than UCLA. Located in tiny Palo Alto, an hour away from San Francisco, it had its own large Spanish revival buildings. It didn't have sororities: some years before Fran arrived, the administration had banned them when a student committed suicide after failing to receive any membership bids. But its fraternities were as elitist and anti-intellectual as anywhere else. Stanford's football team, no less than UCLA's, defined student identity.

Drawing on the energy that had fueled her high school involvements, Fran quickly became a star at Stanford. She took over the position of art editor of the college yearbook. She became a writer and illustrator for the alumni magazine (the *Stanford Review*), and she was elected secretary of the all-campus Associated Women Students. In winning these positions, she completed unfinished business, since many of the leaders of her class were the sons and daughters of Lydia's wealthy Los Angeles friends. In Fran's childhood they had patronized her; now they deferred to her. She challenged them and won. Finding Stanford as exciting as her parents had led her to expect, she wrote in the *Stanford Review* her sophomore year: "I want to explode about this place!"

Fran majored in an art and humanities program that trained her in aesthetics and art history as well as in artistic technique. The program was partly designed to prepare students for careers in college teaching. Fran's professors encouraged her diverse talents and singled her out as a student with great promise. "I was treated as very special at Stanford," Noura told me. "I had no sense of inferiority because I was female. If anything, I felt embarrassed because I dominated class discussions. Just as in our high school debate competitions, in my college classes I could easily win any debate with any student—male or female."

Fran's appearance—her height, her large body, her air of masculine competence—contributed to her success. In every way, she stood out. Her roommate contends that even Stanford slotted undergraduate women into fields such as Education or English—fields that led to elementary and secondary teaching—because of the assumption that women came to college to find husbands and sought career training only as marital insurance. Fran, however, was exempt. "She wasn't condescended to like the rest of us women," her roommate asserts. "She seemed to have been chosen as the exceptional woman who would prove the rule of female inferiority for the rest of us. Because we presumably couldn't match her achievements, we would become docile, willing to do what they told us, resigned to a domestic future." (Ironically, Fran now teaches English as a Second Language, while her college roommate is a well-known computer graphics artist in the movie industry.)

But Fran's drive for college renown quickly faltered. A well-to-do aunt gave her the money for a tour of Europe as a high school graduation gift, and she took the tour the summer after her freshman year. Being abroad affected her profoundly. She experienced firsthand the art and architecture she had studied in books and that was so important to her mother. She encountered new cultures, languages, and lifestyles. She initiated conversations everywhere—on the streets, in restaurants, and in museums. "I met new people of all sorts and in all walks of life," Noura told me. "I felt free in strange lands to be myself. I had been so long controlled both by the strength of my mother and my aspirations to get into college that far away from it all I felt liberated. I began to change, to have much less concern with fitting in, and to be more self-assured and confident of my own style."

Once she returned to Stanford, Fran changed her appearance. She began to mix fabrics and colors in ways that her mother, with her understated style, found garish. She stopped dating fraternity men and started dating men outside the mainstream: students from overseas and men living off campus. She managed to break her attachment to her Pasadena boyfriend. She wouldn't become a second Lydia, a member of the student elite, with her friends campus leaders from the Greek system and her steady boyfriend a tennis player and a football cheerleader. She would now deal with university life differently.

Postwar national pride and the anticommunist frenzy influenced Stanford professors toward moderation no less than the professors at UCLA, although Noura remembers taking a course from an economics professor who was a Marxist. The political protest absent in my experience at UCLA appeared, however modestly, at Stanford. During Fran's sophomore year, several students went South to participate in civil rights protests, and Fran almost went with them. To this day she feels guilty about staying behind, but she recalls with pride her participation in a march against nuclear weapons. Noura thinks that it was the first political demonstration ever held at Stanford. (On the other hand, the university had a long history of Quaker influence with its pacifist orientation, dating back to the days of Augustus Murray and Herbert Hoover.) "I made posters and walked around with a placard advocating banning the bomb," Noura told me. "The fraternity men threw tomatoes at us. It was a small gesture but the first of its kind at Stanford, and it placed me definitely in the camp of the left in a school not known for its radicalism."

Fran seized the chance to return to Europe the middle of her sophomore year. She wanted to go back to the places abroad where she had felt so free. Noura now contends that "the idea of getting out of Inglewood grew in me to the point that I longed to get out of the United States altogether." Stanford had just established a semester program in Germany, and

Fran eagerly enrolled in it. Although most colleges offer study abroad programs today, this was the first in the nation. The program was launched with media fanfare, and Fran was often designated its student spokesperson. Her sense of being special deepened.

Located in an estate on a rural hillside near Stuttgart, the program was small, with six professors teaching sixty-three students. Community leaders from Stuttgart and elsewhere conducted seminars, and the students were welcomed into local homes. They used the nearby city, with its museums and cathedral, as a living laboratory for study. On long weekends they extended that study throughout Europe. The program was intense. Living and studying in one building with a small group of professors and students, Fran came to relish its communal life. The students ate, studied, played, and traveled around Europe together.

Fran responded positively to the program's rural location; she has always liked best being close to nature. In a letter to her parents she described the fields in the valley below the hill as "Van Gogh green and gold and brown." "From an old rebuilt Norman tower I can see all over the valley," she continued, "with about eight little towns and Stuttgart in the distance. The other evening we watched the sunset as the villagers went home from the fields walking, riding tractors—whole families. The women are as big and work as hard as the men." Fran was attracted by the scene, with the women beside the men, participating equally in the work of caring for the fields.

The students at Stanford-in-Germany were a self-selected group. Most had outstanding academic records, and many were fledgling artists and writers who regarded themselves as different. Yet even though they might have marched in Stanford's antinuclear demonstration, they weren't that far to the political left. Fran wrote several articles about Stanford-in-Germany for the *Stanford Review*. In these articles she condemned communist governments for their authoritarianism, and she criticized modern technology for having caused the devastation of World War II—striking in the major destruction of Stuttgart. But she didn't extend the latter critique into a full-scale attack on the West. Instead, she extolled the Western free enterprise system for its role in winning the war, in supporting European postwar economies, and in undergirding democratic systems of government. She concluded that she was proud to be an American.

Noura calls her time at Stanford-in-Germany her first experience of "dropping out," of leaving mainstream society and middle-class conformity to live in a small community. She met her first husband, Hans von Briesen, at Stanford-in-Germany, and that isn't surprising: the intense experience created strong ties among the students. "At the end of our six-month program, three or four of us, including Hans and me, kept on traveling by one of those classic Volkswagon beetles through Italy, Southern France, Spain, Austria. We lived on about a dollar a day by drinking coffee in the morning with a great deal of sugar, and subsisting largely on bread and cheese." Finding pleasure in such an escapade was typical of Fran, as it is of Noura. Traveling, making do, existing on little but enthusiasm and comaraderie, creating an adventure out of every day—that's always been part of my friend's makeup.

Once back at Stanford, Fran moved into a dorm where the artistic and literary crowd lived. She didn't end her campus activities, but she confined them to the art community. She became art editor of the undergraduate literary magazine and president of the Student Art Association. She continued working hard at her studies and her art, and she become seriously involved with Hans.

There were similarities between Fran's and my college experiences. Both of us achieved good grades, and we both aspired to college teaching. We both thought of ourselves as unconventional and were attracted by the bohemians on our campuses, although I didn't join the beat community in Venice and Fran didn't search out the beats in San Francisco. But there were differences. In her childhood Fran hadn't identified with women who worked, and in college she didn't meet women who were determined to have careers. Such women might have inspired her toward a profession and away from marriage, as my sorority sisters did for me. Above all, however, Fran was deeply influenced by the Zen Buddhist doctrines that were then sweeping college campuses and that I rejected.

A lecture course in comparative religion her freshman year introduced her to the subject of Zen. Her professor was dynamic. A Jew from Germany who had escaped the Holocaust, he graphically communicated suffering and spirituality in his manner and speech. In the course he covered the world's major religions, from Christianity to Zoroastrianism and Manichaeism, from Judaism to Confucianism, Taoism, and Shinto. A scholar of Tibetan Buddhism, he focused especially on the religions of India. He held Fran's class spellbound with his stories of his travels in Nepal. He described how he meditated in one Buddhist monastery after another, prostrating himself in front of huge gilded and lacquered Buddhas.

On the roads he saw individuals turning prayer wheels, both large and small, with written prayers to Buddha attached to circular frames. He brought a small Tibetan ghost catcher into class. A spiderweb maze mounted on a treelike structure, it was designed to trap invisible demons. Ghost catchers, he explained, were remnants of an ancient shamanistic folk religion.

Fran never forgot that course or its professor. Its impact on her was as profound as that of my freshman philosophy course on me. Through it she began to doubt her Christian faith and to explore other spiritual paths. She began to question elements of Christianity like the triune God and original sin, and she puzzled over the religion's base in the sadistic killing of a young man. Yet I doubt the influence of that course on her would have been so striking without the popularity of Eastern religions on college campuses. Many students read about Buddhism and Hinduism outside their classes. Authors such as D. T. Suzuki and Alan Watts were well known. Servicemen stationed in the Far East during World War II had brought a knowledge of these religions back to the United States, and beat writers like Allen Ginsberg spread that knowledge through their works.

Fran read Suzuki and Watts and the texts of Eastern religions. "I can't tell you the source of all the influences," Noura told me. "They seemed all around—in references from professors, in conversations with friends, in books I saw in bookstores." For a time Fran carried Paul Reps's *Zen Flesh, Zen Bones* with her everywhere. Reps's work contains Zen stories about masters and students designed to teach the virtues of humility and tranquility; in one story a master gives a robber his clothes because the master has no money. Then, sitting naked in his hut admiring the full moon, he wishes he could give the moon to the robber as well. Fran dipped into Reps's book slowly, savoring the stories, reading them again and again.

"In my classes I read the authors you read: Barzun, Brinton, Hofstader," Noura remembers. "But I didn't respond to them. They wrote about the external realities of politics and society, and those weren't my primary interests. I was already engaged in an internal quest to find meaning in myself, to find my personal faith." Fran was attracted to fields of study such as art, literature, and religion that focus on ethics and aesthetics and pose questions about intuition, imagination, beauty, and spirituality. Fran was beginning to question her rationality and to doubt the logical side of herself that had brought her such success.

Though Fran studied the same Western thinkers that I studied in my introductory course in philosophy, they didn't impress her. "All that logic chopping of theirs didn't reach me at all. Descartes sitting in front of a fire and finding reality in his intellect—that didn't interest me. Reality for me lay in emotions, in intuitions. I wanted to leap into Descartes' fire and recreate myself. Descartes' famous statement defining the Western rational tradition: 'I think, therefore I am,' I found boring. I might have liked him better had he made his fundamental truth, 'I feel, therefore I am,' or 'I imagine, therefore I am,' and founded a philosophy on that idea."

"Philosophy is bunk—too much categorizing." Fran made that statement in a letter to her parents in which she expressed her preference for intuitive analysis. But she still was engaged in the life of the rational mind, and she still was caught up in the intellectualism of the university. She attempted in this letter to integrate the approaches, but I'm not certain she was entirely successful; for she sounds as confused as definitive. "Art is neither all for art's sake, or for man's sake, neither totally intellectual nor totally sensory. The true life of art is its wholeness, its completeness, and these qualities come only from the whole man and his grasp of everything."

One text from the Western tradition fascinated Fran: Goethe's *Faust*. She took an entire course on the sprawling work. *Faust* is the story of an alienated intellectual who, through a pact with the devil, gives up the life of a scholar to explore other paths to self-fulfillment. During his quest he experiments with sexuality, love, adventure, wealth, government, social engineering, and religion. A Renaissance figure cast in a modern mode, Faust personifies the epic hero. His hubris lies in his larger-than-life desires—which invariably have destructive consequences. His salvation lies in aestheticism and spirituality. He finds fulfillment in recognizing the connectedness of nature and humans and the redeeming power of spiritual love.

"I identified with Faust," Noura told me. "I saw my quest as akin to his quest. I gained courage from that work to cast loose from my moorings, to experiment in both my exterior and interior lives, to journey wherever my yen for adventure took me." Self-confident, Fran could relate to a male figure. But she ought to have exercised caution in identifying with Faust. All the female figures in the play—Marguerite, Helen, the Mothers—serve mainly as guides to Faust in his quest for self-understanding. Goethe identifies aestheticism as female in *Faust*, but the women in the work are muses, not artists in their own right. Yet no feminist scholarship existed in the 1950s to suggest such an interpretation. Looking for success in masculine fields, young women like Fran and me had to identify with the male figures such as Faust that we studied and trust that we would be permitted to follow their paths.

Hans von Briesen shared Fran's interest in Eastern religions, and that interest drew them together. Hans was a physics major, and his study of the structure of the universe stimulated his search for a spiritual path. Influenced by mystics' appreciation of intuition and by their belief in the interconnectedness of the universe, he questioned scientific rationality as well as the truth claims of science and the dualisms it drew between man and nature and mind and body. He studied the critical hypotheses of modern physics—such as Einstein's relativity and Planck's quantum theory. As some scientists have throughout this century, he interpreted these critical schemas as supporting the claims of mystics that a force flowing throughout the universe links humankind and nature.

In their senior year, Fran and Hans were drawn to a teacher named Krishnamurti. With headquarters in Ojai, near Santa Barbara, he frequently lectured in Northern California. Krishnamurti first became prominent in the 1920s as a leader of Theosophy, an esoteric movement based largely on Hinduism that grew out of the spiritual revival in Europe and the United States at the turn of the twentieth century. Following the Hindu belief in the periodic appearance of avatars (gods incarnated as humans), Theosophist leaders searched for such a being. They found their avatar in the form of a boy in India named Krishnamurti. They educated him, groomed him for leadership, and worshipped him as a god.

As an adult speaker, Krishnamurti was a phenomenal success; the Theosophists had been correct about his potential. His lectures drew audiences of tens of thousands. But he detested the adulation of the Theosophists, and he broke with them. He established himself as an independent speaker, and he became even more popular. When Fran and Hans found him, he had been lecturing worldwide for over twenty years. As the 1960s approached, his condemnation of modern society was gaining him a new audience among disaffected young people such as Fran and Hans.

Like the Zen masters and the spiritual leaders Fran later followed, Krishnamurti stressed the unity of humankind and nature and the need to free the mind from social conditioning through contemplation. He charged his audiences to find their intuitive selves in order to end their bondage to materialistic values and to bring about a revolution in consciousness necessary for their own contentment as well as for world reformation. Krishnamurti's emphasis on self-transcendence is standard among Eastern mystics. In contrast to most, however, he never developed a precise system for achieving it. Nor did he form local groups to study his ideas and further his message. His lectures were his only pulpit, and that probably was an error on his part; for he was too intellectual to be an effective revivalist. He called his way to enlightenment "total thinking," but he never really defined the phrase. He contended that no human practice could produce it. A sudden vision of the divine had energized Krishnamurti to break with the Theosophists, and he assumed that his hearers could experience the same swift transformation simply by listening to him.

Krishnamurti also refused to represent himself as a guru, even though such teachers are central to Eastern spiritualities. Hindu masters and Sufi shaykhs may preach sermons, but their most important roles involve acting as interpreters of doctrine and as guides who inspire by their example. They possess what is called *baraka*, a spiritual presence so profound that it can transform lives. Krishnamurti may have had such a presence, but he didn't exercise it. In fact, he rarely admitted that any of his followers had achieved anything. His detached attitude grew out of his rebellion against being worshipped as a god by the Theosophists, but his refusal to give others any guidance that might be seen as self-centered on his part made it difficult for neophytes like Fran and Hans to know how to follow him.

If Fran read Suzuki and Watts, why didn't she take up Buddhism? Buddhism offers a well-thought-out path toward transcendence, involving precise techniques. These include breathing exercises, body positions, mantras, koans, and varieties of meditation techniques. Buddhism has teachers as guides and monasteries as retreats from the distractions of the outside world. Yet in the late 1950s the Buddhist movement in the United States didn't possess an institutional structure among non-Asians. Even if Fran had tried to find a Zen organization, she probably wouldn't have succeeded. Buddhist temples existed, but they served Japanese Americans. Not until 1961 did a Zen Center for non-Japanese open in San Francisco, the first of such centers nationwide. Not until 1966 did the San Francisco Zen Center buy a resort in Big Sur and turn it into Tassajara, a well-known West Coast monastic retreat. Suzuki and Watts wrote books. They didn't establish institutions or lead movements. Nor did any of the Beat writers, who practiced Buddhism mainly as part of a hedonistic lifestyle.

Among the Eastern spiritualities she studied during those years, Fran didn't encounter Sufism. Her professor in her comparative religion course covered Muslim mysticism briefly, and in her course on *Faust* she learned that Goethe wrote about Muhammad and spirituality in *The West/East Divan*. But she didn't learn much more. The fad for Eastern spiritualities on college campuses didn't include Sufism. The Beat writers didn't mention it, and interpreters of Sufism didn't become popular.

During those years my friends and I read Omar Khayyam's romantic *Rubaiyat*, and we always recited its famous passage to our lovers: "a glass of wine, a loaf of bread and thou / sitting beside me in the wilderness / ah wilderness were paradise enow." We knew that Khayyam was Middle Eastern, but to us the *Rubaiyat* seemed nothing more than a love poem. We didn't know that Khayyam was a Sufi and that the work is primarily about the individual's search for union with the divine and only secondarily about romantic love. The "thou" of the passage refers to Allah, and the wine symbolizes the ecstasy of the mystical experience. Over the centuries, metaphors of love and wine have been common in Sufi poetry. Sufi poets often write of being "drunk" with the presence of God, and they refer to the divine as "the beloved" and to humans aspiring to grace as "lovers." As college students in the 1950s, we read the poem and didn't realize it had a spiritual meaning.

Fran's ventures into spirituality were important to her, but her courses and her social activities took up most of her time. In her senior year the head of the art department appointed her a teaching assistant, an unheard-of honor for an undergraduate. She wrote her senior essay on a comparison between the styles of Goya and Picasso, and she began to sell her paintings locally. Her future as an artist seemed bright. Then during Christmas vacation senior year, she married Hans.

The summer before, Fran phoned to tell me that she was engaged. The phone call didn't surprise me, for I had guessed the announcement was coming. She would stay at Stanford until she graduated, she told me, and then follow Hans wherever he went. She was radiant; I couldn't spoil her happiness by speaking my negative feelings. I feebly murmured: "I guess you won't be going to New York City with me." She blurted out some garbled words about hoping that I would still go there on my own, and I sensed guilt in her voice. She offered me a consolation prize: she asked me to sing at her wedding. I accepted. What else could I do? I didn't want to lose her completely and, after our separation in college, I was grateful she was including me.

Lydia orchestrated the wedding with panache. The sumptuous prewedding parties matched the elegant china, crystal, and silver given as gifts. The ceremony was held in the Episcopal church behind my Hillcrest house. Guests crowded the pews, and many were Lydia's wealthy friends. Fran wore a floor-length white satin dress with a long train. Her six bridesmaids wore matching dark green silk dresses, appropriate to the Christmas season. Six groomsmen wore white dinner jackets.

But I don't describe the wedding from my memories of it. I didn't sing at the ceremony, nor did I attend it. Several days before, I came down with bronchitis and was confined to bed. Home for the holidays, from my sick bed in the Hillcrest house I listened to the church bells tolling the hours, as I had in the winter of 1950 when my grandfather died and my mother was very ill. But this time the tolling didn't trouble me; for I wasn't upset I was missing Fran's wedding. I had reconciled myself to her marriage. Whatever our grand schemes, I knew that marriage was the ultimate destiny for both of us. I was envious that she'd found a husband, and her marriage influenced me to marry three years later. But I'd summoned up all my courage, and I was determined to go ahead without her to New York City. I was proud of myself.

A month later I applied to Columbia, and I was accepted that spring. In June, at the Stanford graduation, Fran won the award for the most outstanding woman graduate of her year. The next September I flew to New York City to begin my training. Fran remained at Stanford for another year. She worked for an M.A. in Art History while Hans completed his B.A., and her first child, a daughter, was born. In September of 1961, a year after I had gone East, she went with Hans to Rochester, New York, where he entered the Ph.D. Program in Physics at Rochester University.

Many years after, when I wrote a biography of Elizabeth Cady Stanton, I learned that, during her collaboration with Susan B. Anthony, she had lived in New York City while Anthony was living in Rochester. But even though Fran and I lived in those same cities, we couldn't replicate their partnership. We knew nothing about feminism or its history. Involved in early marriage, Fran crafted a life in Palo Alto and then in Rochester, while I plunged into graduate work.

CHAPTER SEVEN

Going East

1960–1966

A journey motif characterizes the outpouring of feminist fiction and autobiography in the 1970s, and this motif is often expressed through the metaphor of flying. In 1973 Erica Jong's first novel was *Fear of Flying*. Kate Millett called her 1975 autobiography *Flying*. The theme occurs in Lila Karp's *The Queen is in the Garbage*, in Alix Kates Shulman's *Memoirs of an Ex-Prom Queen*, and in Lisa Alther's *Kinflicts*. Second wave feminism seemed to liberate these writers to abandon the classic woman's plot enclosed by home and family. Like male heroes, their protagonists now pursued heroic or picaro quests.

Yet in this feminist work flying isn't an unmediated metaphor for freedom. This isn't the world of Allen Ginsberg or the Beatles, where "flying" signifies the ecstasy produced by drugs. Nor are these journey narratives always upbeat. The airplanes Kate Millett takes to speaking engagements symbolize both her excitement and her dread at being independent and famous. They are "my hospital, my Bowery, the hell I carried with me everywhere." For Lila Karp flying means fleeing dependency on men. Take "boats-planes-trains-trucks" so that there won't be "enough time together with any man to be afraid of being left alone." In *Kinflicts* Lisa Alther's heroine's airplane ride to Louisiana returns her to an oppressive 1950s past.

Many young women were traveling in the 1960s. They were going to college and graduate school, South with the Civil Rights movement, to San Francisco and New York City to explore those places of jazz, the beats, Greenwich

Village, and North Beach. But all wasn't flawless in these lands of dreams. Fran and I both found flying liberating, and we both left California for far-away places. But neither of us reached perfection. As for the heroines of so many of these feminist works, our initial adult freedom proved ambiguous and frightening. Each of us fell apart, until we regrouped again. But our indecision and our questing brought us back together for a time.

I found New York City as exciting as Lydia had described it. I explored Central Park and the Fifth Avenue stores, and I went to museums and Broadway plays. After the urban sprawl of Los Angeles, the density of Manhattan fascinated me, as did other East Coast differences, such as snow and the changing seasons. And Columbia University was different from UCLA. A short subway ride uptown from Times Square, Columbia had a real urban campus. It didn't have sororities, powerful fraternities, or much of a football team, and it had a strong intellectual tradition.

I remained a student at Columbia on and off for ten years. Finishing my master's degree in history in 1962, I married a fellow graduate student and took up high school teaching. In 1965 I reentered the doctoral program. The next year my husband and I moved to Princeton, New Jersey, where he joined the history department at Princeton University and I found part-time history teaching at Douglass College. I received my Ph.D. in 1970.

Lasting for a decade of my life, my Columbia experience had a powerful impact on me. I learned how to be a scholar and an intellectual at Columbia, and I met my first husband and many lifelong friends there. Yet what perhaps influenced me more than anything else at this male-dominated institution were its many women students. In a sense we constituted a community. Our community didn't resemble Lillian's and Melba's Inglewood variation or that of my college sorority. Neither self-conscious nor separatist (for there wasn't yet any feminist movement), my women friends and I came together at Columbia around our pride in being intellectual women at an Ivy League school.

My first year at Columbia I lived in a large, multi-story dormitory for women graduate students. The number of women in that dorm and in my classes surprised me, for I had assumed that the all-male undergraduate college would influence the graduate departments to accept mostly men. I hadn't realized that the graduate school was large and autonomous, with its own administration and faculty. I didn't know that women had long been admitted. In fact, from the 1910s through the 1950s, Columbia

Fran Huneke and Lois Wendland, Inglewood, 1956.

The house on Hillcrest, c. 1948.

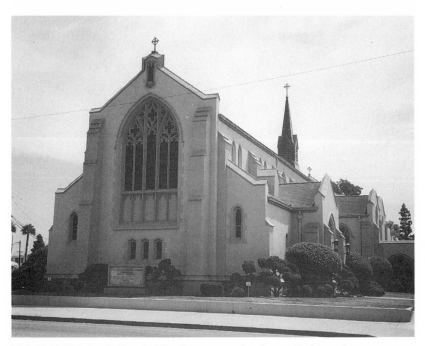

Holy Faith Episcopal Church, "the finest example of pure Gothic architecture west of the Mississippi."

The Wendland family, c. 1947. Photo taken in living room of Hillcrest house, with "two overstuffed chairs in faded burgundy damask and a sagging couch in dark green brocade."

Wedding photo, Charles and Lillian Parkes, 1905; "she impulsively married a stranger."

Climbing the Chilkoot Pass; "a chain of ants on a field of white."

September 1908. Charlie, Lillian, and Melba embarking from Valdez by sleigh to Fairbanks, with other members of the Reid party.

Melba's students' piano recital, Inglewood High School auditorium, "playing by twos the pianos loaned by a local company."

Little Miss Hollywood contest: Lois Wendland, bottom row, far right.

The Inglewood women's world: widows and single women living on Hillcrest Boulevard; church and bridgeclub members. Magdelena Krause, end of row, far left; Lillian Parkes, second from end, far right.

Fran's house in Inglewood, "a house for a working farm." Photo taken in 1997, with Lydia's flowers and plantings no longer there.

Lydia and Albert Huneke, just after their marriage, c. 1930.

The Huneke family: Al and Lydia, Albert, John, Betty, and Fran.

College girls in the late 1950s: Lois at UCLA, Fran at Stanford.

Fran and her father at her wedding, outside Holy Faith Episcopal Church, 1959.

Wedding photo, Lois Wendland's marriage to James Banner, 1962, with Fran as matron of honor, Scarsdale, New York.

Columbia: statue of Alma Mater. "Women symbolically dominate Columbia's main campus."

Lois Banner and her children, c. 1983. Publicity photo, *People Magazine*, for the book *American Beauty*.

Preparing to give a lecture at the University of Bath, England, 1996.

Zome building at the Lama Foundation, "one of the finest examples of contemporary communal architecture in America."

Zome building, Fran leading Dances of Universal Peace, "rituals of worship and individual transformation."

Learning about Islam: Fran as a participant in Lama's Intensive Studies Program, "getting to a place of internal freedom."

Just before leaving Lama for Makkah, "a spiritual explorer who journeyed through many territories before finding a home in Islam."

The masjid al-haram, Makkah, the center of the Muslim world, containing the Ka'aba, a cubic, granite structure forty feet long, thirty-three feet wide, and fifty feet high, and covered by a piece of thick black cloth embroidered with bands of Arabic verses from the Qur'an; embedded in a wall is the pre-Islamic black stone which is the Ka'aba's most sacred object.

Masjid at Dar-al-Islam, in Abiquiu, New Mexico. "Islamic architecture blending into the indigenous architecture of the Southwest."

Noura in Venice with her two youngest children, c. 1983.

Noura (Fran) Durkee and Lois Banner, 1992, in front of Quitbay Fort, Alexandria, Egypt, with the Mediterranean Sea in the background.

awarded more doctorates to women than any other university in the nation.

The graduate school faculty included few women, and the history department had none. No history professor paid attention to women in his scholarship. Yet my professors displayed little overt sexism: my one glaring experience of it stands out. When I returned to the doctoral program after my several years away, I asked the department's senior European historian to serve as my advisor. He responded by delivering a diatribe against female graduate students. "They always marry," he claimed, "and give up their research interests. They never fulfill any professional promise." Yet his openly harsh attitude was the exception not the rule.

The presence of Barnard, the undergraduate women's college at Columbia, fostered respect for women's abilities. So did the celebrated women writers—such as Mary McCarthy and Diana Trilling—who were part of the New York City intellectual community near Columbia. Exposure to achieving women doesn't guarantee that a man will adopt egalitarian gender attitudes, but such exposure can help. William Leuchtenberg, then a history professor at Columbia, told me that teaching at all-female Smith College and working in the campaign of a local woman politician in Massachusetts before joining the Columbia faculty had convinced him of women's abilities. Marriage to a career woman can have a similar influence, and several history professors had career wives. Robert Cross, who chaired the department during much of the time I was there, was married to Barbara Cross, a Barnard history professor who wrote about women in education. Richard Hofstadter was married first to critic Beatrice Swados and then, after her death, to Beatrice Kevitt, a skilled editor who help him shape his mature style.

As many as a third of the students in my classes were women. In my master's degree seminar, with eight women and two men, women were even a decided majority. This high percentage of women testifies both to women's ability and also to the undersupply of new history professors nationwide in this era of expansion of higher education after World War II. To meet the shortage of professors, identified by many commentators as a serious crisis, Columbia continued to admit many women. Besides, the history department needed the tuition revenues generated by large numbers of students to support the salaries of its many professors. Thus most applicants with high grades and good recommendations were accepted, regardless of gender, although some of the women wound up in a terminal master's degree track. As one of my Columbia professors stated to me: "Tuition revenue was crucial; the admissions door was open." Thus women gained entrance.

Tuition wasn't high. I paid for my first year with several thousand dollars I'd saved from summer work and for subsequent years with savings from my salary. Yet I didn't receive fellowship support nor did many other women. The rationale for what today seems like discrimination was that, because women dropped out more often than men, it was risky to invest in their potential to produce dissertations and books. The argument was a variation on the statements made to me by scholarship examiners in college and by Columbia's senior European historian that women always put marriage and family above careers.

Most history professors probably weren't conscious of drawing unfair distinctions between the genders, and no feminist movement existed to raise their consciousness about gender inequity. Yet they must have perceived, however dimly, that research universities didn't hire women; the absence of women in their own department offered striking proof. Their women students most likely would find jobs at state and junior colleges. The problem was that the heavy teaching requirements at such institutions made it difficult for their professors to find time to do the scholarship necessary for professional acclaim—and that acclaim enhanced a graduate school's reputation and the reputation of its professors. Thus women didn't win fellowships. Nor did our professors single us out for special attention, as they did the male students whom they identified as future stars. A gender hierarchy existed in college history teaching; one could hardly expect men to challenge it in this prefeminist era.

Neither was I myself conscious of the discrimination against women. I noticed the numbers of women at Columbia as well as the special attention given to male students, since I married one of the favored men. My analysis, however, ended there. The senior Europeanist's diatribe against women upset me, but I didn't complain to anyone. Afraid of him, I changed my specialization from Europe to the United States. The professors in that field seemed kinder and more appreciative of women.

My shift plunged me into the "consensus" school that then dominated the writing of American history. Influenced by the U.S. victory in World War II, some consensus historians celebrated the American past. Others, alarmed by fascism and communism as well as by internal anticommunism, were suspicious not only of mass movements but also of class analysis and even of reform idealism. Columbia historians, prominent members of the school, mostly stood in the second camp. They primarily studied the workings of politics (presidential administrations and parties), and they criticized Charles Beard and other Progressive historians of the early twentieth century for focusing on class as the motivating force behind politics. In contrast, they located its base in contention among competing groups— economic, regional, and social. They viewed the nation's major parties as generally similar and the heated partisan rhetoric of U.S. politics as little more than the posturing of politicians focused on advancing themselves and their group. Hofstadter's cynicism influenced some of them to suspect even reformers of ulterior motives. I was encouraged to regard the abolitionists as fanatics bent on martyrdom, the Populists as crypto-Fascists, and the Progressives as quasi-businessmen.

Some students took up the new technique of "quantification." This method involved the mathematical analysis of statistics from sources such as census records and city directories to give a more precise determination of political and social participation. Historians of my generation such as Jessie Lemisch and Staughton Lynd applied the method to issues of class and ethnicity. Influenced by the civil rights and student protest movements, they wrote about labor and race in what was called the "new social history" or "history from the bottom up." But the courses I took mostly overlooked class and race (aside from the subject of slavery), and I wasn't yet independent enough to challenge my professors' approaches.

For the master's degree, we mostly took large lecture classes, but the doctoral program was more individual. Following the European system, each student was mentored by one professor, with a yearlong research seminar the only course required. By the time I reentered the doctoral program I was commuting to Columbia and also teaching and caring for a home. With my many responsibilities, I couldn't have handled the numerous courses required in most American history doctoral programs. The flexibility of the Columbia system allowed me to complete my degree. But some of the professors supervised so many students that they couldn't give anyone much time. One of my female classmates at Columbia recently dubbed the situation she experienced "equal opportunity discrimination." No less than the women, many of the male students received limited attention.

Yet the Columbia program had its own rigor. Without any explicit directive, we felt obliged to produce not only dissertations but also publishable dissertations, appropriate to our stature as students in one of the nation's leading history departments. That magical phrase "publishable" floated in the air, and it influenced us women as well as the men. Yet we women were naive about our employment prospects as well as our future ability to publish our research in a gendered scholarly world that didn't have a feminist movement to point out its inequities.

Columbia's graduate student body was large, and many of its professors and students commuted to the campus from a distance. These factors further isolated students from the faculty and from each other. Not until recently did I learn that Jessie Lemish and Staughton Lynd were students at Columbia when I was there, several years ahead of me. I didn't meet Kate Millett or Ti-Grace Atkinson, founders of the radical feminist movement in New York City, even though they were Columbia graduate student contemporaries of mine (Millett in English, Atkinson in Philosophy). I met few of the other women graduate students later influential in women's history. I knew Linda Kerber because she was in a student discussion group with my husband, and I met Regina Morantz (now Morantz-Sanchez) in my doctoral seminar. But I didn't know any of the others—such as Gerda Lerner and Carroll Smith-Rosenberg—until I met them later at women's history gatherings and discovered that they had been graduate students at Columbia when I was there.

None of my female graduate peers wrote dissertations on women, with the exception of Gerda Lerner, who was older and already studying the subject of women before she came to Columbia. My dissertation subject was the antebellum Protestant ministry and reform; I stumbled on the topic in desperation after I couldn't find a topic in political history that another graduate student somewhere hadn't preempted. The only person in my doctoral group to write a dissertation on women was William Chafe, and his focus on women, unrelated to anything I was studying, at first seemed bizarre to me.

I've often wondered why so many women trained in United States history at Columbia later took up women's history and emerged as leaders of the field. The answer partly lies in the many women Ph.D.'s trained there; by virtue of our size we stood out. Yet I'm convinced that our training at Columbia played a role, and I use the term "training" with reservations. It was actually our professors' aloofness, which we grumbled about at the time, that ironically had the greatest positive impact on us. Left without direction, we learned to be independent. To get through the history Ph.D. program at Columbia required special skills: self-reliance, calculation, perseverance. Through our doctoral seminars we formed small discussion groups, and we taught one another. The more advanced students mentored those more naive, with no distinction drawn between men and women. (Bill Chafe was in my doctoral group.) The result was that once feminism appeared we were able to realize the opportunities in women's history, and we had the nerve to invent the new field of scholarship.

The isolation at Columbia was similar to that at UCLA, where my professors had also mostly left me alone. Farther back in my past was my high school, where education meant memorization and reading condensed books. Yet such consistently weak training encouraged my boldness. It produced anger in me at my professors for their distance, mixed with relief that I didn't have to interact much with them, for they intimidated me. Eric McKitrick, a nineteenth-century specialist who was my advisor at Columbia, didn't talk much in the doctoral seminar I took with him, and he had students lead class discussions. But what might seem indifference on his part benefited me. Required to participate, I found my voice. After all my silent years in school, I began to speak in a class. It was still some years before I was confident enough to speak in faculty seminars or at professional meetings. Yet talking in that class seemed to me a breakthrough toward overcoming my shyness.

I took that course in 1965, when I reentered Columbia for a Ph.D. But even then I remained blind to gender as a category of experience, just as I failed to see that three personifications of Columbia as Athena, the goddess of wisdom and war, stand on the university's central campus. Even though I walked across that campus daily for several years and then periodically for over a decade, only when I recently visited the university did I realize that women symbolically dominate Columbia's central campus.

The largest figure—in the form of a large classical statue—is in front of Low Library, a massive Baroque structure which stands across a large square from the neoclassical Butler Library. The statue in front of Low Library is of Alma Mater, Columbia as protector of the university and muse to male rationality. Behind this Athena, just inside the entrance to Low Library, is a small, neoclassical bust of the goddess. Placed on a tall pedestal, she looks you straight in the eye. Across from the large Alma Mater, down the steps and across the huge square where students protested in the uprising of 1968, is the third Athena. A giant, realist 1930s figure guarding a group of workers, she dominates a fresco in the foyer of Butler Library. By this point in my life I understood the meaning of scaling a mountain pass in Alaska and flying across a continent. I had even begun to master the arcane world of intellectuals. But I didn't yet understand the gender implications of any of it.

After a pressured first year at Columbia, I burned out. I'd been in school for too many years without a break. The enthusiasm that had propelled me into graduate school was waning, and I was withdrawing into the desire for a simpler life. Given my weak training at UCLA, I couldn't keep up with the other students, and I earned only passing grades. It was easier to get married than to continue struggling with my graduate work. I studied hard at Columbia, but I also dated many men and received several marriage proposals. The 1950s imperative toward early marriage still influenced my generation.

I chose a man with much to offer. Jim Banner was a graduate student in history; we shared a passion for studying the past. Sophisticated and assertive, he shone in class discussions. Richard Hofstadter nominated him for awards and for a prestigious first job at Princeton. His dissertation, on politics in postcolonial Massachusetts, was published by Alfred Knopf—a signal honor for a graduate student. Hailed as a rising star of the "new" political history grounded in quantification, he won major fellowships: a Social Science Research Council grant, a Guggenheim. When I sought advice from my Columbia professors, they often told me to consult him.

For high school Jim had gone to Deerfield Academy, an elite boarding school for boys in Massachusetts. For college he'd gone to Yale. He'd lived in Europe; been an escort at debutante balls; knew Rockefellers and Tunneys. He came from Scarsdale, the archetypal upper-class New York City suburb. His family's large house was filled with antique mahogany furniture, Crown Derby china on stands, and sterling silver candlesticks and ashtrays. An enclosed porch off the living room was reserved for cocktails before dinner. The cuisine at the Banner house resembled that at Lydia's: it was simple and low in calories. But here a Black maid in a white uniform cooked and served dinner every evening. This "faithful family servant" (as they described her) spent every day cleaning the house before she cooked dinner; the interior always looked immaculate. My childhood family had eaten dinner no later than five o'clock, but here the evening meal was at seven—a sure sign of upper-class behavior, I concluded. As we sat around the well-polished mahogany dining-room table, the maid brought the food on silver platters and offered it to each of us in turn.

Jim's father sat at the head of the table, his mother at its foot. Elegantly coiffed and dressed, she had a lacquered quality, even when she adopted the fashion of wearing shirts and pants during evenings at home. She wore a huge diamond solitaire; she summoned her maid by ringing a small silver bell. I'd never witnessed anything like this, except in movies about the upper class. Lydia's house didn't have this elegance, and I'd never been to dinner at the homes of her wealthy friends.

Jim's mother, of Irish descent, had attended Smith College. His father, a Yale graduate, brokered commercial real estate at one of New York City's major realty firms. He was the descendant of German Jews who had made a fortune in the garment business early in the century, although much of the family money had been squandered by a spendthrift heir. Jim's mother spent her time arranging their social life, overseeing her servant, and doing volunteer work. She didn't approve of her son marrying a nobody from Los Angeles, but Jim liked my looks and my love of learning and he thought, as did I, that my sweetness and shyness complemented his outgoing nature. In choosing college teaching, he rebelled against his family's preference that he enter law; marrying me was part of that rebellion.

I married a man who seemed destined for success. I could retire from scholastic competition and realize my aspirations through him. I captured the best prize Columbia had to offer to a young woman from the hinterlands whose energy had faltered: marriage to a graduate student with great potential. Entering that marriage was like entering a moratorium. It offered a retreat from my grandiose dreams of professional achievement and from the rigors of graduate school. Through marriage to Jim Banner I resolved my childhood issues concerning class and wealth. I captured a man who seemed to me a scion of an elite Eastern world equal to that of Lydia's; I countered my rejection by her wealthy friend's son who hadn't liked my Inglewood background.

When the *New York Times* printed an announcement of my engagement, I achieved what seemed to me the height of social recognition. I sent a clipping of the announcement to Fran. Understanding my need to triumph over a wealthy world like the one she'd spurned, she wrote to me that the announcement, duplicated in the *Los Angeles Times*, "would show Los Angeles and the people therein." That's precisely what I wanted: to prove that I was a success. I didn't realize that I had used my looks and brains in a classic female maneuver to achieve upward mobility through marriage. But I wasn't that calculating, for at the time I viewed my actions through the haze of romantic love.

With my anticipated marriage, the elements of my life seemed to fall into place. I found a job as a high school teacher at Rosemary Hall, a girls' boarding school in Greenwich, Connecticut, where Columbia graduate students were often hired as teachers. I wasn't displeased to follow my mother into high school teaching. At that point in my life I welcomed combining domesticity and a career in the same way she had. At Rosemary Hall I would again find myself in a community of women, but once again feminism didn't exist to stimulate me toward considering gender as a tool of analysis. Involved in teaching and caring for my home, I didn't join the civil rights or student radical movements of the early 1960s. Yet within a few years I would tire of my retreat into marriage, and I would return to graduate school.

When Fran moved East in 1961, the year after I came to Columbia, our friendship revived. Far from California, with our lives again parallel, we renewed our closeness. Both our partners were graduate students, and both of us were questioning what to do with our lives. That Fran would leave the academic world while I remained attached to it wasn't yet clear. We exchanged letters, and I visited her in Rochester. When I married in the spring of 1962, she was my matron of honor at my wedding, held at my in-laws house in Scarsdale.

At first Fran seemed happy in Rochester. She and Hans rented a house in the country, and she liked decorating it. "It is exceedingly meaningful to make a place a home," she wrote me, "to make it warm and secure and a personal bulwark or cave or whatever." They painted the interior and bought curtains and plants. "We have worked like hell for the last three weeks trying to transform somebody else's turquoise and mauve to our white, beige, and orange. We feel far freer and far more ourselves than previously, and Rochester offers, at the moment, more than I have time to do."

Rochester was a regional art center. With a university, an art museum, an institute of technology, and the Eastman Photography Center, the city offered Fran many opportunities to continue her art. Soon after she married, she had children: a daughter born in Palo Alto; a son born in Rochester a year after she moved there. Even with the demands of childrearing, she seemed as energetic and optimistic as ever. Her children enthralled her. In her letters she described them to me as creations akin to her art. She thanked me for the rattle I sent her daughter as a gift, writing me that her baby liked to shake it wildly, "beating about her head like an evangelical preacher. She is an identity now—astonishing and a mystery."

Her letters to me in those years radiated her confident, excited temperament. Her handwriting, dark and firm, covers all available space. She continually counseled me about marriage, books, art; she still was the leader in our friendship. She wrote me about being "sort of" an art consultant for a new international quarterly publishing "names of the future." Modeled after the journal which first published T. S. Eliot, Dylan Thomas, and Archibald MacLeish, "it could be very, very big," she enthused. She also took classes in photography. So pleased was she with the results of her venture into this art form that she considered arranging some of photos she'd taken into a book and trying to find a publisher for it. She landed a part-time job as assistant to the director of the Rochester Museum of Fine Arts. At the museum she did administrative tasks and gave public lectures on the permanent collections and shows traveling through. She liked the challenge of becoming an instant expert on whatever the museum was featuring—American folk art, ancient Greek vases, medieval Japanese painting.

She continued her painting. Praising Michelangelo and Van Gogh in her letters to me, she presented herself as following successfully in their masculine tradition. She adopted a male heroic stance when she mused that her feeling about a bare canvas before her first brush stroke must be similar to how some men feel about virgins, about the excitement and power of conquering innocence. She described the figure of a large, abstract human that dominated one of her paintings as having a searching, Faustian presence. She declared: "Faust is the most powerful image in literature. I want to make some shape that meaningful in my painting." She wrote me that the Dallas Art Museum was exhibiting her work and that a Dallas collector had bought some of her drawings; she was confident the rest would sell.

Were Fran's hopes for success foolish? At the time I was certain she could achieve anything she wanted, but perhaps I was wrong. In 1965 artist Eva Hesse wrote that women needed "fantastic strength and courage" to make a mark in the misogynist art world. Having good connections was crucial. Almost all acclaimed women artists in the prefeminist years, Hesse pointed out, had a major male artist, gallery owner, or critic as a husband or lover— like Georgia O'Keeffe and Alfred Stieglitz. Fran had Hans, a gentle, supportive man who praised her work but couldn't help her advance her career.

Yet young women artists who in the 1970s would explode on the art scene were being trained in the 1960s, some in places like Rochester and some without male patrons. And Fran didn't have to become an artist. She could become a college professor or a museum administrator, for she had shown talent in both fields. In her listing in the 1966 roster for our tenth high school class reunion, she sounds like a young woman on the road to achievement: Frances von Briesen, married, with two children, Assistant to the Director, Rochester Museum of Fine Arts. Even when I read that entry today, I imagine someone poised on the brink of a brilliant career.

Problems existed, however. On the surface Fran seemed as assured as ever, but her internal self was confused and unhappy. Her paintings reflected her disorientation. Her large human figure may have seemed a Faustian adventurer, but Faust's escapades often ended in disaster and Fran knew it. For she also described that large figure to me as a man "fighting his fate or the organization or whatever." Was Fran fighting her fate? What was that fate? She described another of her paintings as having a monster head with a huge, hawklike bird hovering over it. That image hardly suggests confidence. In our interviews Noura told me that, in fact, those paintings reflected her sense that she was falling apart. "The art I painted in Rochester," she said, "was a cry for help."

Noura's portrayal of her Rochester years in our interviews differed from the positive version I had constructed in my memory, in which Fran remained my high school comrade, my better self who could never change. On the contrary, Noura remembered her years in Rochester as lonely, even despairing. "It's hard to think back and imagine how I suffered," she confessed to me. Much about her life discouraged her. The malaise began with her art and spread. Like me, Fran had burned out. For many years, ever since high school, she had been on a youthful high. Faced with the reality of forging a career as an artist on her own, she didn't know how to do it— or even if she wanted to paint any longer. Perhaps she had always succeeded too easily. Perhaps she really hadn't developed the toughness she thought our high school experience had taught us.

The loneliness of the act of painting and the difficulty in being recognized discouraged her. The Dallas Art Museum returned most of her paintings unsold, and the failure to find buyers was a blow. A professor at Rochester University expressed interest in sponsoring a show of her work at the university, but the exhibit didn't materialize. She didn't find buyers in Rochester either. "I am painting," she wrote me. "But it is hard, very challenging, very frustrating, very depressing, always there driving me mad. It would, therefore, be easier not to do it. But I must." Why "must" she paint? She still thought of herself as a professional artist in the making; she wanted to demonstrate achievement; she was always passionate about her involvements, even at the point of abandoning them.

Fran did have a connection to the New York art world. Stephen Durkee (her brother-in-law, married to Hans's older sister Barbara) was an artist with shows and museum purchases to his credit. In 1964 *Art News* featured him—along with Andy Warhol, Jim Dine, Jasper Johns, Robert Indiana, and Roy Lichtenstein—as a leader in the new movement known as pop art. Stephen was given equal billing with the others. Claiming that its coverage offered the "first published documentation" of the new movement, the journal classified Stephen as a "legatee," a younger leader who could take pop art in new directions.

Stephen and Barbara and their avant-garde life style in New York City fascinated Fran. In her letters to me, she referred to them with admiration and envy. She liked to visit them. "On Christmas Day," she wrote me, "we all drove up to Stoney Point, an artist's colony in the country. We sledded by moonlight, and saw old Chaplin films, and ate soup from a great cauldron over an open fire, and slept in a *round* bed." Fran liked the comaraderie of this artist colony, whose members displayed the closeness she had responded to in communal environments before. She also liked getting away from her regular life at home.

Yet Stephen Durkee's success intimidated Fran, as did the competitive and sophisticated New York City art world. Despite her artistic gifts, she was still a young, unknown woman raising two small children in Rochester. Besides, selling her work wasn't Fran's only worry; she couldn't decide what syle of painting to adopt. Abstract expressionism was still in vogue and pop art was coming in, yet she wanted to develop her own personal style. The decision was difficult. No matter how much the style she chose might satisfy her, it might be overlooked by the art world as unfashionable; and Fran wanted public recognition and sales.

In fact, realism appealed to her more than abstraction. She especially liked the work of Kathe Kollwitz, the early twentieth-century German lithographer. Above Fran's desk in Rochester hung a small Kollwitz etching of a mother and infant; it was a prized posession. Fran admired the strength and spareness of Kollwitz's work, the way she captured the human form with a few bold lines. A committed socialist, Kollwitz often drew proletarian women. She found beauty in their rugged bodies; she saw them as history's true heroes. Enduring war, poverty, and sexual abuse, they kept their families together through sheer force of will. Kollwitz's vision of the dignity of poverty and of motherhood impressed Fran. The last painting I saw Fran do was of a mother and infant.

Kollwitz associated with radicals, but she considered herself an artist not an activist. Her form of resistance lay in depicting oppression. She didn't lead revolutionary forces. Nor did Fran. Like Kollwitz, Fran had a strong social conscience. She watched the emergence of student radicalism and the growth of the civil rights movement in the early 1960s. She observed the formation of the Students for a Democratic Society in 1962 and the 1964 participation of students in the "freedom summer" voter registration drive in Mississippi. Again as in college, she wanted to join them. But she was homebound, a hostage to domesticity, unable to participate in a distant public protest. And she faced personal conflicts that went beyond her dissatisfaction with her art.

Like her mother, she had children soon after she married. After they were born, she continued her classes in art and her work at the museum. But she found combining childrearing and a career deeply conflicting. Daycare centers were few in Rochester, and she had difficulty finding competent babysitters. Even when she found individuals she trusted, she felt guilty leaving her children with them. She couldn't quiet her mother's voice in her head, a voice that repeated again and again that her family should come first. She didn't know how to resolve the discontent or where to turn for help. During one of my visits to Rochester she confided in me. I chided her for martyring herself to her family and advised her to find more babysitters. She did so and felt better. "Old friends are the best friends," she wrote to me. But so strong was her guilt that she didn't follow my solution for long.

Fran read Betty Friedan's *The Feminine Mystique* soon after it was published in 1963; but she didn't respond to Friedan's attack on domesticity nor to her advice that fulfillment lay in careers. Fran liked taking care of her home and children, and working at the museum was only making her anxiety worse. She didn't know what to do. "There was no one in Rochester who could help me," Noura said, "no one to whom I could turn for advice." Indeed, before the formation of the National Organization for Women in 1966 spurred organizing, local feminist support groups were few.

Hans did what he could to help, but he was preoccupied with graduate study and teaching and Fran seemed able to handle her problems on her own. Schooled by her family in hiding negative feelings, on the surface she seemed in control. Hans's training was grueling; Fran's needs had to take second place to his. Thus she wrote me about tiptoeing around the house and keeping the babies quiet while he studied for his Ph.D. exams. "My aim is to keep myself and children out of the way, silent, and available only when called." She tried to be humorous, as though her enforced silence didn't matter. But being left alone, with a husband absorbed in his work, was doubly discouraging; for his absences echoed the main problem in her mother's marriage.

Fran's dissatisfaction extended to the university. She found Hans's graduate student peers and the professors she met pedantic. They seemed obsessed with their specialized research topics and self-absorbed in their search for fellowship support and scholarly acclaim. She continued to read scholarship in art history, her academic interest, but the more she read in the field the more it seemed to her dry and scholastic. She found it focused on narrow topics dealing with genre and form rather than with human content. Even the possibility of projects such as her college honors essay comparing the styles of Goya and Picasso bored her. She began to lose interest in art history as well as in the possibility of a career as a college teacher.

Fran had to do something about her depression. She took a radical step: she gave up painting. She couldn't continue identifying with the lives of masculine artists who didn't have to clean houses or raise children. Even Kollwitz's example wasn't enough. The act of putting her ideas on canvas had become symbolic of all her difficulties: finding a personal style as well as public recognition; reconciling homemaking with a career. Fran didn't renounce her art completely. Instead, she redefined it in terms of homemaking. She learned to weave and to pot, and she redirected her creativity toward making household artifacts. Weaving and potting don't require the concentration of painting; she could more easily oversee her children while doing them.

In the 1960s such crafts were experiencing a renasance, as the advent of the modern ecology movement and the radicals' critique of capitalist materialism inspired a new emphasis on craft production at home. I remember the term "earth mother" as a positive designation for women who expanded homemaking into such areas as gardening, canning, and crafts. Fran found pleasure and a new rationale for her art in "simple domestic activities." "The only thing that kept me sane in those Rochester years," Noura told me dramatically in Alexandria, "was baking bread."

By this point Fran no longer thought much about public achievement. Yet other women artists in this same period were refashioning domesticity to create a revolutionary feminist art. Through constructing doll's houses, using fabric and lace, and employing the techniques of women's crafts, artists such as Judy Chicago and Miriam Shapiro were celebrating domesticity. They created high art out of what Shapiro had previously dismissed—"my homemaking, my nesting." Their art would be as important as pop art in challenging the postwar vogue for abstract expressionism—a style that some feminist art critics dismissed as rooted in a tiresome linearity that was intrinsically male.

Not until the 1970s did Chicago, Shapiro, and other feminist artists gain public acclaim; not until that decade did women artists protest the sexism of the art world. In 1970 the newly formed organization called Women in the Art World publicized the lack of art by women in major museum collections. In 1972 a Women's Caucus on Art was founded in the College Art Association. In 1977 in her pathbreaking essay "Why Have There Been No Great Women Artists?" Linda Nochlin first exposed in print the masculine bias of art history. Judy Chicago finally completed her germinal work, *The Dinner Party*, in 1978.

Long before then, Fran had renounced bourgeois life and individual artistic endeavor for a communal life and art in New Mexico. Perhaps if she had remained in Rochester or moved to New York City she might have met feminist artists and been transformed. Perhaps if she had read Nochlin's critique she might have become angry enough at the masculine bias of art history and her own celebration of male artists to find her own style within the new feminist modes. Perhaps she would have been inspired toward college teaching again. In concentrating on her home and family she acceded to her mother's teachings and her lifestyle; she did so even in her employment outside her home. She continued working part-time at the Rochester Art Museum until she left the city; once she moved to Boston with her family in 1966, she gave up museum administration to keep close to her children by teaching art part-time in their schools.

Fran was moving through her life cycle out of chronological step with public feminism as well as with student radicalism. If she had been a few years younger—if she had come to maturity and married later in the 1960s—she probably could easily have found women in feminist groups to advise her about childrearing and to assuage her guilt about having a career. Participating in feminist "consciousness-raising" might have helped her toward better understanding her guilt. She left regular society for Lama in 1969, just when second wave feminism was beginning to receive major attention. Yet being younger might not have mattered. For once again, as in college, she turned to alternative spiritualities to find meaning in her life.

Responding to an invitation from an artist friend, Fran joined a Gurdjieff group. Such groups had existed since the 1910s, when Gregory Ivanovich Gurdjieff, inspired by that era's spiritual revival, developed a system of spirituality combining Eastern religion with Western thought. Born and raised in the 1880s in Armenia, a cauldron of nationalities and creeds, Gurdjieff was as charismatic as Krishnamurti. But he differed from the Indian teacher in stressing individual instruction, specific practices, and self-sustaining groups. In the 1920s he established a community near Paris that attracted well-known writers such as Katherine Mansfield, Jean Toomer, and A. R. Orage. He died in 1948, but his disciples carried on his movement.

Compared to the simplicity of Zen Buddhist doctrines and of the teachings of Krishnamurti, Gurdjieff's system is complex and elusive. Yet that complexity attracted Fran, disenchanted with Western intellectualism but still attracted to paradox and ambiguity. In his writings Gurdjieff used playful parables and stories, and he framed his major work, *Beelzebub's Tales to His Grandson*, as a science fiction adventure. He combined complicated theory with the fantasy that had always appealed to Fran. Gurdjieff's life was also fantastic. As a young man he journeyed for over a decade around mountains and deserts in Asia and the Middle East to find ancient texts and practices, before spending a number of years getting by on his wits. Critics called Gurdjieff a charlatan; his supporters thought him a holy man. His mysterious life contributed to his appeal.

Gurdjieff liked numbers and systems, and he devised laws and diagrams explaining the connections between humans and the universe. (Gurdjieff's Enneagram, a nine-pointed figure inscribed in a circle, which he derived from Sufism, has recently been popular as a tool for analyzing personality.) In his psychology Gurdjieff drew from Sufism and Tibetan Buddhism to portray the individual psyche as an internal world of epic dissonance. He posited that thousands of conflicting ego drives within the individual bombard a number of "mental centers." Each of the centers is located in a different place in the body and each controls a specific mind or body function, such as intuition, rationality, or the sex drive. There is no connection between them. Most individuals, unable to cope with their internal chaos, turn off all awareness. In Gurdjieff's arresting phrase, they "sleepwalk" through life. They act like "robots," with no perception of who they are.

To both calm and stimulate the self, Gurdjieff devised two main practices: a series of movements and an exercise called "self-observation." Some of the movements draw from yoga and ancient Sufi dances and are strenuous, while others, more controlled, resemble tai chi. "Self-observation" involves focusing all one's awareness throughout the day on one's thoughts, emotions, facial expressions, and body movements. The goal is to figure out the drives, as well as the contradictions, between the mental centers, in order to pull them together into some sort of harmony. Then one is on the way to finding the elusive spiritual center in the self that remains uninfluenced by social conditioning.

Once Fran, along with Hans, joined the Rochester Gurdjieff group, their lives centered around it. Its founder, Louise March, had been Gurdjieff's secretary at his community near Paris. After his death she became a leader of the movement in the United States. Following Gurdjieff's example, Mrs. March (as Noura called her) established a craft collective on a farm in Rochester; pottery from her Rochester Craft Guild gained a national reputation. The acclaimed photographer Minor White, a founder of photography as an art form, taught at Eastman Kodak and participated in Mrs. March's group. His presence validated Gurdjieff's system.

Fran and her family didn't move to the collective; she wasn't ready to give up her regular life completely. Nor did Mrs. March require her to do so. Although Gurdjieff favored communalism, he also encouraged living in the world, and he critiqued the monasticism of spiritualities such as Zen. "Be in the world and yet not of it." He borrowed that concept from Sufism. "I have been desperately in need of a teacher," Fran wrote her parents, "because I was wandering around not knowing how to go about understanding myself, let alone other people, and the universe." Fearing they might suspect that this sect was nothing more than a cult, she described Gurdjieff's approach as "a direct, practical way." Fran did the movements and the "self-observation," and she accepted the powerful and spiritual Mrs. March as her teacher. As such, the older woman was an instructor in doctrine, a spiritual guide, and a psychologist who intervened decisively in Fran's life.

Gurdjieff was often harsh on his pupils, reasoning that only drastic measures could wake them up from sleepwalking through life; and Mrs. March was harsh on Fran. She insisted that Fran give up every nonessential activity—even reading and listening to music—to focus exclusively on self-observation. Again following Gurdjieff, Mrs. March applied one of his central teachings about human behavior to Fran. Extending his fondness for paradox to human personality, Gurdjieff had contended that what seemed an individual's greatest strength was in reality his or her greatest weakness. In Fran's case, Mrs. March diagnosed that weakness as her sense of being special, her belief in the superiority of her talent. Mrs. March saw the solution to Fran's depression in challenging that central trait of self-pride to refashion her internal self completely.

Mrs. March's diagnosis—and Fran's willingness to follow it—baffled me when Noura told me about it in our interviews. I'd always found Fran self-confident, but never vain or overbearing, and I'd always envied her assertiveness. I couldn't believe that she would question her artistic talent, much less her entire self. But she felt fragmented, without a core, and Gurdjieff's practices and his personality analysis held out the promise of integration. Perhaps Fran, like me, simply needed time off. Perhaps Mrs. March astutely found a way for my intense friend to take a moratorium. Perhaps the criticism about her egotism offered her a reason to live her life for its intrinsic pleasures not for external rewards. Many Eastern spiritualities identify the search for humility as the first stage on the mystic's journey; as a psychological quality humility can soothe a tortured self. But the level of meekness given Fran as a goal seems extreme to me. Nonetheless, the Gurdjieff regime probably provided Fran with an additional rationale for giving up painting and for interpreting her commitment to homemaking as part of the needed reconfiguration of her being.

Along with others from the Rochester farm, Fran went to a retreat at a Gurdjieff community near New York City. In a letter to her parents, she described the experience. One hundred and fifty people stayed together for a week, building a house and practicing self-observation. "Among the teachers were some people who, if you could only see them, could explain with no words why the work is important. There is in some of them a bearing, an awareness, I haven't seen before." She wanted to achieve that awareness. She liked doing physical labor with men and women, "all of whom are sincere and serious, helping each other with great sympathy. Nothing is phony here. And what a relief. We have to act so much of the time." She described a new technique for self-control she was learning. "One of the tasks given at Armonk—a task being something you work at privately while doing whatever outside job you have—was this: relax your face. That was all. But in doing it not only did I collect myself and become more alert every time I remembered it, I also learned about what situations inside and outside cause me to get tense. In the end I may get to know some of the tense reactions well enough to ward them off before they happen."

Among the spiritualities Fran has followed, the Gurdjieff system holds out little appeal to me. I find it too austere, too focused on self-criticism. Like most mystics, Gurdjieff aimed at finding the place in the psyche free from social conditioning. But like Krishnamurti, he doubted that anyone could attain enough self-understanding to actually connect with that interior wholeness. He called himself a skeptic and a materialist, and he didn't write much about ecstasy and joy. He had little conception of a God aside from a force he called the "ray of creation." He often criticized intellectuals, and he dismissed Western art as self-indulgent, preferring the more controlled art of the East. After a number of years with the Gurdjieff movement, Fran was ready to move on to a spiritual persuasion that might be more life-enhancing.

In 1967 Fran and Hans moved to Boston because Hans had completed his Ph.D. and had been hired to teach in the physics department of Northeastern University. Finding part-time work at the schools her children attended, Fran taught art at a primary school after-school program and designed the arts and crafts program for a local Montessori School. She continued her Gurdjieff involvement, but her life would soon take a different turn.

The year before, Jim and I had moved to Princeton, New Jersey, where he began teaching at Princeton University and I part time at Douglass College. My life seemed to be proceeding predictably. Then with the explosion of feminism on the national scene, the community at that women's college took a course different from anything I'd previously experienced. Fran and I would continue our friendship for a time, but it would break apart once again when we began to live very separate lives.

CHAPTER EIGHT

Feminism
1966–1982

I visited Fran during Easter vacation the year after she moved to Boston, but the visit wasn't a success. To begin with, I didn't feel comfortable in her home. I'd liked her bohemian taste in Rochester: thrift shop furniture, burlap curtains, and Indian madras throws. But this house, with pillows for sitting and mattresses on bedroom floors for sleeping, seemed rumpled and "hippie" to me. Fran seemed to be ridding herself of her possessions, and I couldn't understand why. My husband and I were slowly acquiring antiques, signed lithographs, and metal and leather furniture to achieve an eclectic look popular among young urbanites—a look I considered avant-garde and elegant. Even though I liked Fran's pots and her weaving, her decor didn't suit my new taste.

I wondered what had happened to the china, crystal, and silver given her as wedding gifts, but I didn't ask. Even if she still had those gifts, I thought their formality would have been out of place in that house. In our interviews Noura told me that she not only still possessed them in Boston but used them for dinner parties. She had begun to collect oriental rugs, she said, and they were on the floors of her Boston house. Taking a different life direction, I didn't notice those rugs, even though my eclectic style often included them. I saw only what I wanted to see.

Much of the visit replicated my visits to her in Rochester. During the day we sat in her kitchen drinking coffee and talking, while she prepared meals and made bread—the thick whole wheat variety then becoming popular. In the evenings we drank wine and listened to music. We played with her children and took them to the park. A loom was set up in the living room, with a piece of partly woven material on it, but I didn't see any paintings in progress. Fran didn't seem interested in painting any longer. We talked a lot about cooking and about her children. As in Rochester, we discussed the books we were reading, but our conversation lacked intensity. The technical works I was reading for my Ph.D. didn't interest her, nor was I drawn to her mix of novels and criticism. She still talked about the aesthetics of art. She still touched me on the arm and pointed to objects or to the sky with a dreamy smile on her face. But she seemed aloof, detached from me.

She didn't cut me off completely. She took me to see a friend of hers, a woman who lived nearby. I didn't attach much importance to her friend, who appeared middle-aged and ordinary to me. Even when Fran told me her friend knew herbal and homeopathic medicine and practiced astrology, I didn't respond, for my marriage had brought out my conventional side. (In our interviews Fran described her friend to me as a gifted psychic, who possessed powers like those of Edgar Cayce, the Virginia clairvoyant who went into trances and made medical diagnoses. She also taught Fran the medicine she knew, a knowledge that was invaluable when Fran lived in remote New Mexico.)

Perhaps if I'd shown more interest in her friend, Fran might have told me about her Gurdjieff involvement; but she never broached the subject. For my part, I had complaints with Fran that prevented me from opening up to her any more than she revealed herself to me. I was concerned that she wasn't painting. I didn't understand why she was teaching at her children's schools rather than doing museum administration. I thought that in living an ordinary life she was wasting her talent. I wanted my high school soulmate back, the girl whose energy and ambition had sparked mine.

We didn't exchange any harsh words during my few days in Boston, and we didn't part with any bitterness. But after I left, she wrote me a letter that at the time seemed to me a continuation of an ongoing dialogue about intellect and creativity we often engaged in when together. It now reads to me like an epitaph to our friendship. "A natural awareness of my surroundings," she wrote, "is in me stronger than this thing of cerebral concentration which you have." She identified a difference between us as "the age-old distinction between scholars and artists." I think she regretted that

I had given up singing for scholarship; I think she felt that I had betrayed our joint artistic interests. In becoming a scholar, not a singer, I had closed down that part of me she most admired. In joining the university I had accepted its values, which she questioned, and in working for a Ph.D. I was displaying the pedantry she had come to dislike. "How much does it really matter," she concluded, "when there are songs needing singing, and yes, even meals to cook for someone you love? To me history and all the other academic disciplines are to be valued because they show what man is. But one must go on from them and be a man."

I paid no attention to her sentiments. I liked my growing intellectualism; I didn't respond to her criticism. As part of a married couple, no longer single, I had to craft a joint persona with my husband. Everyone I knew observed that requirement in those more traditional days, when married couples lived less independent lives than now. As a pair, my husband and I didn't mesh with Fran and Hans. Jim found them too bohemian, while his upper-class East Coast formality and his pointed intellectual conversation, with references to scholarly works and academic theory, puzzled them. They must have found our antiques and signed lithographs much too bourgeois.

For his part, Jim didn't like Fran's paintings. When he objected to hanging on our walls the one she gave us as a wedding gift, I stored it in a closet. A large watercolor she painted in college, done in muted grays, pinks, and blues, it depicts wavy trees blowing in a storm or being consumed by fire: either interpretation fits its fluid forms. Jim preferred hard-edged, geometric work. We collected lithographs of his favorite painters, Calder and Vasarelly. I accepted his taste, for he seemed much more knowledgeable than me. But I didn't always remain under his influence; today Fran's picture hangs in the living room of my house in Santa Monica. I took it out of the closet when Jim and I divorced.

Absorbed by my dissertation, by homemaking and teaching, I avoided the estrangement between Fran and me. When my daughter was born in 1969, Fran sent me a warm note of congratulations about the joy of having a child. Soon after that she moved to the Lama Foundation, and I didn't reply. Our lives were simply too different, and I didn't know how to respond. I was learning new social skills which I found difficult: to make small talk at cocktail parties, to call by their first names the eminent Princeton professors who were my husband's colleagues, to host dinner parties. Mastering Princeton society and my husband's sophisticated taste at times seemed overwhelming. I was too busy to think about Fran.

Princeton was a small, New York City commuter town, with few theaters or good restaurants. Since most of the professors at the university were married and living in nuclear families, our social life revolved around giving and going to formal dinner parties with other professors and their wives. In our dinner party potlach, the wives did the cooking; over my years in Princeton I became expert in preparing meals of many courses, from soups to desserts. My ability wasn't unique; most professors' wives had the same skill. We took as much pride in our cooking as our husbands did in teaching at an elite university.

Living in the country, with farms and woods all around, we were isolated from the day's social ferment. It was like existing in a time warp, with Princeton's colonial past and the university's Gothic design underscoring the traditionalism of our lives. Occupying the bottom rung of the academic ladder, my husband and I imitated our faculty elders and submitted to our socialization to the academic world. Like many of our peers, we aspired to live in one of the university's large homes, lined with bookshelves, that were reserved for senior professors.

Rebellion seemed far from our lives—until the protests on college campuses against the Vietnam War began in the late 1960s. In 1968 I applauded the Columbia uprising. Although I didn't participate in the protest, I was well acquainted with the university's aloofness. By then I wasn't often at the Columbia campus, and as a faculty member at Douglass and a faculty spouse at Princeton, I was involved with the faculty response to the student protests at those institutions. But we never abandoned the dinner-party ritual or our middle-class lifestyle.

The university's intellectual life was its main feature. Because of Princeton's isolated location, eminent scholars from elsewhere regularly gave lectures and seminars, and everyone at the university with any intellectual pretensions attended them. Faculty members were devoted to research and writing, and the impulse was powerful: I absorbed their zeal for scholarship as if by osmosis. They talked incessantly about their "work." I saw how "great" scholars did their research and how they presented it in public forums. I wanted to be like them, even though they intimidated me.

When we first came to Princeton, the student body was all male, with no women graduate students and, to my knowledge, only one woman on the faculty. A senior professor in sociology, she was especially articulate and toughminded. Yet despite the university's overriding maleness, to my surprise my husband's colleagues were cordial to me. My position as a graduate student at Columbia, studying with scholars they admired, seemed to gain me their respect. Their wives, on the other hand, viewed me with suspicion. Most of the wives my age stayed home and had babies, while the older women with grown children tended their homes or did research for their husbands. My teaching and graduate study perplexed them; they assumed I was keeping busy until I had children. They came to my dinner parties and I went to theirs; we talked guardedly about recipes and babies. As a woman entering the academic profession, I challenged their husbands' status as well as their own need and desire to stay at home.

At a dinner party one evening, the wife of the history department's most eminent professor took me aside and scolded me for not attending the monthly luncheons for faculty wives. "As a wife," she declared, "you have the responsibility to support your husband in every way." I answered her in confusion: "My husband doesn't attend spouses' gatherings at Douglass; why should I go to ones at Princeton?" "It's not the same," she replied. "Wives' careers are secondary to their husbands'. They must help their husbands, but the men don't need to do the same for them." Despite her criticism, I still didn't attend the wives' lunches. I may have been shy, but her intervention angered me. I didn't accept her insinuation that my actions might hurt my husband's career; by then he was tenured and couldn't be fired.

I'd also made friends by then with other faculty wives who didn't go to those lunches. Like me, they also were Ph.D. students at universities elsewhere, and they also were married to men they'd met in graduate school who now taught at Princeton. We numbered no more than four or five. We banded together, providing mutual support to each other. Those women reminded me of my independent and career-minded sorority and graduate school friends. Involved with them, I didn't need Fran.

Some of the Princeton wives taught at Douglass along with me, and that women's college influenced all of us. The Douglass faculty included many women. As I recall, the history department alone had seven full-time women, nearly half its members. Three were tenured, and two were full professors. Today these figures seem remarkable to me, especially in light of the decrease in women faculty in history departments at the other Eastern women's colleges since the 1930s. Given their numbers and cohesiveness, the women faculty at Douglass offered a fertile ground for feminism.

So, too, did the Douglass undergraduates. Mostly drawn from the large working-class Polish and Italian populations in New Jersey, they were upwardly mobile in goals and attitudes, even if they expected to marry and forgo careers for a time. Nonetheless they lacked the sense of privilege that went with attending a private, elite women's college and that could foster complacency about future prospects. The Douglass undergraduates didn't expect career attainment to be easy, but they expected it to be possible. Early studies by feminist scholars that uncovered barriers to women's achievement in all the professions, as well as in laws, attitudes, and social mores, made them very angry. Douglass would be one of the first colleges in the nation where a militant feminist movement would emerge.

I finished my Ph.D. in 1970, and I began teaching women's history the next year. Before then feminism hadn't interested me, for it hadn't seemed relevant to my life. I read Friedan's *The Feminine Mystique* soon after its 1963 publication but, like Fran, I didn't respond to the book. I liked taking care of my home, and I had a job. Friedan seemed to have in mind women different from me. It took the militant radical agitation of 1968 and 1969 to shock me into awareness: the sit-in at the *Ladies' Home Journal* offices; the Atlantic City protest against the Miss America Pageant.

The decisive event for me was Kate Millet's photograph on the cover of *Time* magazine in 1970. The accompanying article revealed that her bestseller, *Sexual Politics*, had been her doctoral dissertation at Columbia. Intrigued, I read her book. Millett's extension of politics to the realm of the personal resonated with something inside me. She led me to see that women's problems went much deeper than domesticity; she persuaded me that gender inequality was embedded in laws and institutions. She introduced me to such terms as "feminism" and "sexism," and she convinced me that a system of male dominance called "patriarchy" ordered most societies. Her ideas were fresh and exciting.

At the time the metaphoric term "click" was coined and widely used to describe the turn to feminism. Like the sudden illumination produced by turning on an electric switch, taking up feminism suddenly shifted my whole perception of the world. The ideology enabled me to see that gender functioned as a universal organizing principle. I realized that the dearth of female faculty members at UCLA, Columbia, and Princeton wasn't an accident. I realized that I wasn't the only woman refused jobs and scholarships because of my appearance or called a "dumb blonde" by my colleagues. I finally understood how gender stereotyping functioned as a constricting force in high school, college, and graduate school. I understood more fully why the Princeton faculty wives were suspicious of me and why my career ambitions threatened these women who identified with their husbands.

I responded to feminism's rallying cry: "The Personal is Political!" Not only did the phrase ring out with my anger against my own situation but it also enabled many of us, women raised in the 1950s, to counter our socialization to dependence. Recent analysts contend that the feminists of my generation were shrill women motivated by unjustified anger. On the contrary, the noise we made came from anger over the hidden nature of the gender discrimination we had experienced all our lives with no understanding of it, as well as from the need to overcome timidity to become actors on an unexpected historical stage.

Among my Princeton friends who taught at Douglass was Elaine Showalter, a professor of English married to a French professor at Princeton. Early in her graduate studies, Elaine focused on women writers. Her dissertation, on women writers in Victorian England (published as *A Literature of Their Own*), became a founding text of feminist literary studies. In subsequent years she developed a theoretical stance known as "gynocritics," based on the premise that women's writing should be studied in terms of female experience and not male models. Elaine was a founder of the Princeton chapter of the National Organization for Women and of the women's studies program at Douglass. Like me, she enjoyed domesticity. She gave dinner parties and managed her home. When I met her, she already had a child. When my daughter was born in 1969, she helped me find babysitters and counseled me about mothering.

The timing of my decision for motherhood is important. In contrast to Fran, I waited to have a child until my husband's professional situation was secure. By then, feminist support networks for mothers were in place. Fran had felt isolated and guilty as a working mother, but I didn't. I had my mother's example to guide me and also feminist friends and a feminist community I could turn to for support.

Elaine Showalter and I commuted together by car to Douglass. During those rides, she urged me to study women's history. In the spring of 1970 she asked me to give a lecture on the subject for an evening series on feminism she was organizing for the Princeton community adult school. Finished with my Ph.D., I had time available. "But my dissertation focuses on men, not women," I said to her. "I know nothing about women's history, and I can't pretend to be an expert." "That's all right," she responded. "You have several months to prepare, and you don't have to be an expert. No one knows anything about the history of women. Whatever you say will interest your audience." She persuaded me to give the lecture.

I no longer possess that talk. But I remember speaking about the discriminations against women in law and social customs; about how women were excluded from the professions and struggled to open them up again; about women as witches and warriors; about many of the subjects of women's oppression and autonomy that I have taught and written about ever since. I remember that the lecture left me both pleased and angry. I was pleased because I had discovered a past for women and angry because this past had been hidden from me—and from every other woman I knew. And to my knowledge, it had not been hidden out of malice but simply because of neglect and the presumption, in the patriarchal academy, that only men's activities mattered.

Once I experienced that initial "click," the rest of my transformation happened quickly. I joined the Princeton NOW chapter, and I enlisted in Elaine's campaign to create a women's studies program at Douglass. Because a number of the careerist faculty wives and other women staff and administrators at Princeton University had children, we pressured the university to open a daycare center. In 1971 I enrolled my two-year-old daughter in the center. She was among the first children to go there.

Even without Elaine's influence, the feminist movement would have found me, for I couldn't have avoided its relevance to my life. In university circles and among my friends, we talked about it constantly. At one of the dinner parties my husband and I gave, I became angry when a sociology professor who was a guest insisted that, although we faculty wives could cook well, we could never be great chefs. Throughout human history, he contended, women had never created fine cuisines. According to accepted sociological theory, he informed us, women were incapable of genius in any field of endeavor. To prove him wrong, I read histories of cooking and memoirs of chefs. My research resulted in an article I titled "Why Women Have Not Been Great Chefs." In that article I concluded that women in fact had often been culinary innovators as well as head cooks in noble homes, while their exclusion from restaurant cooking resulted from male chefs' fears that admitting women to their occupation would worsen its already ambiguous status. It was my first publication in the new women's history.

By 1970, as the Vietnam War escalated, student radicalism was flourishing. At Douglass, students demanded a curriculum more relevant to their lives. They wanted to study leftist ideologies and ideologues. In response, the history faculty devised a series of new courses. One was on the history of women; I eagerly volunteered to teach it. In the day's feminist agitation, however, I didn't participate in much activism outside the academic world. I preferred to read a book rather than go to a rally, to take care of my house rather than stuff envelopes. By 1969 the birth of my daughter made attending demonstrations difficult. I could use these reasons to excuse myself; but in truth I was more a loner than a joiner, more contemplative than active. In those days I called myself an "armchair radical." Group participation still triggered my shyness, and displaying that trait embarrassed me. To take part in the agitation at Princeton and at Douglass was all the assertiveness I could muster.

Sympathetic to lesbianism and feminist separatism, I sometimes felt guilty living a conventional lifestyle. If I'd lived alone, I might have joined a commune, but my husband didn't like the idea of group living and there weren't any communes in the Princeton area. I had fleeting thoughts that Fran's communal life was more in keeping with my feminist ethics than my life in a nuclear, middle-class family, even though most of the feminists I knew lived in the same sorts of families. I was never against men or the nuclear family. I always supported individual choice: the choice to stay at home with a family or to go out to work; to live a conventional lifestyle or to espouse alternative ones. I always believed that an important part of achieving gender equality was to allow men to have the same choices as women. That's what I absorbed from the feminist writings I read; that's what I taught in my classes.

If I'd remained in New York City after I married, I might have more readily taken up activism. Radical feminism, with its militant attacks on patriarchy and capitalism, was especially strong there. But in Princeton we weren't very militant. We pressured the university to establish a daycare center, and we successfully overturned the men-only policy at lunch at the town's main hotel. We established consciousness-raising groups, and several members of our NOW chapter initiated a suit against Princeton University for discriminating against women. But for demonstrations and media attention we had to go to New York City.

I may not have been much of an activist outside the university, but the feminist movement transformed my life. Buoyed up by feminism, I realized that, despite my mother's career, I had been socialized on many levels to accept female inferiority. I began to think I really might be capable of becoming a scholar. The change was swift. Feminist historians today use the image of an ocean wave to characterize the impact of the feminist movement of the sixties on individuals like me, and that's what it felt like. In 1966, when my husband and I came to Princeton, I was vaguely aware of the existence of feminism. By 1970 I was in the thick of it.

Throughout my years in Greenwich and Princeton I struggled with anxiety and depression. My teaching at Rosemary Hall improved my intellectual confidence and critical skills to the point that I could hold my own as a doctoral student, but I found advanced graduate work emotionally draining. Nor was dealing with the East Coast social world and my husband's sophistication easy. Sometimes my shyness overwhelmed me. I never spoke at university seminars, and when I gave dinner parties I often escaped to the kitchen to avoid the heated intellectual debates among the men.

Behind these anxieties lay the traumas of my childhood. I now lived far from from Los Angeles, and I rarely went back to visit. By now Lillian had died, and my father and his new wife had sold the house on Hillcrest. My older brother and sister were married and involved with their own families; my younger brother was in college and involved with his friends and his studies. Not much of my childhood remained to draw me back. But my family still lived in my memory: the past had a powerful hold on me. Like Fran, I often felt fragmented, and I turned to psychologists for analysis and advice. But none of them suggested a retreat to domesticity as a solution; nor would I have accepted such advice had it been given to me. In fact, perhaps the most helpful therapies I underwent in those years were feminist consciousness-raising and assertiveness training, for they quickly led me to realize the extent to which my social conditioning was partly responsible for my self-doubt.

I also turned to my husband for support, and he often provided it. He encouraged my career; he helped me with housework and childcare. He supported feminism, and he tried to incorporate it into his own life. I edited his writing, and he edited mine. He was a model to me of how to act as an academic; I drew from his self-confidence to bolster mine. As Fran had been in high school, he was another confidante who stimulated my energy and helped me find self-definition. When we divorced, I kept his last name to honor his encouragement.

We forged a successful academic partnership but not a workable personal one. Fran guessed the problem in a letter she wrote to her mother shortly before my marriage. "Lois is emotional and needs Jim's constancy and support," she conjectured. "But the real problem is that Jim is an 'unromantic' realist; he is not a poet, not the sort of mysterious, unstable neurotic type who would have more appeal to Lois." Fran implied that I might have been happier with my romantic, bohemian college boyfriend, and she may have been correct. Jim's stability moderated my emotionalism, but his "constancy" could turn into what seemed rigidity to me. Where I was playful, echoing Charlie and Eddie, he was sensible; and he didn't like my childish moods. Accustomed to casual housekeeping from my childhood, applying the lessons I'd learned from Lillian and Lydia, I often put off dusting or mopping while I read a book. Jim didn't regard household order that casually; he wanted consistent neatness. What he defined as my messiness irritated him.

I was absent-minded, always losing keys and glasses, but Jim never misplaced anything. He had an unerring sense of direction; I could get lost a block from our home. I saw multiple causations and connections in any situation; Jim always kept to a logical, linear argument. "Stick to the point!" he would say to me. "You are wandering all around the subject." I would reply, "There isn't any point. It's all complexity."

A psychologist once suggested to me that I married a man who, like my father, closed himself off emotionally from me. That may have been the case, but Jim had sophistication and charm, and my father didn't. Jim didn't bury himself in his work and, in contrast to Harry, who deferred to my mother, he was powerful and controlling. He would never have permitted a wife to dominate him. I, rather than Jim, was the workaholic in our marriage. I never stinted time in caring for my children; college teaching allowed me to spend many hours at home with them. But I immersed myself in my scholarship, and I often retreated to my study when they were at school or in bed. In retrospect I realize that I was avoiding both the conflicts in my marriage and my despair over the deaths in my family, but at the time I thought my scholarly projects required total involvement and I may have been right. In my preoccupation with work perhaps I did pattern myself after my father. He, after all, had survived my family's disasters. I prefer to think that I inherited what has always felt to me like a passion for creation from my mother and her love of music.

What about Jim? What happened to him? Perhaps he achieved too much at a young age. His early fellowships and awards were followed by tenure at Princeton when he was only in his mid-thirties. There wasn't much more for him to attain. I increasingly enjoyed spending long hours alone in libraries, for I found doing research an absorbing detective game. He, on the other hand, increasingly disliked the loneliness of being a scholar. He became restless, wanting different challenges. The possibility of a more public life intrigued him. He founded the New Jersey branch of the reform organization Common Cause, and he served as its New Jersey state chairman and as a member of its national board. Unfortunately, however, his colleagues at Princeton discounted such activity. It slowed down his scholarly productivity, and that was what they expected from him. The criticism bothered him, but he continued on his own way.

The instability of my career, in addition to Jim's discontent, was hard on both of us. Yet feminism seemed to be operating in my favor. The women's movement had created a demand for books on women, and there weren't many academic women in the preceding generations to write those books. Publishers had to turn to young scholars like me. An editor was looking for someone to write a history of U.S. women in the twentieth century. My husband knew him and persuaded him to offer me a contract. On the basis of that book, another editor asked me to write a biography of Elizabeth Cady Stanton. I won a regular position at Douglass when someone hired to teach quit just before school began one year. That stroke of luck launched me on a real scholarly career.

In 1971, soon after I began teaching full-time at Douglass, I attended the annual meeting of the Berkshire Conference of Women Historians. A small group of women who taught in Eastern colleges founded this organization in the late 1920s in response to their exclusion from gatherings of male historians. Once a year they met at an inn in the Berkshire Hills of Western Massachusetts. I went to the 1971 meeting with my colleague, Mary Hartman. Like many of my women friends during those years, she was married to someone at Princeton University (a graduate student, in her case). She also had been a graduate student at Columbia, several years behind me. For some time older women in the Douglass history department had told us about the Berkshire Conference, and we felt honored when they invited us to its yearly meeting. Once there, to our consternation we found the other older women at the meeting cool to us. They seemed to want to talk to each other, not to us. They didn't show any interest in women's history, the subject rapidly becoming our passion.

As assistant professors, young and insecure, we coveted their tenured faculty positions. We knew nothing of the struggles they had gone through to attain those positions nor of the loneliness many of them felt in living isolated lives, without husbands and children. It was a classic case of the politics of generations: we younger women begrudged our elders their status without understanding them. We might have bridged this gap at the meeting, but they accidently failed to invite Mary and me to their traditional late-night drinking session. Away from the formalities of the daytime events and relaxed by liquor, they were then in a confiding mood.

Mary had the original idea to hold a separate meeting on women's history and to locate the meeting on a college campus rather than in the Berkshires. In that way we could explore women's history and still respect the older women's interests. I suggested holding the meeting at Douglass, for through my work in women's studies I knew of a small conference center on the campus. We wrote the president of the Berkshire Conference proposing our plan. She approved it and appointed us joint program chairs for the organization to give us authority in planning our conference.

At the time Mary and I didn't think we were doing anything unusual. Feminist scholarly conferences had already been held. We projected ours as small, with scholars delivering about ten papers and an audience of seventy-five or so. With over a year to plan, we solicited widely for papers. The response was overwhelming. Unsuspecting, we had tapped into a rich vein of scholarship. Many women faculty and graduate students, inspired by feminism, were doing research on the history of women.

Five hundred people attended the conference, and seventy-five papers were given. The subjects of the papers ranged widely. They included the participation of women in reform in Argentina; domestic technology in the United States; Muslim women in India; women in the Chinese revolution; women in the Native American family; women's activism in the French Revolution; and stereotypes of Black women in American literature. The diversity of the papers pleased us, for even in those early years we were concerned that the categories of gender, race, class, and national difference be included in our work. We didn't want our new women's history to focus exclusively on white, middle-class women. (In fact, at one point we worried about the lack of studies being done on middle-class women.) Participants in our conference came from the Northeast, the Midwest, and the South. In the final months before it began, registration soared. Planning became hectic. Again and again we searched for additional hotel space, larger rooms for the conference sessions, and extra microphones and audio equipment.

One commentator has suggested that the modern field of women's history should be dated from that first large Berkshire Conference meeting. (Since that first one in 1973, the conference has been held biannually at one of the East Coast women's colleges, always with a large attendance.) However flattering to Mary and me, that suggestion isn't really accurate. Women historians had already founded a number of organizations, including the Coordinating Committee for Women in the Historical Profession (CCWHP), the activist arm for women historians, and the West Coast Historical Association (now the Western Association of Women Historians). Both organizations were founded in 1969.

By the early 1970s women's studies programs were also appearing. They were a culmination of the movements for the inclusion of women in all the disciplines. I taught my first women's history course in 1971; by 1973 I was teaching in the new women's studies program at Douglass. Although without job security, I and my young colleagues, including Elaine Showalter and Mary Hartman, summoned up the courage to press for change. Feminism opened our eyes to the small numbers of women who were senior professors and administrators in most colleges as well as to the absence of women as subjects of scholarship and teaching. We were amazed when deans listened to our pleas for courses on women and faculty departments and senates voted in favor of them. It was a heady moment for young women faculty. We projected effecting an intellectual shift in the history of Western thought akin to those of the Renaissance and the Scientific Revolution. Where others were taking to the streets to demand gender equality, we would be the shock troops of the mind. We would revise whole fields of knowledge, while we transformed the university itself.

We would not, according to an aphorism widely used, just "add, mix, and stir." We would not add women to existing knowledge without changing the theoretical underpinnings of that knowledge. We would uncover a history of women, and then we would rewrite the historical record in terms of that history. No longer would U.S. history revolve around politics and presidents. We would create new schemas—around the family, women's life cycles, the struggles of the dispossessed. The traditional divisions of U.S. history into decades would fall. We would devise new periodizations attuned to such factors as demography, changes in family structure, and women's position in the work force. Nothing would be the same after we achieved our objectives.

As the end of my six years as an assistant professor approached, I suspected that I wouldn't be granted tenure. My initial hurried appointment was part of the problem. Simply present, already teaching part-time in the department and not chosen from a group of applicants, I didn't possess the mystique of newness. Besides, I was too quiet to stand out. But my weak stature doesn't explain everything. I didn't socialize after hours with the male Rutgers faculty members who, in the end, decided my fate. I made a mistake not utilizing my skill at tennis, however rusty, to make friends with those men. My involvement in women's studies was a liability. That frivolous new field, several Rutgers professors told me, isn't grounded on solid scholarship. Your participation in it can only count against you. Behind my back I heard mutterings about finding Douglass professors in supermarkets and in Princeton University faculty housing.

When my tenure decision came due, plans to amalgamate Douglass with Rutgers were under way, and Rutgers history professors were voting on promotions in the Douglass department. The history faculty at Rutgers was all male, and it was considerably larger than the faculty at Douglass. Thus the men at Rutgers effectively controlled Douglass history promotions. They were highly competitive toward the nearby Princeton history department, and they were especially angered by national rankings that rated the Princeton department superior to theirs. I was in the middle of them, married to a Princeton professor. I provided a constant reminder of the irritating rankings.

Even without my Princeton connection, I doubt they would have promoted me. For I didn't publish my dissertation as a book, and that is a standard requirement for tenure at research universities. After four years of work on the antebellum Protestant ministry, I was bored with the subject and eager to move into women's history. One month I took to my desk and turned my three-hundred-page dissertation into a forty-page article. I had no desire to work on it any longer. Eventually I published three articles from the dissertation in scholarly journals, and that seemed enough to me. By the time I came up for tenure, my history of American women in the twentieth century had been published, and I was working on my books on Elizabeth Cady Stanton and on the history of physical appearance in the United States. The Rutgers professors, however, discounted my articles, dismissed my history of women as a textbook rather than original scholarship, and doubted that I would complete my new projects.

Proud of my accomplishments, more and more certain that I could complete the studies I'd begun, I was enraged by the criticism, delivered in a pre-tenure review. Yet I was also devastated by it. A novice in the world of scholarship, I was insecure around those male professors. If the senior scholars at Rutgers were united in dismissing my work, was I really correct in my positive estimation of myself?

Even at the time I realized that my judges were sexist. Given the threat of feminism, I'm certain they secretly enjoyed dismissing a woman. Their attacks were ferocious, and they went beyond my scholarship and teaching. In a confessional moment, one of the Rutgers men told me that my wealthy, Waspish husband was the real problem. I answered him angrily: "My husband is neither wealthy nor a Wasp. Our extra money comes from my working, and he is as much Jewish as Anglo." Their incorrect, insulting assumptions went further: they speculated that my husband wrote my dissertation. Even men in the Douglass department friendly to me displayed sexism. One day at lunch one of them pointedly declared in my presence that the main problem for women's colleges was that none of them had enough male faculty members.

Copies of official letters sent to me attacked my teaching and my scholarship as worthless. Several male colleagues told me to my face that I was incompetent. I might have filed charges of sex discrimination with affirmative action agencies, but Mary Hartman had fought to achieve tenure the year before the decision on me came due, thus preempting the standard argument in such cases of a pattern of discrimination over time. Worn out by the criticism leveled against me, close to falling apart, I was unwilling to undergo the inevitable negative vote on my future, and I resigned. All I wanted was to stop their attacks.

But the anger remained. Once I resigned I had two choices. I could accede to the verdict of my Rutgers judges that I was incompetent and leave the academic profession for another career. Or I could try to prove them wrong by becoming a scholar of note. Without any conscious design, I chose the latter path.

The years after I left Douglass blur in my memory, for I spent each performing similar tasks in a different location. Helped by professional friends, I held visiting positions at seven different colleges and universities.

I took whatever I was offered. While at Douglass I'd taught myself the fields of women's history and women's studies, and in subsequent years I taught myself American Studies. I traveled around the country, and I took my daughter and my son, born in 1978, along with me. Sometimes we lived with Jim; sometimes we commuted. Throughout, we tried to keep our family together.

The longer I failed to find a permanent job, the more determined I became. I finished the books I'd begun during my Douglass years, and I resolved to write so many books that some university somewhere would hire me permanently. Dealing with intense frustration, often despairing, I seemed to develop an iron will. Perhaps I'd inherited that will. Perhaps the difficulties of my life produced it. By my late thirties, my shyness began to retreat more quickly, and I became more self-confident and assertive. No longer would I remain unnoticed, as I had at Douglass.

Meanwhile, Jim and I moved our home base to Washington, D.C. Tired of the academic world, he founded a national organization there to promote the humanities. He secured major foundation funding, and he resigned his tenure at Princeton to head his enterprise. But he was probably overly ambitious. Membership revenues didn't reach a level adequate to support the organization, and when his funding ended he had to disband his venture. I was living in Washington with him at the time, on a year's appointment at George Washington University, when in 1982 I was offered a position as a full professor at the University of Southern California.

I never expected to return to Los Angeles, much less as a professor at the university my mother had attended. But after twenty years of Eastern snow and cold, I welcomed returning to the sunshine of Southern California and to its intellectual and artistic communities, now large and thriving. When I left Los Angeles it had been an intellectual wasteland, but it now rivaled New York City in culture and sophistication.

Leaving the East meant leaving my marriage. I had long considered taking this step, but I'd never had the nerve to carry it out. For over twenty years Jim and I had tried to adjust to each other, but our efforts hadn't worked. More self-confident, I no longer needed him for support, and he wanted relief from me. One could suggest, uncharitably, that I learned all I could from him and moved on, but my success itself took a toll on our marriage distinct from any motivation I may have had. One day Jim came home from a conference to report that someone had asked him if he was related to me rather than my being related to him, which had always been our experience. We laughed about the episode, but it distressed both of us. Yet how could we have predicted this outcome, when in the beginning of our marriage I had dropped out of Columbia to become a high school teacher and had been a hanger-on at Princeton? Our careers were suddenly equal, and that was hard on both of us.

Going back to the place of my childhood meant that I could reconnect with my family and investigate my past in depth. I had explored that past in therapy, but it still eluded me. As an historian, I wanted specificity. I wanted to know about Inglewood and its history, about why Lillian and Charlie didn't get along, about what position my parents had held in the community. Reconnecting with my family and exploring that past meant that I had to find Fran and Lydia, for they had shaped me as much as anyone in my early life.

Finding Fran raised the issue of religion, for by then I knew that she had professed Islam. In the years after I left Los Angeles I didn't attend church services nor think much about the personal practice of religion. In actuality, my studies in feminism pointed me toward religion again. For what captured my attention most in the flood of feminist publications during those years, what I found the most fascinating idea in all the new approaches, was that God might be female not male. If that was the case, then the awful God of my childhood was only a patriarchal fantasy I could laugh at and forget. I eagerly read the work of feminist scholars of religion as well as the large body of literature on the existence of prepatriarchal goddesses preceding male gods.

More than that, I liked the focus on rites and rituals within the new feminist spirituality. The seriousness of many political feminists put me off. I wanted an aesthetic, theatrical content to my feminism; I wanted my life and my work, difficult for so long, to be amusing and fun. After years of suppressing my playful, expressive side to conform to my husband's expectations and the solemnity of the male academic world, I wanted to express that playful side publicly. I wanted a means to connect with others that went beyond the rational. Perhaps I wanted to bridge the "age old division between artists and scholars" that Fran had written about to me many years before.

In coming to USC, I came to one of the few universities in the nation that valued feminist spirituality and scholarship on the goddess. No less than three scholars in our gender studies program studied prepatriarchal goddesses. The rational university suspects such research interests, but I was now a full professor with tenure and I could do what I wanted. I participated in goddess groups; I explored Wicca (witchcraft). I attended a local Episcopal church, and I joined its women's group. I wrote a paper for that group on Mary Magdalene, and I found evidence that disputed her identification as a prostitute and suggested that she was one of Christ's major disciples.

I didn't find the early years back in Los Angeles easy. I had brought my fourteen-year-old daughter and my five-year-old son with me, and I was a single parent. For a time I became involved with a man eighteen years my junior, but that relationship ended after a number of years. Intrigued by our difference in age and by the process of aging itself, I wrote a book about the history of aging women and age-disparate relationships. I was happy with my tenured position and with the group of supportive female faculty around me, but in the midst of my crowded life I broke down. That breakdown coincided with the age at which my mother had died. I now regard the breakdown as therapeutic, for it helped me to come to terms more fully with traumas that had plagued me all my life.

Beginning my life as a pious Lutheran I had come full circle, back to the place of my childhood faith. That faith seemed dead in me. But I wondered what I could find by reconnecting with Fran. For many years I hadn't especially thought about her. Given my new interest in spirituality, our lives seemed to be coming closer again. With my curiosity as an historian in operation, by 1990 I decided to find out what had taken her to Islam. At that point I had no idea that she would profoundly influence me once again.

IV

NOURA
1967–1990

CHAPTER NINE

Lama
1967–1971

In 1967 Barbara and Stephen Durkee, along with their friend Jonathan Alt-
man, founded a spiritual community in New Mexico. They called it the Lama
Foundation. That summer Fran and Hans drove from Boston to spend a few
days with them. What Fran saw impressed her deeply. Lama lies at 10,000 feet
in an awe-inspiring physical setting, twenty miles north of Taos, in the Sangre
de Cristo mountain range. The few people there were living in open A-frame
cabins they had built themselves. They didn't have daily electricity, only a gen-
erator that they occasionally used for power tools. They cooked over open
fires and with kerosene stoves, and they bathed in a nearby stream. They spent
time in spiritual study and practice. Lama was meant to be not only a community close to nature but also a "Center for the Awakening of Consciousness."

Over the next several years, Hans and Fran completed their life in Boston
and decided to move to Lama. In a very real sense they were now dropping
out. They had gained all they could from the Gurdjieff movement; yet Fran
was still looking for a life in which work and family, art and spirituality could
be integrated into a creative whole. She had no professional commitments to
hold her to a career, and she didn't want to continue to live a variation on her
mother's life. Hans's interest in physics had long been connected to spirituality, and he hadn't received tenure at Northeastern. He was also looking for a
new life.

Noura traces her final disenchantment with academic life to a cocktail party she and Hans attended. The guests were from Boston universities, and some were Hans's colleagues. "Through the Gurdjieff work, I had become accustomed to closely observing myself and others. In a clear moment of insight at that party, I saw all these 'intellectual' people competing with one another in quoting the latest magazines, in one-upping their partners in cleverness, in showing off their egos. The moment convinced me of what I had felt for a long time, that the university life was shallow. I had always succeeded in being the best in school. And for what?" Noura left the party convinced that her quest to integrate her mind with her surroundings was the real way to find meaning in her life. "I was looking for Lama long before Lama happened to me."

The civil rights and student movements had passed Fran by, as she coped with marriage and children. Public feminism hadn't attracted her. Despite my reaction to her Boston house, she wasn't a hippie. She didn't go to rock festivals or take drugs, and she lived in a nuclear family. But through her involvements in spirituality she had participated in the cultural rebellion of the 1960s. A woman of strong convictions, she was critical of political radicals for failing to realize that without changing themselves they might not have the staying power to sustain their activism. Her work at Lama could provide a blueprint for the personal transformation she believed necessary. She might no longer paint pictures or administer museums, but she could help create a new lifestyle for others to follow.

The year 1968 was tumultuous and depressing, with the assassinations of Martin Luther King and Robert Kennedy, race riots, violence at the Democratic convention, the continuation of the Vietnam War, and for leftists like Fran, the election of Richard Nixon. The spring of 1969 was calmer, as Nixon hinted at ending the war. But the student rebellion escalated, provoking stern reprisals: students were teargassed at Berkeley and arrested at Harvard. National guard troops occupied the University of Wisconsin's Madison campus. Fran didn't see much hope in regular society. "Hans and I both feel that the only way to find peace is an inner way," she wrote to her sister, "and that no outer securities in the form of jobs, people, and ideas will, in the end, suffice. If we become embroiled in the outer things, they have us trapped. It is not that things, people, and life are bad, but that our attachment to them, our dependence on them, keeps us enslaved. To live passionately yet to be able to let go of it all . . . that's the ideal."

She remembered her relatives pioneering in the West: her grandfather on the Alaska goldrush and her grandmother teaching school in Montana. She thought of Augustus Murray founding the classics department at Stanford, and she remembered his reply to family and friends who questioned his leaving the settled East for a new university with a chancy future: "I think there's hope in it." His statement repeated itself again and again in her mind. She remembered the excitement of her experiences at the intimate communities where she had been—at Stanford-in-Germany, Mrs. March's in Rochester, the artists' colony near New York City she had visited with Barbara and Stephen. She thought of the garden in her childhood home and of the Girl Scout summer camp so many years before where she'd liked living close to nature.

Lama itself resonated to the American past and, despite Fran's alienation from the nation's present, she respected that past. As a spiritual community in the West, Lama stood in the long American reform tradition of utopian societies created as models for personal transformation and social change, often on the frontier. These societies began with the seventeenth-century Puritan "City on a Hill"; they continued with such communities as Brook Farm, Oneida, and the Shaker communities in the nineteenth century and the Catholic Worker Communes and the Quaker retreats after World War II. Between 1965 and 1970 over a thousand communes were founded in the United States, more than the total number in the preceding three centuries. Many of those 1960s communes failed; Lama stands out for its success.

Fran wasn't without apprehension about moving to Lama. She expressed her fears in a letter she wrote to her mother just before she left Boston. "Why am I so dissatisfied? Always, with everything? I'm always wanting to move, to do something unusual, to have things other than the way they are." Would Lama be different? Would she find stability and peace there, as well as creative excitement? She thought so. "The only certain thing with me is Lama," she continued. "It's with me much of the time: the air, and the space, and a free-swinging walk my body remembers." She concluded: "How beautiful to have an earthly paradise one can go to."

Thus she and Hans sold all their unnecessary possessions, stored the rest, and set across the nation with their children to an uncertain future on a mountain in New Mexico.

Like many other sixties communalists, the Lama founders were drawn to New Mexico, to its deserts and mountains and its multicultural population of Anglos, Hispanics, and Indians. On New Mexico's uninhabited land one could still approximate the pioneer experience. Besides, property was cheap and readily available. With twenty thousand dollars donated by a friend, the Lama founders bought one hundred and thirty acres on their mountain near Taos.

The town of Taos held its own appeal. In 1918 art patron Mabel Dodge went there for a vacation and stayed permanently. She married a Native American, Tony Luhan, and she persuaded writers and artists such as D. H. Lawrence and Georgia O'Keeffe to join her, thereby establishing a major art community. The high altitude of Taos lowers the oxygen in the air and raises the hydrogen level. This mix produces cobalt blue skies, and it can also alter brain chemistry, causing an intensified sense of reality. "It is as though all kinds of ethereal essences and elementary perceptions creep through from beyond our usual plane," Luhan wrote, "and we become aware of the life in things—in trees, and rivers." D. H. Lawrence, equally seduced by the region, lived in the lowlands near what would be Lama's site. "In the magnificent fierce morning of New Mexico," he wrote, "a new part of the soul woke up suddenly."

Place and space demarcate lives. Just as the university world defined my adult life, Lama defined Fran's. Although she spent less than a decade there, she still considers it her home. When I visited Noura in Alexandria in 1993, she took me with her to a lecture she gave on the United States to a class at a local university. She titled the lecture "The Land." In it she expressed not only a deep affection for her country of birth but also reverence for Lama. Like everyone I've met who has lived there, she spoke of the mountains—of their beauty and majesty. She described mists rising out of the valleys and streams flowing down from the snowline. And the space! The space around the Lama mountain encompasses a vista of unlimited forests and deserts as far as the eye can see. For the Lama mountain overlooks a part of the Rio Grande Valley preserved for posterity in its natural state through its designation as national parkland. Looking out from Lama over the valley gives one the sense of being on the edge of the world.

"People go west for the space," Noura said in her lecture. "Space empties you out, and you become aware of the sun and the earth and yourself. Small details impress themselves on you: the scent of a flower, the twitter of a sparrow. One lives a quiet, peaceful life in the midst of nature." In that Western setting, away from the confusions of civilization, transcendence is everywhere. It waits to be found, through oneness with the natural world.

"The landscape is the real United States," Noura concluded in her lecture. "The built environment represents its exploitation."

By 1969 nearly thirty communities had been established in the vicinity of Taos. Aside from Lama, the best-known were Morningstar East, New Buffalo, the Hog Farm, and the Family. Most of the Taos communes were "hippie" in nature, with little ideology or structure beyond an anarchic romanticism which was antibureaucratic, anti-industrial, and in favor of sharing property. Their inhabitants often took mind-altering drugs and rejected any work ethic, acting on values formed at folk and rock festivals and in the hippie communities of the late 1960s in places such as Haight-Ashbury in San Francisco. Not surprisingly, such behavior often led to internal conflict and financial failure. Disgruntled, well-to-do backers withdrew support, while the Taos authorities, overwhelmed by the influx of indigent young people seeking utopia, pressured the communes to disband. By 1973 only two remained: New Buffalo and the Lama Foundation, and New Buffalo closed down a few years later. Lama survived because it wasn't a "hippie commune." It had the structure and discipline typical of the "intentional communities" of today.

Baba Ram Dass, the New Age lecturer and author, is often identified as the founder of Lama, but that identification isn't correct. A close friend of Barbara and Stephen Durkee's, he often visited Lama, but he didn't participate in establishing the community. Its origins, however, can be partly traced to similar reactions he, Barbara, and Stephen had to the use of mind-altering drugs, central to sixties cultural radicalism. As Richard Alpert, Ram Dass had been a professor of psychology at Harvard, where he had assisted Timothy Leary in his famed experiments with hallucinogens. Barbara and Stephen had lectured with him on these drugs in California shortly before founding Lama. For a time the three of them promoted the use of LSD and other hallucinogens; for through them they underwent the sensation of time dissolving and experienced the bliss of feeling at one with humanity and the universe.

But the high didn't last indefinitely. When the drug wore off, the letdown could be difficult. "After six years," Alpert wrote, "I realized that no matter how ingenious my experimental designs were, and how high I got, I came down." Moreover, the drugs sometimes produced destructive social and personal impacts, and gurus whom Stephen and Barbara respected had taken antidrug positions. These included the influential Hindu leader

Meyer Baba as well as Herman Rudnick, an artist living as a hermit and mystic near Taos, whom Barbara and Stephen had met in visits to New Mexico before founding Lama. Reading extensively in the literature of Eastern religions, they became convinced that individuals could reach enlightenment through their own efforts, without using drugs.

Mystics throughout history have described finding ecstasy on their own—or through the intervention of a force beyond themselves. St. Paul was blinded by a heavenly vision, and the crucified Christ appeared to medieval nuns, who imagined themselves his spiritual bride. The eleventh-century Sufi philosopher Al-Ghazzali progressed from seeing angels and prophets to "forms and figures to a degree which escape all expression." In the thirteenth century Ibn al-Arabi, whom many consider the greatest Qur'anic commentator, had a more precise vision. He saw the throne of Allah, with angels walking around it as humans circumnabulate the Ka'abah in Makkah, on Hajj, the journey required of Muslims to the place where Muhammed founded their religion. Krishnamurti's experience of infinity gave him the strength to break with the Theosophists. Walt Whitman wrote of "the intuition of the absolute balance, in time and space, of the whole of this multifariousness we call the world; a soul-sight of that divine clue and unseen thread which holds the whole congeries of things, all history and time, and all events."

Alpert's growing conviction that transcendence could be self-induced deepened after he read the *Book of the Dead*, a Tibetan Buddhist text detailing practices to enable the soul of a dead person to enter a higher incarnation. He discerned that these practices could be adapted to produce illumination in regular life. Following the example of Leary and others, Alpert went in 1967 to study with spiritual teachers in India. He soon encountered the Hindu master, Neem Karoli Baba, who inspired his conversion into Baba Ram Dass.

Like Alpert, Barbara and Stephen Durkee wanted to transform their lives, but they didn't go to India. With small children to raise and a vision more comprehensive and communal than that of Alpert, they decided to found a community that could function as a school, a spiritual center, and an experiment in ecological and holistic living. In their community they could test both spiritual paths and practical ways to build and provision a community close to the land. They could then publicize their results.

They drew their ideas from their previous experiences in spirituality and in communal living as well as from Stephen's leadership of a group of artists in New York City in a collaboration called USCo. This group designed and produced sound and light shows in what was the first major attempt of artists to meld Eastern spiritualities with modern technology to produce the visionary experiences of hallucinogens without using drugs. Lama was a living expression of that communal artistic vision, focused on spirituality, without the sound and light shows. In its way, it was a work of art.

When Barbara and Stephen founded Lama, she was a Stanford graduate and he a successful artist. Both were in their late twenties. Their previous experience with communes had taught them that the small size of these communities was a virtue but that at many there was a problem keeping residents disciplined and at work. Thus they limited the residents at Lama to no more than thirty, and they emphasized discipline and work as central features at Lama. They positioned the nuclear family as a stabilizing core. They weren't interested in sexual experimentation; in one description of their project they called their community a "family monastery."

The name of their community reveals both their practicality and their visionary intent. Tibetan Buddhist monks carry the title "Lama," and the name fit the Durkees' "family monastery," for they often followed Buddhist practices. Their mountain was already named Lama, as a town once located near their site had been; it made sense to extend the name to their community. And as Noura pointed out to me in our interviews, in Spanish the word *lama* means "mud." This meaning underscored both the hard physical labor their enterprise required and their grounding in the solidity of the earth no matter how high-flying their spiritual ambitions. The derivation of the word "foundation" in their title isn't so complex. It indicates that they obtained nonprofit, tax-exempt status from the federal government in order to attract individual and foundation financial support.

Like its name, Lama's mission statement combines practicality with spirituality. It describes Lama as both a spiritual center and "a School for Basic Studies," and it lists practical skills such as carpentry and adobe-brickmaking as "basic studies." The primary goal of the Lama residents was to refashion their internal selves, but skills such as carpentry were crucial to maintaining their physical environment and they honored such skills in the small, holistic community they were creating. As artists they understood the creativity involved in craft, as against machine, production. Like other communalists, they were romantic anarchists, but they were also pioneers in the day's ecology movement.

Maintaining discipline was important to them. In the first place, they banned drugs. Noura: "From the very beginning, Lama was a place for serious study, and this was affirmed by the rules and regimen which we as members imposed on ourselves. Lama had one central rule which immediately sorted out its membership: no drugs of any kind. Not even coffee or tea were permitted, although residents who once had been into drugs were mostly finished with the drug culture and its laxness and laissez-faire attitudes by the time they came to Lama. (We relaxed this rule when we took peyote as participants in the rites of the Native American Church with Indians from the Taos Pueblo.) We were also vegetarian, respecting Hindu beliefs in the sanctity of animals. Another rule limited the usual drop-in passer-by who could disrupt harmony and take up precious time; no visitors except on Sundays. Many of our neighbors didn't like these rules, and they considered us somewhat stuckup. But we knew discipline was necessary to insure the community's survival, and we wanted it as a way of structuring our lives.

"We instituted a governing arrangement that allowed everyone a voice and yet moderated conflict. We governed by consensus, with a co-ordinator to carry out group decisions. This meant that with regard to any issue regarding practice, work, membership, internal problems, or finances, everyone had to agree or nothing would happen. There was a group meeting every night. Every aspect of the Foundation was regularly discussed, and then all kinds of interpersonal group work would be done, including talk, silence, confrontation, music, or study with a spiritual teacher when one was in residence."

When Ram Dass returned from India, he visited Lama and gave Stephen a manuscript he had written on spirituality. Stephen developed it into several publications which were edited and produced at Lama. One was a book done on heavy brown paper, bound together by thick string, and titled *From Bindu to Ojas*. ("Bindu" designates the beginning stage of the Hindu path to enlightenment and "Ojas" the final one.) The Lama residents worked together on laying out and assembling the book, and Fran drew many of its illustrations. They distributed it mostly through word of mouth, until a commercial publisher picked it up and issued it under the title *Be Here Now*. It was an immediate best-seller; Noura calls it "a sort of Bible of late 60s and 70s spiritual pop culture." Still in print, its sales have totalled nearly a million copies. Its profits helped support Lama.

Beginning with a brief autobiography by Ram Dass, the book combines quotes from spiritual leaders with a short, breezy text exploring the meaning of enlightenment. With profuse illustrations both serious and comic, it has an appealing poster art quality. The text contains words differing in size and spacing, producing an individualized statement on each page. Expressing the ideas of Eastern mysticism simply and with fervor, it has the look of a sophisticated school primer. The message of *Be Here Now* isn't complex. Possessions are a trap, and the real world is a delusion. Don't worry about the past or the future. Live in the present moment and try to reach the center of consciousness in the self that connects outward to the universe. Realize that true contentment lies in union with "the one," the force that connects humans and nature and that most religions call God. The book includes quotes from Gurdjieff, but most of its philosophy comes from the Hinduism and Buddhism Ram Dass studied in India.

Be Here Now was one of many such Lama projects. The residents fashioned prayer flags and greeting cards, and they produced one or two books by hand each year. They opened the premises on Sundays to visitors, and in the summers they organized seminars conducted by visiting spiritual leaders. Eventually they advertised their seminars through brochures and charged fees for attending. In the summer of 1969, at the first seminar, Ram Dass came and brought with him thirteen monks and seven yoga teachers.

Lama's ambitious program took root, despite the harsh mountain climate, with a snow season lasting from late November to mid-March. The work load was staggering—clearing paths, constructing and maintaining buildings, cooking meals, teaching children at home or taking them to local schools, with only an unpaved road connecting Lama to the main highway. In their isolated setting, Fran's herbal and homeopathic knowledge was invaluable, and she was often Lama's healer. They struggled to grow their own food supply, and Stephen invented a type of mountain garden ecology by building greenhouses into the mountainside to obtain winter heat for plants. (Stephen named them "growholes.") It was a difficult technique, never entirely successful, and they never completely weaned themselves from depending on outside provisioning. Unlike the residents of other communes, however, Lama members never applied for welfare or food stamps. Their projects brought in money; they landed several grants; they lived simply.

Fran wrote to her sister enthusiastically about their life at Lama, envisioning herself as a pioneer. "And where does it fit into our family scheme that a Ph.D. and his family live in a one-room house and walk a quarter of a mile through snow to an outhouse? I just began to see how trapped my mind was, and here I am on the frontier." Away from mainstream America, Fran felt the same sense of freedom that she'd experienced years before in Europe. She identified with the vagabond young people she met in Taos and at Lama during Sunday visiting. "People keep showing up here who've hitch-hiked to India and back with no money . . . who have no jobs and eat somehow . . . who are in search of life and their souls, and the rest is by the way. And they are beautiful to meet because they make me know that almost anything is possible and most of the excuses we offer ourselves rise from fear of the unknown." She felt in harmony with the people living at Lama. "I've always known somewhere I was a different kind of animal from most of the people I knew. So few of them had my passion. It then led to excess in school, to the constant desire to achieve. Well, now I know a few others of the same species."

In letters to her parents, Fran proudly described their successes in communal living. She liked the barter system that evolved at Lama and among the Taos communities, for it brought people together and eliminated the alienation of commercial transactions under capitalism. She appreciated that Lama residents shared housekeeping and childcare. "I used to look down our street in Boston and see all those big houses with all those walls and inside each one there was some woman working all day long to keep it clean and fixed up and all those walls washed. And I realized what a waste of time and energy that was when all those women could get together and simply by sharing a washing machine or baby sitting for each other could save hours of their lives for living together."

Feminism wasn't absent at Lama. Noura: "We couldn't avoid it. By 1970 it was everywhere, and it was publicized in magazines like *Time* and *Newsweek* that we read to learn what was going on in the outside world. We didn't stay on the mountain exclusively. We went to Taos and Santa Fe and occasionally to conferences and gatherings outside of New Mexico. But feminism didn't grow at Lama as a reflection of something happening outside the mountain. It grew out of relationships, elements of communal living, the constant questioning and examination of all life process. Moreover, we never adopted traditional gender roles. Work assignments were by rotation; there was no division by gender. Decisions were made by consensus, and everyone—male and female—had an equal voice." Stephen and then

Hans served as Lama's first coordinators, but a long line of women eventually held the position.

During Lama's first years, its residents built individual dwellings and community buildings. Families lived together in small wooden cabins or A-frames. They shared meals in a communal kitchen and dining room in a building they constructed in the form of a two-story octagon covered by a peaked dome. A dome also topped the large meeting hall, the interior of which was hexagonal in shape. Applying the ecological and aesthetic principle that architecture should reflect its surroundings, they used adobe bricks, native to the Southwest, in building it. Stephen Durkee and Steve Baer, a builder and mathematician, designed these two structures. Stephen named the domed form they invented a "zome."[1] One historian of 1970s communities calls the main Lama zome "one of the finest examples of contemporary communal architecture in America."

Noura: "We made ourselves the subjects of our experiment in how to work and how to live. Six days a week we built Lama. We constructed a huge central dome over a space big enough for dance, music, and any kind of meeting. A prayer and meditation room was built for the obligatory early morning meditations, which were led in turn by the members, and included chanting, prayer, and silent sitting. On one side of the central dome was a 'living room' with a fireplace, called the 'only room' because its foundation was the only structure on the land at the beginning. We also had a wash room and bath house, and over time the original A-frames were insulated and enclosed.

"Eventually small domes were built in the forest, one high on the mountain for hermitage and retreat, as well as several permanent houses: but all that was in the future. In the beginning we lived a very primitive lifestyle, but one of great beauty, in constant communion with the earth and sky and one another. The beginning was a time of immense inspiration and hope."

Much of this description of Lama would fit other communities. Working hard, attempting to attain economic self-sufficiency, crafting a governing

---

[1] Noura: "A zome is related to a geodesic dome, but is considerably different. In it a combination of polygons tile with one another to cover spaces of various sizes and shapes. A geodesic dome is based on regular hexagons and always makes a circular space. A zome can be taller, squatter, longer, thinner, or take many different forms. The zomes at Lama are slightly peaked and have skylights. They are made of sealed plywood touching down on adobe walls."

structure—these were standard requirements. Lama's success was unusual in Taos, but other communities succeeded elsewhere. Nor was it the only spiritual community in this era. But it was unique in its members experimenting with a variety of traditions, in their persistence in constructing an effective system, and in their publications, summer workshops, and connections to spiritual leaders worldwide.

Soon after they arrived on the Lama mountain, the founders became friendly with the Indians of the Taos Pueblo. Noura: "Lama land sits astride an ancient Indian highway going from New Mexico into Colorado. The Indians came up to visit the new settlers and made it clear to them that, by Indian belief, the land did not belong to them, and that they should use it respectfully. They also offered their help, physically and spiritually, in the development of the Foundation. They taught us how to work, slowly and steadily, cleanly and consistently. They taught us how to make adobe using a pit of mud and straw mixed by people and horses, formed into bricks, and dried in the sun. Although they insisted that there was no way we could become Indians, they did invite some of us to participate in the rituals of the Native American Church. These rituals were held from time to time in teepees set up in different places in the Taos Valley.

"Some Lama members took to the Indian ways more than others, and for some the Native American Church, with its strict form and earthy comaradarie, and incredible visions through the use of peyote, became their spiritual path. There were even a few marriages with Indians and some very strong friendships. We often visited the pueblo, for dances and holidays and feasts. But the true Indian religion, based on lifelong tribal initiations and meetings in the kiva, was closed to us."

Native American spirituality isn't included in the Lama pamphlet, *Cookbook for a Good Life*, written in 1970 to publicize their early experiments in spiritual practice. *Be Here Now* isn't precise about spiritual practice; *Cookbook*, as its name implies, is a detailed and practical guide to spirituality, containing numerous "recipes" for how to achieve enlightenment. Demonstrating the richness of the spiritualities that have developed over the centuries in the East, it seems predicated on the sensible notion that different individuals may prefer different practices. It also documents the spiritual experimentation at Lama, especially the explorations into Hinduism and Buddhism. These paths predominated during the community's first years.

Many spiritual leaders visited the mountain, especially as teachers in the summer program. They represented many faiths and many sectarian variations on those faiths. Each teacher had new practices or new texts to share, and each left a mark on the community. Noura: "We were always experimenting with ourselves, with diets, chants, meditations, dances, psychoanalyzing one another. As teachers came, we would add or subtract practices. Ram Dass was one teacher among many, and he influenced us, but so did the Native Americans, Rabbi Zalman Schacter, Hari Dass Baba, the Tibetans, Zen Buddhist teachers, Vipassana Buddhist teachers."

The Lama residents did yoga exercises and breathing techniques, called *pranayam* in India, to calm anxiety and produce peacefulness. They also did tai chi to center themselves. They sang spiritual songs in the evenings (called *bhajan* in India), and they performed the Hindu practice of *kirtan*, which is a singsong, repetitive chanting using the names of gods, such as the deities Ram or Krishna. As individuals, they silently chanted those names while moving strings of prayer beads through their fingers. (Hindus call the prayer beads *mala*.)

Meditation was a central practice, and *Cookbook* details a number of varieties, some with mantras and some without, some sitting and some walking. Meditation is important in all Eastern spiritualities; the goal is to silence one's stream of consciousness—the "monkey chatter of the mind" Buddhists call it. That act of mental self-control is preliminary to finding the place of quiet contemplation in the self from which transcendence can be reached; many religions define that internal place as the "soul." To meditate successfully isn't easy. In one recipe, *Cookbook* recommends using mantras throughout the day, even when doing ordinary tasks like taking showers, washing clothes, or cooking. Included in *Cookbook*'s recipes for meditation is Gurdjieff's self-observation technique, which Fran had practiced for many years.

To someone uninformed about Eastern religions, life at Lama may sound like a silly child's game. But as anyone who has tried to reach enlightenment can report, the path isn't easy. Westerners not versed in Eastern techniques can find them boring; continual backsliding can occur. There is also the issue of achieving not simply ecstasy but also a constant sense of contentment in everyday life, and this state of equanimity may be harder to achieve than ecstasy. Because of these difficulties, commentators note that Eastern religions train their members for spirituality as rigorously as professional athletes are trained in the West. Thus the Lama residents emphasized practice: chanting, meditating, exercising, dancing. All these techniques are designed to further self-control and to awaken in individuals the subtle connections between mind, body, and soul.

High on the mountain above the central buildings the residents built small cabins as meditation retreats to which they went alone, sometimes for days at a time, away from the distractions of family and community. Those cabins exemplify Lama spirituality. The foundation's members wanted a sense of the divine to extend up and down the mountain to permeate everything they did. They called it *sadhana*, which they defined as the discipline of the spiritual life. They included even work as a spiritual exercise. They called it, in Hindu fashion, karma yoga. Digging in the garden, cleaning up the property, cooking meals—they visualized these work activities as exercises to aid them in self-overcoming.

In addition to discipline and spirituality there was laughter and joy. Both *Be Here Now* and *Cookbook* have a comic strain, and *Cookbook* recommends practicing cosmic humor as a part of the spiritual journey. Lama spirituality also had a feminist side. The women at Lama knew the female traditions in the religious texts they studied, and they drew on those traditions as readily as did followers of mainstream feminist spirituality. The Lama summer programs included workshops for women, and the men and children in the community left the mountain during those workshops. Fran taught a class in feminist spirituality at Santa Fe, naming it "Sherose." The term was a wordplay on Christ's resurrection, combined with the word "hero."

When I lived at Lama, I met a a woman who had attended a Sherose retreat at the mountain community. She gave me a description of its rituals she had published in a Sufi newsletter. "We did explorations into the nature of Mother May," she wrote, "the queenly loving beauty of Venus, and the awakening curiosity of Eve. There was a dance to Inanna [the ancient Sumerian goddess] and the snake and the ability to shed our skin. On Saturday night we held a tribute to the full moon. We danced with the sound of tambourines, flute, and lyrical voice. We became the magical moon mother herself." Her description could be used to portray the rituals we did in Los Angeles in practicing feminist spirituality.

Early Lama publications such as *Cookbook* mention Sufism, but they don't emphasize it; it wasn't yet a community focus. But that indifference began to change when, in the summer of 1969, Samuel L. Lewis, a murshid (leader) in the Sufi Order in the West, came to Lama to teach. Murshid Sam (as he was familiarly known) brought Islam to the community. An American, he was born in San Francisco in 1896 to a wealthy Jewish family, who disowned him when he refused to enter their business. He supported himself as a gardener while he studied Buddhism and Sufism. In the mid 1920s he became a murshid within the Sufi Order. When he came to teach at Lama, he had been studying Eastern spiritualities for over forty years.

What is the Sufi Order in the West? Hazrat Inayat Khan, among the first Sufis to lecture in the United States, founded it around the time of the First World War. A member of the Chisti Order in India, after several years in the West he widened his religious perspective to embrace an ecumenical vision of the equality of all religions.[2] Disregarding the Muslim conviction that only Muslims can be Sufis, Hazrat Inayat Khan opened his order to non-Muslims. He contended that the mysticism of Sufism had existed in religions that predated Islam—like Judaism and Christianity—and that Islam had borrowed it from them. Muslims find this stand incomprehensible. They trace the origins of Sufism to companions of Muhammad, and they regard it exclusively as part of Islam.

Murshid Sam followed Hazrat Inayat Khan. He wasn't a Muslim, and he didn't expect his students to profess Islam. Short and energetic, brash and outspoken, he didn't fit any stereotypes of a guru as emotionally distant and reserved. Yet his appeal was great. Everyone I met who knew him described him to me not only as dynamic and with a penetrating insight but also as witty, with a captivating sense of humor. "He was a very great comfort to me," Fran said, "like a second father to me. I never spent that much time alone with him; it was just the way he was. He was so funny, and he had such insights; he could look at you and you wouldn't escape it."

I understood Fran's reaction when I saw Murshid Sam in *Sunseed*, a movie about him, Ram Dass, and Pir Vilayat Khan, the son of Hazrat Inayat Khan and his successor as head of the Sufi Order in the West. In the film Murshid Sam at first appears to be a small and unkempt man, brusque and loud. But then you discern that a lilt modulates his stern voice and that he radiates joy. His body has the energy of a young man, although he is in his late sixties. "He was sturdy, and he could outwalk everyone on the Lama mountain," Noura remembers. People called him Puck, or the pied piper,

---

[2] Sufism is organized in terms of orders established by masters, like Muin ad-Din Muhammad, who founded the Chisti Order in India in the twelfth century, or Jelaluddin Rumi, who founded the Mevlevi Order in Turkey in the thirteenth century. The central relationship, however, is between the shaykh and his follower (or mureed); thus the number of orders in any period can vary. In 1966, for example, there were sixty Sufi orders in Egypt, and in 1989, seventy-three. Shaykhs characteristically trace their lineage (or *silsila*) to Muhammad.

for in San Francisco, his permanent home, he attracted many followers from among the transient young people who thronged the city in the late 1960s.

Like Hazrat Inayat Khan, Murshid Sam espoused religious universalism. He preached that all religions are one religion. "Know that Allah has sent many messengers," he wrote, "with variations of one spiritual message. And *dharma* [the spiritual teachings of India] and *din* [the spiritual teachings of Islam] are essentially one." What matters most is the mystical path, the process of self-overcoming to attain self-realization. Central to this attainment is the awareness that nature and humans are one, that one great consciousness flows through everything, touching all things and creatures with its spirit. Beyond that typical mystical perception, Murshid Sam stressed love—as the binding force in the universe, as the true way to reach God. He drew that element of his belief, as well as other parts of his practice, directly from Islam.

Murshid Sam instructed the Lama residents in traditional Sufi practices as well as in new ones developed by Hazrat Inayat Khan and by himself. He taught them *dhikr*, the Sufi variation on the Hindu practice of *kirtan*. Like *kirtan* (and the dovening of Orthodox Jews), *dhikr* involves chanting the name of Allah again and again on a repetitious melodic line. Sometimes it is done standing and sometimes sitting, sometimes individually or in a group, sometimes loudly or silently. Often the body sways and the head moves backward and forward in a rocking motion. The word *dhikr* means remembrance, and it refers to remembering Allah. As a practice, *dhikr* is meant to produce a coming out of self and an awareness of the presence of God, in an ecstatic experience. Sufi texts suggest that individuals doing *dhikr* may lose control of themselves. On one occasion when doing *dhikr* with a group, I witnessed a participant exhibit such frenzied behavior.

Murshid Sam also instructed the Lama residents in Hazrat Inayat Khan's Universal Worship Service. In this ceremony candles are lit and verses are read from texts of major religions: Islam, Christianity, Judaism, Buddhism, Hinduism, Zoroastrianism, Shinto. Murshid Sam advocated walking meditation, and he had the Lama residents walk around the property and up and down the mountain while doing Hindu and Sufi chants. He also taught them a practice he had himself created called the Dances of Universal Peace, or more simply, "Sufi dancing." (The name is something of a misnomer, since the dances include singing and chanting.) In creating the dances, Murshid Sam drew from the practice of *dhikr*, from ancient Sufi

dances like the whirling of the Mevlevi "dervishes," and also from American folk dances. When a young man, he had studied dancing with Ruth St.
Denis, a pioneer in modern dance who based her choreography on folk
dances as well as on ancient spiritual tales from the East. Most of the
Dances of Universal Peace are slow and stately, with individuals moving
alone or with changing partners in geometric patterns centered around a
circle.

In fashioning his dances Murshid Sam also drew from the texts and
hymns of numerous religions, although in my experience Islam predominates. Two moving dances, which I've often performed, are based on
Qur'anic passages central to Islam: "La illaha illa Llah;" (There is no god but
God); and "Ishk Allah Mahbud Lillah" (Love, lover, and beloved are one).
Murshid Sam intended the dances as rituals of worship and of individual
transformation as well as of brotherhood and sisterhood promoting peace.
With the enthusiasm of a believer, he hoped they might spread throughout
the world.

Murshid Sam deeply impressed the Lama community, and Fran was his
major supporter. Among the quartet of Lama leaders (Fran, Hans,
Stephen, and Barbara), she was the first to move toward Islam; she was the
first to take initiation in the Sufi Order. She was Murshid Sam's first
mureed (disciple) at Lama. After Murshid Sam's visit, *dhikr* and the Universal Worship Service didn't replace Hindu and Buddhist practices in
Lama spirituality. The Dances of Universal Peace were done only on Sundays, during visiting hours, when Fran led them in the large domed room.
They were very important to her; for she needed to establish her own spiritual path as a way of bolstering her sense of identity. Dissension had
appeared at Lama, and she was in the center of it. She needed Murshid
Sam.

For his part, the Sufi Order leader admired the Lama community and
thrilled to its mountain setting. On one occasion he compared the Sangre
de Cristo mountain range to the Himalayas and Lama to the Buddhist
monasteries there. Like everyone at Lama, he responded to the beauty of
the mountain and to its sacred quality. The visionary imagination of these
young people attempting to create a world center for spirituality also
deeply impressed him. When he suddenly died in San Francisco in 1970,
his body was brought to Lama and buried there, as he had requested.

Located in a forest clearing a mile up the mountain from the central
Lama buildings, Murshid Sam's grave has become a shrine where visitors

to Lama leave offerings, as they might at the shrines of Sufi saints in the Middle East. Carved into a wooden memorial over his grave is a brief, elliptical saying: "And on that Day the Sun Shall Rise in the West." The adage comes from a hadith, and the original statement concludes: "all men seeing will believe." It points to Murshid Sam's cosmic optimism in hoping for world peace, as well as to Lama's location in the West and to the community's aspirations for world regeneration through personal transformation. When I was at Lama, I placed on Murshid Sam's grave a ballpoint pen given to me at a Berkshire Conference convention the month before. Inscribed with the name *Journal of Women's History*, it seemed an appropriate tribute from an historian like me.

Murshid Sam's death played a powerful role in Noura's life, and she remembers vividly the day she heard the news. Noura: "When the news of Murshid's death came it was fall and I was at a meditation class off the mountain. Stephen came down to tell me. At that time I was Murshid's only initiate at Lama, although he had many friends there. I was very hard hit. I ran all over the mountain through scrub oak and thorns, scraping on pine trees, trying to find a suitable place to bury him. In the end, others found the place. When the men carried his body up the mountain they found him to be very, very heavy. They couldn't understand it. They had to dig his grave through the frozen ground.

"It was the first death in the community. I had been scheduled to go out later that winter to act as Murshid's secretary. It was a time when my life was in real confusion. I was questioning many things, including my marriage relationship, and I was looking forward to being near Murshid and his guidance. When that possibility was removed I felt great sorrow and realized how much courage he had given me. Later, when Pir Vilayat came to fill in the gaps left by Murshid Sam, I felt a new resonance and took initiation with him in turn. But he was a completely different person. Where Sam Lewis was down to earth, the Pir was ethereal; where Murshid Sam was witty, the Pir was cultured; where Murshid Sam moved with animal magnetism and energy, the Pir moved with taking people with him to exalted states of soul. They were compliments to one another, and I am thankful for both of them. Murshid Sam taught me to say the name of Allah. Pir Vilayat taught me the meaning of *La illaha illa Llah*. Later, in Jerusalem, I learned the meaning of Muhammad."

Barbara and Stephen, Fran and Hans—they were the linchpins of Lama. Each was tall and beautiful, statuesque. Each was committed to Lama.

"They were four spiritual titans: we all looked up to them; we all revered them." That's how a woman who was at Lama in the early years described them to me. But Noura has her own response to that statement. "That was a problem, titanism, thinking yourself important and powerful, and others supporting that image so it's even harder for you to cut through it. It is the opposite of Islam, of surrender. That was the lesson, however painful, we all had to learn, how to overcome our inflated images, each in his and her own way."

CHAPTER TEN

Dar-al-Islam

1971–1990

Involving personal communion with God, mysticism easily leads to spiritual independence, to individuals finding their own teachers and religious paths. Many people who came to Lama, Noura told me, stayed for a time and then left, following teachers with whom they had studied at Lama or had met elsewhere. Writer Natalie Goldberg lived at Lama during the summer of 1976; the next year she went to Colorado to study with the Tibetan Lama, Chogyam Trungpa Rinpoche. In 1993 I met a married couple at Lama who called themselves Mary and Joseph. They told me they had lived at the community one summer ten years before but hadn't stayed. Instead, they went to New York City, where they attended a lecture given by a Buddhist guru named Ma. She swept them away; they followed her to her ashram in Florida. They've lived there as her disciples ever since.

Lama encouraged this individualism. When I was there, the people at the community for summer workshops followed a number of spiritualities: Buddhism, Theosophy, Jewish and Christian mysticism, the Sufi Order in the West. They had come to Lama for its ecumenicism in its impressive mountain setting. "What is your spiritual practice?" I was repeatedly asked. Noura: "Lama was never intended to be a permanent home for many people. Only a few were ever allowed—or had the inclination— to stay over the winter. Whenever a teacher came who attracted someone deeply, that person would want to follow the teacher. This certainly happened to us in following Pir

Vilayat Khan. For spiritual discipline you need to spend a period of time close to your guide, serving him or her, learning from the presence of the person in many situations."

Fran also followed her own path; she moved from the Sufi Order of Murshid Sam and Pir Vilayat Khan to Islam. Why did she take this direction? Why did she give up the undemanding Sufi Order for a rigorous faith? Childhood experiences pointed her that way: her Episcopal faith and the exotic splendor of her Inglewood church; the fairy tales she read set in far-off lands; her mother's aestheticism and her grandmother's stories of adventure. To someone as passionate as Fran, who began studying Eastern religions her freshman year in college and who searched for fulfillment through them for more than a decade, Islam had the appeal of finality, of being at the end of a path. Besides, to a Sufi Order member, Islam isn't that distant.

Wait a minute! That may be your response when you know the whole story. You may suspect that Fran professed Islam because she fell in love with Stephen, and he became Muslim. (When he professed Islam he changed his name to Nuridin.) To win Stephen, Fran had to follow him. No, I would counter, the truth is more complex. To apply Western standards and to assume that romantic love takes precedence in human motivation, especially for women, is reductive. The people at Lama were living deeply spiritual lives, and they must be viewed from that vantage. Fran's movement to Islam was parallel to Stephen's, but her growing commitment was independent of his. It took years for his marriage to dissolve, just as their paths to Islam were gradual and not always smooth. Along the way it was never certain they would wind up together.

Fran broke with Hans because she didn't find him sufficiently committed to her brand of spirituality. Although he seemed drawn to the Sufi Order, she sensed a strong streak of agnoticism in him. Stephen was willing to go all the way to Islam, and that's what she eventually wanted. Hans and Fran differed in temperament. Like his sister Barbara, Hans was gentle and serene; Fran was passionate and dramatic. And so was Stephen. He was a charismatic leader at Lama. A "Lawrence of Arabia," one Lama resident described him to me. Another called him "a profound prophet" and a "gruff, crazy man." With admiration for his eloquence, Hans described him as "a tongue dancer from the New York City streets," for Stephen was largely self-taught. Fran and Stephen tried to stop their involvement. To cause dissension was deeply troubling to Fran; to undermine the community and their close family relationships violated all her conceptions of honor and duty. Children were involved: Stephen and Barbara had four young daughters; and Fran and Hans had had a third child soon after they moved to Lama. *Cookbook* reveals the desperation which all the adults at Lama felt; passages in the pamphlet caution against gossip, small talk, and "hanging out" and recommend turning families into shrines by conceptualizing the family as a union like the one between the individual and the divine. But nothing seemed to work; the attraction between Fran and Stephen was too strong.

"The Lama drama." That's what people who lived there at the time now call the breakup. It was just as melodramatic as a soap opera, they say. Such wry humor staunches their hurt over what happened years ago, when the bonds between the founders of their community, their leaders in spirituality who were related by blood and marriage, seemed to disintegrate.

Noura: "The end of my marriage was combined with the end of Stephen's, and his took a long time to sort itself out. With the intimacy and proximity at Lama, everything was blown far out of proportion by our being so few, so comparatively isolated, and observing one another so closely. The judgments, the ostracisms, and the occasional understanding were all part of divorce in a hothouse setting. Hans and I were incompatible in certain very deep ways and even with ten years of successful marriage, with much good in it, these ways became too much. Then he went through a long period of religious and personal introspection, and he withdrew from me just when I wanted strong emotional and physical companionship. Stephen and I resisted the magnetism between us for a very long time. Even after we accepted it, we all continued to work toward the same spiritual goals for a number of years, both at Lama and elsewhere."

Noura remembers two experiences as the beginning of her movement to Islam. A Hindu teacher, Hari Dass Baba, came to Lama to conduct a workshop. Seeking him out, Fran asked his advice about a matter that was troubling her. She was committed to Lama, she told him, but she disliked Hindu and Buddhist meditations. She found them boring; even with a mantra, her mind wandered. Hari Dass Baba had maintained a vow of silence for eighteen years. To answer her he wrote with chalk on a slate, which was his way of communicating: "Don't try to squeeze oil out of sand." She took these words to mean that she should seek out a practice that felt right to her, rather than blaming herself for not feeling moved and refreshed by the practices that worked for others.

Then Murshid Sam came to Lama, and he held individual spiritual conferences with the residents. (Hindus call these conferences *darshan*.) He gave different advice to each person who saw him. He counseled one to study Christianity, another Buddhism, another Islam. Noura: "Murshid's *darshan* was hardly traditional. He explained that the teacher should give a small gift to the student at the end of the sitting. He had been working hard in the garden, and there was an overabundance of swiss chard, quite large and with heavy heads. He piled these up and handed one to each person as they left. People came out of the room looking bemused, having just been given often surprising spiritual advice that could change their life, holding in one hand a limp bunch of chard like a green, day-old bouquet. I went in to him and sat, and we stared at each other. Rather he stared, and I tried to back through the wall. Then he told me, quite simply, to say 'Allah' over and over and to read the Qur'an and the hadith. He also taught me to say: subhan Allah (s-b-h in Arabic means 'to swim'), alhamdulillah (praise to Allah), and adahu Akbar (Allah is greater). I took my chard and left. I remember coming out into the sunshine and thinking something had altered dramatically in my concentration."

Noura doesn't know why Murshid Sam sent her toward Islam rather than one of the other belief systems he recommended that day. Spiritual teachers can be ambiguous in giving advice, for they want their disciples to discover for themselves if a suggested path is right for them. Fran desired a new meditative practice, and Sufi forms may have been more suited to her active nature. In spiritual practice Sufis are often in motion, chanting, doing *dhikr*, meditating on the "ninety-nine beautiful names of Allah," the attributes of Allah identified in the Qur'an. Fran was in emotional turmoil; submission to a new kind of discipline, one that Murshid Sam himself followed, might offer a way for her to regain balance. Besides, Fran was a wife and mother, and Sufism doesn't stress asceticism. Muslim shaykhs usually are married. "Be in the world and not of it." That is a common Sufi—and Muslim—admonition.

Noura recognizes that at the time she didn't know why she followed Murshid Sam's advice. Noura: "Murshid Sam's death was part of the turmoil of my life. Once I no longer had his wisdom to lean on, everything fell to pieces. I had gone through this vast process of education, and it didn't seem to have gotten me very far, and my new love was impossible, and

Murshid Sam had taught me to say the Name of Allah although I really wasn't a Muslim. I was just doing what my teacher told me to do, and it helped direct me." Once Fran began her spiritual odyssey, I don't think she could have stopped it. She was too intense, too driven to finding the ending once she had begun the journey. She had studied spiritual texts for years. She had put all her ambition into the search for spiritual truth and personal transformation, and those goals had proved almost impossible for her to attain. Some individuals find enlightenment easily, like St. Paul on the road to Tarsus or Ram Dass in India. For others it can take a lifetime.

"I so often say that what I'm after is real union with God," Fran wrote to her mother after her breakup with Hans. "Which is what I'm after, I say—but I so often forget." She continued: "I watch myself traveling through the lattices of my mind, into room after room each with a different voice: you feel sad and lonely; you're the queen; you're lost and stupid; you're capable of self-sufficiency. Somewhere in my being I hear all of the sirens calling, and I then know I'm nobody, and I know it's possible, and all right as long as I say yes." She concluded: "Oh, I'd like it if getting to a place of inner freedom were easier."

Inner freedom—what does that term mean? Equanimity, transcendence, ecstasy—all are part of this state that lies at the end of the mystic's path. For Sufis, surrender is key. "Die before you die." That is a key teaching for Sufis. My teachers in the Sufi Order in the West regard the surrender as internal, not external. They see it as giving up negative drives such as vanity and jealousy to overcome the ego and to create an integrated personality. But that may be only the beginning: I'm still not far along on my own path. Noura's own words express her sense of liberation through surrender. "What may appear from outside Islam as a set of strictures, even a trap, a series of limitations, appears from inside to be an infinite expanding geometry, a crystalline structure of great beauty which not only insures safety and orders chaos, but allows the soul freedom to soar."

Using the scientific term "geometry" along with the aesthetic term "beauty" to characterize Islam isn't unusual, for the faith includes a cosmological and symbolic system that can take a lifetime to comprehend. (A relevant, although oblique, analogy from the West might be Jung's "archetypes.") With my Sufi Order group I study the Qur'anic commentaries of the thirteenth-century Moorish philosopher, Ibn al-Arabi. His vast synthesis of alchemy, astrology, Neoplatonism, Pythagoreanism, and different viewpoints within Islam is considered definitive to Islamic mysticism. He is called "the greatest shaykh." As we ponder each word and phrase in Ibn Arabi's work, trying to tease out hidden meanings, his system sometimes seems scholastic to me. Yet I also find such exegesis fascinating, like a game or a puzzle.

I also find it profound, as when I read that everything in creation is a symbol and that all those symbols are recreated in me, if I can only find them. Every verse of the Qur'an, according to one commentator, conceals a minimum of seven hidden meanings, and the number can reach to seventy—or seven thousand. Seyyed Hossein Nasr writes that "the sacred history in the Qur'an is the epic of the life of the soul. The forces of good and evil in it are to be found within ourselves, and even the prophets are the objective and external counterparts of the inner intellect." Thus Noura describes Islam as crystalline, and that is another common descriptive adjective for the religion. It refers to the transparency and clarity of the crystal, absorbing and refracting light, with its regular plane surfaces reflecting an ordered internal arrangement of molecules. All gems (except for the opal) are crystals; no two crystals are exactly alike.

What do I make of the angels, archangels, and jinns in the Qur'an? Are they real or metaphorical? Are they beings who control me or whom I create? How do I interpret the seven heavens through which Muhammad ascended on the night journey, with each heaven containing a Ka'abah directly above the earthly one in Makkah and directly below the throne of heaven? There are volumes of Islamic writings on questions like these, and the commentaries date to the time of Muhammad. How do I deal with the common complaint that Ibn-Arabi's work has never been adequately translated? Noura contends that his translators always emphasize the universalist elements in his thought and downplay the Islamic.

In their teachings, some Sufis apply age-old systems of metaphysical speculation mixing the sounds and letters of Arabic with numbers, with a numerical value for each letter of the alphabet. There are learned treatises on *dhikr* which examine the meanings of its movements and its chants. This exegesis is multiplied through including the ritual prayers and Qur'an reading as forms of *dhikr*. Sometimes I think that all of Islam can be reduced to one word, "Allah," and to God's divinity and humanity's submission. That exacting monotheism troubles me, until I realize that the word extends outward to a complex cosmology, metaphysics, ethics, and psychology. The Sufi written tradition also includes the love poetry, which proposes that love is the true way of reaching illumination. Annemarie

Schimmel writes that love is "the power that separates true mysticism from mere asceticism." There are aphoristic stories, dating back for centuries, still told throughout the Middle East. The stories have an earthy, peasant quality, for Sufism has been a way of life for ordinary people as much as for intellectuals.

But its intellectual side appeals to me, as it does to Noura. By intellect Sufis don't mean only rationality; they include intuition and imagination as components. They speak of understanding through *ma'arifa*, the "eye of the heart," the gnosis of ancient Eastern philosophers. Centuries ago the Western intellectual tradition split these elements of human understanding apart and privileged the rational mind. That split between intuition and rationality contributed to the ending of Fran's and my friendship, when I followed my rational bent to became a college professor and she went to Lama on a spiritual quest.

The other day I remembered that Fran's grandfather, Augustus Murray, was a classical philologist and that his uncle, Lindley Murray, was the most eminent grammarian of the English language a century ago. Both these forbears of Fran's studied the structure and meaning of language, and Noura follows in their path. The study of language comprises a major part of Islamic learning, since the Arabic language—with no written vowels, many verb tenses, and words with a variety of meanings—adds another layer of analysis to an activity such as Qur'an study. The literary style of Semitic people is filled with embellishments and indirect figures of speech as well as with metaphor and allegory. One commentator calls that style "musical calligraphy." The focus in Islam on the Qur'an, the words of Allah, and on calligraphy, the visible expression of those words, is, on one level, a concentration on language. The complex language, the literary style, and the calligraphy have an aesthetic element appealing to artists such as Nuridin and Noura.

Can I be so certain that Fran's spiritual journey is the key to understanding her? I suppose one could choose to overlook the years she spent in religious study and contemplation to posit that I've never really understood her. One could claim that the free-spirited girl I've depicted was an illusion and that throughout her life what Fran really wanted was to be controlled. I suppose one could speculate that she came under the influence of powerful gurus or that she had some sort of life crisis and that those are the real reasons she became Muslim. But I wouldn't agree. Like practiced psychologists, effective gurus reflect their pupils as much as they lead them, and Fran's spiritual teachers whom I've met are subtle and skilled. She did have a life crisis, triggered by the breakup of her marriage, but she struggled through it to reach a stable life plateau in Islam. I had a similar crisis when I reached the age my mother died, and I also worked through it to reach a new maturity. Fran has always liked drama in her life. I think of her as a spiritual explorer who journeyed through many territories before she found a home—and the internal drama and peace Islam provides her.

Noura: "It was finally the collapse of my life that allowed me to make the leap into faith. The end of my marriage produced such tension at Lama that I could hardly bear it; the chaos around that ending destroyed any predetermined picture I had of what my life should be like. This devastation finally undermined the 'I' enough so that I could finally say, OK, there is something to these doctrines of personal transformation through practice and belief in a higher being. I had always sensed that something, but until well along my journey to find it I didn't have a name for it or a way of addressing it that felt right and natural to me. Islam gave me a doctrine and a practice that felt right and natural."

Islam also offered absolution for transgressive behavior. Muslims, unlike Christians, don't believe in original sin. Human error is forgiven if there is true repentance, and guilt doesn't linger. For Muslims the framework of faith is not sin and salvation but error and guidance. From an Islamic framework Fran was able to ask forgiveness in the expectation of receiving real absolution for having ended her marriage and caused others such pain. Many years later, Fran's youngest son, a Muslim, called his mother from Georgetown University where, as a freshman, he was taking a required course in Western thought which was heavily weighted with Christian writers. "I don't really understand what's bothering them," he said. "What is their problem?" He didn't understand the troubled spirit of writers like Kirkegaard, for it wasn't part of his Muslim experience.

With their marriages breaking apart, the four Lama leaders began leaving the mountain. They would come back at various times and in various combinations, but for a while they needed to be away from each other to sort out their lives. Hans went to California and worked with the followers of Murshid Sam; eventually Barbara also joined the Sufi Order. Fran and Stephen followed Pir Vilayat Khan. As is standard Sufi Order practice, the Pir renamed Fran. She became Shahidah, meaning witness. (Hans, Barbara, and Stephen also took new names: Hans became Siddiq; Barbara, Asha;

Stephen, Shanaz). After her years of spiritual searching and her renunciation of mainstream society, Fran no longer felt she was the woman who had grown up in Inglewood and graduated from Stanford. A new name was appropriate to her commitment to a new spiritual path.

Noura: "Stephen and I, along with Barbara, bounced all over the place for a while. We all three and all of our children spent a year together near San Francisco editing and illustrating Pir Vilayat's book, *Toward the One*. During three summers we built a meditation camp for the Pir high in the French Alps overlooking the Mer de Glace, the glacier over Chamonix. We worked on Nuridin's book, *Seed*, a collection of many images, experiences, and spiritual teachings. We lived off and on at Lama in various combinations, with Stephen sometimes with Barbara and sometimes with me." At times Fran's children were with Hans, at others they were with Fran; in the winters they mostly remained at Lama, with its community of adults who were like kin to them and with their schools nearby.

Fran began studying the Qur'an and the hadith, as Murshid Sam had advised. At first she found the text of the Qur'an nearly incomprehensible, and that isn't surprising: it is very difficult for non-Muslims to understand. But she slowly responded to it. Stephen's book *Seed*, published in 1973, indicates their growing acceptance of Islam. The book weaves quotations from spiritual and secular texts with Stephen's writings and includes many quotations from Muslim sources. It ends with excerpts from the Qur'an, in addition to the words of the Muslim prayers and a list of the ninety-nine names of Allah. The names begin with Ar-Rahman (all merciful), Al-Rahim (all compassionate), and al-Malik (sovereign, lord of lords). *Seed* also extols the *salat*, the Muslim prayers, as "the realization of one's subsistence in God & Being essentially one with God."

During those years Pir Vilayat taught Fran a new chant, one of great authority within Islam and one that profoundly moved her. The chant helped her to better manage the emotional upheaval she was undergoing. Pir Vilayat taught her to say "La illaha illa Llah" (There is no God but God). Noura: "That phrase is really the basis of Islam. There are libraries on that phrase. One of the things it means is that any person, or any idea, or any ism, or any concept which may be your ideal or goal is as nothing compared to Allah. That over all these ideas and isms is a greater power which created them all in the first place. You know this from before you were born, and you will know it after you die. You must acknowledge this and say, I surrender. That is what separates a Muslim from a non-Muslim, because Islam means surrender."

The summer of 1975 was a turning point in Fran's journey to Islam. Noura: "Then one summer I went alone to Chamonix. I was running the kitchen for sometimes two hundred people, and it was a daily miracle that food was served which had come up the mountain by mule, human backs, and *telepherique* [gondola cars on a cable], and which had been transformed into meals." Fran read many Sufi authors that summer, and she talked with students at the camp who had studied Islam in Turkey, Afghanistan, and India. Those students had found that the Sufis in those countries were all Muslim. Fran began to realize that only several Western orders, such as the Sufi Order in the West, allow non-Muslims to be members. She began to feel that the Sufi practices they were doing—*dhikr*, meditation on the names of Allah, Murshid Sam's dances—were only a prelude to a deeper understanding that was inside Islam. She felt as though a breeze was blowing over her from the Islamic world like the one from India some ten years before, which had drawn Richard Alpert to India and influenced the founding of Lama.

Fran's final decision to profess Islam occurred in Jerusalem, the ancient crucible of Judaism, Christianity, and Islam. After the summer camp in 1975 Fran went there to join Stephen and others from Lama and Chamonix. Noura: "While at Chamonix, I received a letter from Stephen inviting me to meet him in Jerusalem to collect material for a book of interviews and photographs about the three great monotheisms which meet in that holy city. I had just enough money to get a ticket. I took the Orient Express to Athens, spent an hour at the Parthenon in honor of my mother, and then flew to Palestine. We stayed there for four months, with ten other people, in a big house on the Mount of Olives. There, through observation, experience, and long discussions with real Muslims, many of us became Muslim."

Jerusalem was magical to Fran. "It is the same as when Christ was here, the same as when the Prophet came here from Mecca on the Night Journey," she wrote to her mother. "I look out of the window of our house, and I see the hills of Jordan; the Dead Sea; the hills between here and Bethlehem." She was exultant. "The church over the stone Christ stepped on to mount the ass on Palm Sunday is across the street. Yesterday I walked in the Garden of Gethsemane." But there was fear. It was a dangerous time, with an open state of war between Israel and neighboring Arab states. "Planes were flying overhead," Noura told me in our interviews, "and the atmosphere was very tense, and people were getting killed."

In the midst of the elation, the fear, and the pressure of doing the interviews and photographs for the book, she responded strongly and positively to the traditional Muslim culture around them. In the mid-1970s, Muslims still predominated in Jerusalem; Jews migrating there weren't yet in the majority. It was still a city of domes and minarets, dominated by the Quabbat al-Sakhra, the Dome of the Rock. This structure was built in 691 on the rock from which Muhammad is said to have ascended to heaven for communion with Allah, in what Muslims call the Night Journey. Sufis revere this event, for Muhammad's ascent to heaven symbolizes their mystical path. Muhammad's footprints, Noura told me, still show in the rock.

In Jerusalem Fran experienced a non-Western culture for the first time. She had liked living simply at Lama, and the simple way of life of the Palestinians impressed her. She liked the closeness of their extended families, their lack of a focus on time, their deeply felt hospitality to strangers, and their public culture of bazaars and open markets, with streets filled with people until well into the night. As she penetrated more deeply into the Arab culture which supports Islam, she began to feel that the supposed superiority of Western modernization over ancient folkways was an illusion. This identification of hers with a non-Western, Middle Eastern culture would play an important role in her professing Islam.

The classic narrative of the conversion of a Westerner to Islam is that of Muhammad Asad, a leader of the emerging state of Pakistan in the 1930s. To understand why she became Muslim, Noura recommended that I read Asad's autobiography, and I did so. Born in Poland to Jewish parents, Asad had been a member of the turn-of-the-century generation that, like that of the 1960s, questioned Western values. Influenced by the ancient Chinese philosopher Lao-Tzu, Asad first followed the Taoist path of controlled serenity. Then a visit to Jerusalem brought him into contact with Islam. There he found exactly what Fran found fifty years later: great human warmth, an organic coherence, and a kin community. He, too, began to identify with this non-Western, Islamic culture. He became convinced that the Muslim Palestinians had none of the "painful cleavages of the spirit; those phantoms of fear, greed, and inhibition that made European life so ugly." Asad became Muslim in 1926.

Important to Fran's path toward accepting Islam was a Sufi shaykh whom Stephen met by accident on a local bus in Bethlehem. The shaykh was the Qadi (judge) of the city. Both he and Stephen had red hair and beards. They began by joking with one another on the bus about the similarities in their appearances, and they ended by establishing a bond. For a time the shaykh came to their house daily to pray, chant, and study with them.

Noura: "Our meetings with him in that stone house in that ancient place were out of time, beyond history. He began them by saying what I had long wanted to hear: 'Ask me anything you want. If I can't answer your questions, I'll find someone who will.' So we asked all kinds of questions, and at last after many days he turned to me and said: 'You've got it all wrong. You think that there are all these religions, and they are equal, and they are all around in a circle leading to the center on paths like the spokes of a bicycle wheel. This is not the way it is. It is not a circle, but a spiral, growing up like a plant from the first man, Adam, who had the first guidance from Allah. His descendants followed that guidance for a time, and then misused it, and so another prophet, Noah, was sent. People followed his teaching for a time and then the same thing happened. Every time a new prophet was sent he brought the same message. Every time, some of the people followed for a while and then built walls around what they knew and stood behind them and said that they were the chosen people and knew the truth. And they stayed behind their walls and misused the original teachings to the point that a new prophet had to come. This is the real history of the human race until the time of the last one, the Seal of the Prophets, Muhammad. He brought a message which Allah has promised will not be altered, and which is sent not to one tribe or people but to all the world. We still have it today, word for word. That is Islam. It is the same message sent to Adam and to all the other prophets, including Moses and Jesus. There is only one message: Surrender to the Creator, Allah.' "

Then came Fran's first experience of Ramadan, the month-long fasting from sunrise to sunset that is a central Muslim rite. The holiest time of the Muslim year, Ramadan celebrates Muhammad's initial reception of Allah's revelations, and the fasting symbolizes the submission to Allah at the center of the faith. Fasting requires great self-restraint; it can produce faintness, tranquility, and even ecstasy, as the body contends with the absence of food and water. Through its discipline Fran found a way to break through what she saw as her resistance to Islam.

Engaged in this physical experience of dedication to Allah, Fran felt a change occurring in herself. She seemed to move beyond her ego and her body to an internal place she had experienced before only as sudden surges of feeling, and she seemed to give up her will to a force beyond her self.

This turning to Allah wasn't a sudden mystical experience, focused on an intense epiphany. She didn't see visions or speak in tongues. The change was gradual, involving feelings of peace and joy. She had reached a new stage in her spiritual journey. Over the centuries Sufi commentators have written many treatises specifying the exact number of stages on the road to illumination: often the depiction is of seven, sometimes of a lesser or greater number. Whatever the stages Noura traveled in her years of searching, she was moving toward the state that Sufis call *fana*, the final stage of annihilation of self in union with Allah.

Not for several years more would she finally commit to professing Islam. Noura: "In fact, I reached a place of exhaustion after that Ramadan in Jerusalem where I had to lie down in the hot afternoon sun because I couldn't do anything. And I realized that all my life I had thought I was 'doing'—when in actuality Allah had been in control from the beginning. And at that point, I gave up. For Ramadan had not been simply a practice; it was a reality I came up against that I had never experienced before. It was as though my whole image of myself shifted planes suddenly. I had entered the world of Islam; I felt a deep, abiding sense of the presence of Allah."

As they had for centuries, the traditional Arabs in Jerusalem wore long robes which concealed their bodies, and the women covered their hair with scarves. Feeling part of them, Noura also put on clothes which covered her body, and she also tied a scarf around her head. Wearing the scarf seemed strange to her; at first she put it on as an experiment, to see what her reaction would be. She found that she liked wearing it. She liked the sense of security and freedom it gave her—security in being part of a community of believers and freedom in no longer fearing unwanted male attention. When she wore the scarf, men didn't stare at her on the streets; she avoided male comments and whistles.

When I was at Lama I spoke to a woman who had been in Jerusalem with Fran and Stephen and who was drawn toward professing Islam there. "I was swept away," she told me. "I was overcome by the beauty of the traditionalism of the Arab culture and the intensity of our experience together. It was like taking a ride on a magic carpet to lands of peace and joy." Noura wasn't naive about the potential costs of her radical change in belief and lifestyle—to her family, to Lama, to her ability to function in the regular world. Her years of work and travel had exhausted her, and she had to be absolutely certain she was doing the right thing. She may have been swept away, but after the Jerusalem experience, "I felt like a beached Jonah, just out of the whale's belly."

Once Stephen and Fran had completed taking the photos and interviews for Stephen's projected book, they left Jerusalem to come back to the United States, to New Mexico and Lama. They had always meant to return to the place they considered their home. In Jerusalem they'd formulated a grand scheme for Lama: they would establish an international center for Islamic studies on their mountain. Some months after they arrived, companions of theirs in Jerusalem joined them. However, residents who followed the teachings of Murshid Sam and other spiritual leaders were at Lama, still maintaining the community and conducting the summer workshops. Barbara and Hans were among them, and Hans was the coordinator. Both remained loyal to the Sufi Order.

Stephen and Fran had no thoughts of taking over Lama. Yet as founders and early leaders of the community, they felt they had a right to be there. The point was indisputable, and the others agreed not to challenge their presence. The mountain was large enough to provide space for both groups. Lama was meant to function as a center for spiritual experimentation and a "school for basic studies"; its ecumenical mission could extend to Islam. For their part, Fran and Stephen could apply Islamic toleration to the situation. Over the ages Islam has characteristically accepted other religions. Muslims believe that Abraham, Jesus, and other founders of early religions were revered prophets of Allah who preceded Muhammad; the Qur'an teaches that their faiths deserve respect.

Given their differing lifestyles and the personal tensions between them, the two groups couldn't occupy the original buildings together harmoniously for long. The domed meeting space wasn't large enough for the Muslims to pray, worship, and perform their meditative practices like *dhikr* and Qur'an reading, while the non-Muslims did the Dances of Universal Peace and their Hindu and Buddhist chants and meditations. The Muslims needed their own masjid, where they could worship and pray undisturbed. Even preparing food in the same kitchen was difficult, since the non-Muslims were vegetarians and the Muslims, following the Islamic dietary code, ate meat. Once again Stephen conceived a building, as he had in the early days of Lama and as he would later at Dar-al-Islam. Drawing on Lama plans for a study center, Stephen, Fran, and their group constructed his building to serve as their masjid and living space. They called it the Islamic Study

Center (ISC). The building resembles the original zomed structure, on a smaller scale. Noura: "It was a short distance through the woods to the Foundation proper. It was much like a small monastery, with twelve single rooms around a court with a large room for cooking, a smaller one off it for eating, and space for prayer in what was the first masjid in New Mexico. We built all day and studied Islam deep into the night."

No one at the Islamic Study Center had yet openly declared themselves Muslim, although all were studying Islamic texts intensively. As a result, according to Noura, they were being rapidly drawn to Islam. As their religious fervor deepened, conflict between them and the non-Muslims was probably inevitable. The utopian vision of living peacefully together, of raising their children together, slowly broke apart. There were the questions of what faith Fran's and Stephen's children were to be taught and what to do about Barbara and Stephen's reluctance to divorce. The differing lifestyle of each group began to annoy the other. The Muslims wore Muslim dress, the women with scarves over their heads. They called five times a day for prayers, and they observed Muslim ceremonies. They didn't like the statues of Buddha the non-Muslims put in the meeting center zome that Stephen had designed, and they didn't like seeing women on the property wearing shorts, with their legs exposed. Both groups still used Lama's original washroom; the Muslims demanded a special time to take non-communal, nonmixed gender showers.

Minor differences rankled. An important yearly rite for Muslims is the feast of Eid El Adha (the festival of sacrifice). It commemorates God's command to Abraham to demonstrate loyalty by sacrificing his son Ismael and God's retraction of his extreme demand as Abraham prepares to carry out the sacrifice. To Muslims, Allah's demand symbolizes his divinity, while Abraham's willingness to obey shows human submission. The retraction of the command symbolizes God's mercy. In their celebration Muslim families kill a sheep, give most of the meat away to the needy, and feast on the rest. This feasting offended the non-Muslim vegetarians at Lama. As the celebration approached one year, they untied and freed the lamb the Muslims had acquired for their ceremonial meal. This intrusion angered the Muslims.

Throughout this time of growing tension, the two groups managed to compromise their differences, even to maintain Lama's practice of governing through consensus. Lama's 1977 outreach brochure reveals both the comity and the division. It announces that the Islamic call to prayer is sounded five times a day and that some of the residents observe Ramadan. It praises the ecumenicism of Murshid Sam and describes him as a Sufi master with training in "Zen Buddhism, Hinduism, Judaism, and Christianity." It also hints that the non-Muslims may be planning to take control by announcing that the "future use" of the Islamic Study Center is "under consideration." That same year those studying Islam at the ISC put together a brochure for a work camp they intended to hold. On its cover Fran drew a handshake before a palm tree, symbolizing their hope for reconciliation.

But the attempt to live together was proving impossible. Family stress as well as the fervor of religious belief brought each side to solidify its position. The disagreements continued. People who were there at the time now call the bickering, moderated by truces and attempts at reconciliation, "the Holy Wars."

The Lama process of governing through consensus was breaking down. In the spring of 1977, less than two years after the arrival of the Muslims, a three-day meeting was held in the main hall at which both sides aired their grievances. Reconciliation was impossible. Unable to arrive at any decision, they decided to suspend the consensus process and to take a vote on the future of the community. A majority voted against the Muslims, and Hans and the other non-Muslims retained control. Lama would remain an ecumenical center without a strict Muslim component. Shortly after this episode, Hans remarried. He remained coordinator of the community for a time, until he moved to Santa Fe to become first a plumber and then a professor of physics at St. John's University. Barbara, unwilling to share in Muslim polygamy, divorced Stephen as he moved toward marriage with Fran. She left Lama to live in a community in Virginia, where she has remained ever since. She often returns to Lama to visit and teach.

Fran and Stephen left Lama, but they continued their path to Islam. They took the next logical steps: they married and they professed Islam. Stephen became Nuridin (meaning light of the din, or way of Islam), and Fran became Noura, a name that is a feminine form of Nur and that was the name of the mother of the Muslim man before whom she made her profession of faith. Becoming a Muslim involves a simple act: the witnessing, *shahadah*, that there is no God but Allah and that Muhammad is his prophet. Beyond that the faith has four requirements: fasting during Ramadan; praying five times a day; journeying on the Hajj to Makkah; and tithing for the benefit of the community (*zakat*). Finally, Fran found the ending to her long spiritual voyage; she found certainty and freedom through submission to Islam.

Leaving Lama, Noura and Nuridin decided to return to the Middle East. They obtained visas for many Arab countries. Eventually they arrived in Saudi Arabia, in Makkah, the holy city of Islam, and they stayed there. They enrolled in universities to study the Arabic language and Islamic doctrine.

During the time that Noura and Nuridin lived in Makkah, its fifty thousand residents included only eight Western families, for non-Muslims are prohibited from living in or even visiting this sacred city. But Noura wasn't troubled by her isolation from Westerners. She studied at Makkah's separate university for women; she taught English as a second language; she cared for her family. Her two older children chose to stay at Lama, but her youngest son and one of Nuridin's daughters lived with them during one of their years in Makkah. Noura's first daughter with Nuridin was born there. (A second daughter would be born in Abiquiu.) Noura accepted what Westerners regard as restrictions on women in Saudi Arabia. She wore the required dress for women, a cloak of black cloth which covers the entire body from head to feet and which is called an abayah. "It really isn't as oppressive as Westerners think," she told me. "You simply throw it on over your clothing; you can wear anything you like under it; you don't have to change every time you leave the house."

Noura and Nuridin lived only three minutes from the Great Masjid. In that sanctuary stands the Ka'abah, the large black cube that is the center of the world for Muslims. No matter where they are, Muslims face in the direction of the Ka'abah when doing their daily prayers. Noura and Nuridin visited the masjid whenever they could, sharing in the rapture of pilgrims on Hajj. They watched as those pilgrims touch the sacred black stone in the corner of the Ka'abah; circle seven times around the cube; and pray before the nearby stone honoring the prophet Abraham, reputed by some to have built the Ka'abah. Then they drink water from the well of Zamzam, before continuing on to the rites of Hajj elsewhere.

"What did you do for entertainment in Makkah?" I asked Noura. "We went to the Ka'abah," she answered. "We experienced its ecstasy whenever we wanted to; we healed from the hurts we had experienced at Lama. We had broken up two families; our vision for Lama hadn't succeeded. We needed time to rest and regroup. In Makkah we were at the center of the Muslim universe: how could we ask for more?"

Noura also spent part of every day alone in the Haram, the sacred area around the Ka'abah. She prayed and watched the women there, who came from countries around the world. Noura: "One of the strongest impressions I had in Makkah was of the community of Muslim women. I used to sit by the Ka'abah and watch them pass by, from Malaysia, Pakistan, Afghanistan, Southern Russia, Africa, Europe, Egypt. I learned from each one of them, from the walk, the talk, the many varieties of dress. I learned from the women I met in Makkah, from the care we all showed one another. It was the first time in my life I had been in a society of women, where women met, prayed, and studied together—not for just a weekend but all the time. The love and tenderness changed the way I viewed the world.

"It was so different from our high school experience, with its competition, its attention-grabbing, and the continual attraction and polarization between girls and boys. To some degree that polarization continued even at Lama, where men and women were all mixed together in a way that was exhausting. Suddenly, when I came to Makkah, I was in a world of mystery and questions and faith. It was a feminine democracy quite unknown to me in any other context. Its grace and love have continued to amaze me ever since."

Noura and Nuridin's stay in Makkah lasted only three years. It was a time of resting in which they affirmed their faith and studied its meaning. Noura: "From the beginning we knew we wouldn't stay in Makkah indefinitely. Saudi Arabians aren't especially sympathetic to the mysticism of Sufism, which we espoused; their brand of Islam to us was hard and legalistic. The climate is hot and dry. There are few trees in Makkah; few places to experience green nature; few parks where children can play." Yet for the time being, living in their religion's holy city satisfied them. Once they left Makkah, they felt nostalgia for it.

Nuridin met a Saudi businessman in the Great Masjid one day, and the two of them shared their separate dreams of establishing an Islamic center in America. One evening during Ramadan, when Noura was at the sacred space, she observed a group of women praying and concluding the daily fast together. One of them was Moothie bint Khaled, a daughter of Saudi Arabia's King Khaled. She was a philanthropist whose family supported art and education, and her husband was a son of the reformist King Faisal. Noura and the princess fell into conversation. Noura spoke of how she and Nuridin had failed in their attempt to found a center for Islamic studies in the United States and of how they still dreamed of creating such a center.

Noura's story deeply moved the princess, and she decided to back Noura and Nuridin in a second attempt. She donated money of her own, and she persuaded her sisters, her father, and other members of the royal family to contribute. Other Saudis backed the project, including the businessman Nuridin had met. Later fund-raising on the part of Noura and Nuridin throughout the Middle East brought contributions from both the wealthy and the less well-to-do.

In 1980 Noura and Nuridin returned to the United States to launch their new project. They searched for a location in the vicinity of Santa Fe, an area they knew well from their years at Lama, and they bought a large tract of land near Abiquiu, midway between Santa Fe and Taos. Muslims who had been with them at Lama and others they had met in the Middle East joined them. The plans for their venture included a working farm, elementary and secondary schools, a conference center, a university, and a school for teaching and producing indigenous New Mexican and Islamic crafts. They named their undertaking Dar-al-Islam, the territory of Islam, the abode of the faithful. Their scheme was impressive; their center had the potential to become a major religious and educational enterprise.

Noura: "The idea was unique, and we were deeply committed to it. The intention was to build a community in the West where Islam would be lived, not just a masjid or an Islamic center. These centers function more or less like churches all over the United States, serving as weekend schools and places for prayer, particularly the required Friday prayers. But we wanted to build a place where everyday life was touched by Islam, as in other parts of the Islamic world, where school, neighbors, and small businesses all take part in that Islamic character."

To design their masjid, Nuridin contacted Hassan Fathy, a renowned Egyptian architect whose book *Architecture for the Poor* had influenced Nuridin in designing the Lama structures. Fathy was a leading advocate for the use of traditional designs and materials in building. As the plans for Dar-al-Islam took shape, Nuridin and Noura went to Egypt for an intensive visit to study with Fathy at his School of Appropriate Technology in Cairo. In his design for the New Mexico masjid, Fathy employed Byzantine and Sassanid domes, along with old Egyptian barrel vaults. With the help of craftsmen Nuridin executed the design, for which Fathy did only four drawings.

Noura: "We wanted it to be an outstanding example of Islamic architecture blending into the indigenous architecture of the American Southwest, using local materials in a way suitable to its purpose. The architecture was so interesting to so many that when Fathy came to conduct a two-week building seminar on arches and domes, during which time the masjid was begun, adobe builders came from as far away as Europe and Mexico. The buildings have drawn many thousands of visitors. This was part of the intention behind them, that they would be a built example of traditional architecture adapted to modern purposes.

"Nuridin thought of Americans as basically materialists. Therefore he decided that they should be appealed to by means grounded in material reality, namely, by the beauty and power of traditional Islamic art. Americans, especially in New Mexico, he thought, would appreciate a Hassan Fathy structure much more than modern concrete buildings. And the princess was particularly interested in this part of the project because her father, King Khaled, who died during this time, loved traditional life and the old architecture. A place built of adobe seemed a fitting memorial for him."

Noura founded and oversaw an elementary school for the children in their community and others nearby. In 1982 she began the school with one teacher and ten students; by 1987 it had seven teachers and sixty students. In keeping with their community's mission as an Islamic center, Nuridin and Noura held workshops and conferences. These included a 1986 training session for teachers in Muslim schools, cosponsored by the Muslim World League, and a 1987 seminar for architects on traditional Islamic architecture, cosponsored by the University of Florida. As their venture progressed, some thirty families joined the community. But Dar-al-Islam wasn't a commune. Families lived separately.

Once again Nuridin, with Noura's help, had dreamed a dream that was probably impossible to realize. Today Noura laughs ruefully when she remembers the occasion when their Arab supporters asked her to sketch a design for the proposed university. She did so—and then sat back, aghast, for the cost of building it was estimated at some ninety million dollars. Even the wealthy Arabs supporting them were taken aback by this sum.

Other problems arose over finances. Some of the members of the board of trustees were appalled at the high cost of using local adobe bricks. Some of them rejected the entire aesthetic rationale for using indigenous materials. Some preferred concrete and steel, the less expensive building materials of modernity. While Nuridin and Noura thought of their community in terms of a traditional village, like those of the Southwest Indians and of Middle Eastern peasants, the board's model was an American suburb.

When it came to their educational plans, Nuridin and Noura thought in terms of a day and boarding school that would have to be financed for some time by contributions, but their Middle Eastern supporters saw it as a business enterprise which ought to generate profits immediately.

In the end, their Saudi partners, who controlled their finances, held the real power. Once again, as at Lama, Noura and Nuridin lost out. The university, the secondary school, the working farm, the school for teaching and producing indigenous and Islamic crafts—these parts of their plan were never attempted. Dar-al-Islam still exists, led by individuals who were there with Noura and Nuridin. The masjid still functions sometimes; the houses are still inhabited. Conferences are occasionally held. But Noura and Nuridin's utopian plans for a major center for Islamic Studies in the United States have never materialized. To meet expenses, the leaders of Dar-al-Islam have sold three-quarters of the community's original land. The school is closed.

Blocked in achieving their goal, Nuridin and Noura again left the United States, this time to wind up in Alexandria, Egypt. They attended a conference on Islamic education at Cambridge University in England, went on to visit friends in Egypt, and stayed. In many ways, this city is appropriate for them. In contrast to Sufism's weak position in Saudi Arabia, mystical Islam is strong in Egypt. Alexandria, the city of Cleopatra, where the modern library originated and ancient gnosticism flourished, is a place where civilizations have met and mingled. Despite what the guidebooks say, Alexandria isn't sterile and in bad repair. It still has the feel of the exotic city that Lawrence Durrell created in his *Alexandria Quartet*.

In Alexandria Noura has taught English as a Second Language to adults, taught in a private Egyptian grammar school, written school texts for an Islamic publisher, given lectures for the American Cultural Center, and helped Nuridin with his projects. While still in Abiquiu, Nuridin became the Northern American khalifah (representative) of his shaykh in the Sufi order of the Shadhdhuliyyah, centered in Egypt. As a shaykh, he is a respected teacher of Sufism. Several years ago Noura helped him with the publication of his translation and explication of the teachings of the Shadhdhuliyyah Order and of its thirteenth-century founder, Sidi Abu-l-Hasan ash-Shadhdhuli.

It's taken Noura and Nuridin a long time to reach this life plateau—one of religious contemplation and involvement in daily life. Their several years in Alexandria, like those they spent in Makkah, have been a retreat from the turmoil of lives lived dramatically and from the pressures of building innovative architectural and social structures. Individuals with energy like Noura's, who abandon ordinary lives to live on mountains and who travel across continents in pursuit of spiritual awakening, don't end their questing when the original search is completed. They go on to continue the work of redemption in themselves and the task of bringing it to others. But the missionary task is gruelling, requiring retreat and regrouping. Thus the interludes in Makkah and Alexandria. What Noura will do next, whether or not she will continue her visionary activities, I can't say.

"Do you remember all those fairy tales we read together as children?" Noura asked me recently. "Sometimes I feel like Dorothy in the *Wizard of Oz*, who has traveled the yellow-brick road to the Emerald City and found her dream. But unlike Dorothy, I don't want to return to Kansas; I have found my real home."

Abiquiu Revisited

Noura and I continued our conversations in Abiquiu, as we packed her possessions and cleaned her house. We talked about the past and the present,
about our childhood and our families, and about feminism and Islam. The last
topic was perilous, for our renewed friendship could falter on our different
beliefs. In the past, when our lives diverged, we had lost each other. I didn't
want that to happen again. I wanted to understand Noura's Muslim faith and
to reconcile her views with my feminism.

Most Americans don't realize that a deep communal impulse exists within
Islam. For Noura, I think that this impulse provided a continuation of what she
had experienced at Lama. Fatima Mernissi traces Islamic communalism to the
founding days of Islam, when Muhammad preached monotheism, the security
of a monotheistic oneness, against the chaotic world of the preexisting tribes
of the Arabian peninsula. *Ummah*, she notes, is the Arabic word for the united
Muslim community that Muhammad created and that exists. Derived from
umm, the word for mother, it encompasses ties between parents, children, and
kin, and between the individual, the state, and the divine. Moreover, it implies
emotional qualities such as tenderness and forgiveness which apply not only
to the personal realm but also to the social order. Under its umbrella, devout
Muslims display *rahmah*—an intense sensitivity to others, to the group. Individual desire is downgraded. "Democracy," defined as the rights of individuals

over the interests of the group, is a questionable concept to Muslims. In contrast to the West, the Arab world underwent neither a religious Reformation nor a secular Enlightenment to undermine the notion of a unified religion connected to society and the state. Within Islam lies a sense of history as static. This conception is baffling to modern Westerners, with our automatic presumptions about the linear progression of time and the benefits of progress.

Noura: "Muslims believe the best civilization existed when Islam was founded, under the original dispensation offered Muhammad. We have no belief in progress; we only have some hopes for the reappearance of some semblance of those days under the Prophet's direct guidance. Devout Muslims even today pattern their lives after that of Muhammad and follow the original message given him by Allah and transcribed in the Qur'an."

Muhammad not only created a unified community, he also was antimaterialistic. Islam developed among tribes in the Arabian peninsula at a time when enterprising individuals were creating a local trading economy and linking into a transcontinental one. This incipient capitalism produced urban centers and disparities of wealth. Muhammad drew the majority of his first converts from women, slaves, youths, and the least wealthy. Like other great religious prophets—Buddha, Christ, Lao-Tzu—he preached a doctrine of brotherhood and sisterhood and of the virtues of a simple life. In Islam usury is forbidden. According to Noura, in Muslim lands it's practiced but frowned upon. Other systems of profit are preferred, particularly shared risk. One of the five requirements of Islam is *zakat*, tithing for the good of the community.

Devout Muslims fear the impact of Western materialism and consumerism on their cultures. In 1993 I observed that impact in Egypt. Displays of sexuality in movies and advertising are censored in this Muslim country, but huge cigarette advertisements, emblazoned with the figure of the Marlborough Man, were plastered on buildings in downtown Cairo. Everyone I met spoke of a national fixation with the American soap opera, "The Bold and the Beautiful." When it aired on Sunday evenings, I was told, even peasants in remote villages watched it. Since I was a Westerner who studied popular culture, the people I met thought I could shed light on their fascination with that show. In fact, I was asked to speak publicly about the program on several occasions, once on Alexandria's television station.

I'd never before seen this soap opera, but the American cultural attachée in Alexandria had videotaped several episodes. She showed them to me. After watching them, I concluded with dismay that the program concentrated on the worst characteristics of American life. It featured broken families, blatant sexuality, and rampant consumerism. The actors and actresses in it embodied the stereotypes of Western beauty. The women were blonde and Anglo-Saxon; the men had bland, rugged features. It seemed to me almost a satire on other soap operas I had seen, near camp in its frenzied portrayal of wealthy people indulging narcissistic desires.

Well-to-do Egyptian women I met wore Western clothing and heavy makeup. "We are all concerned about how we look," they told me. "We are influenced by Western standards of appearance, especially by your cult of thinness. We don't know what to do about it; we don't know how to stop the influence." The truth is that, as much as in the case of Western women, they have been lured by consumerism into accepting materialistic values and enforcing them on their own bodies. They liked "The Bold and the Beautiful" so much because its melodramatic intensity led them into a realm of outsized fantasy and cast the banality of American consumerism in a larger-than-life, heroic light. Yet they also realized its costs in social disorganization and, for women, in sexual objectification. As much as I may dislike this resolution, it seems to me that Muslim traditionalism offers a way to subvert the obsession by having women return to the strict observance of the law and the wearing of conservative dress.

On many issues concerning gender and women Noura's beliefs are the same as mine. She supports equal education for women, equal access to the professions, and equal pay for equal work. Like many Muslim women with feminist views, Noura contends, in opposition to Islam's Western critics, that Islam extends both freedom and authority to women. She traces those features to Muhammad. She points to the powerful women around the Prophet, especially his wives Khadijah and A'isha and his daughter Fatima. When in his twenties, Muhammad married Khadijah, a wealthy merchant fifteen years older than he. She was his first convert, a major supporter throughout his life, and his only wife until her death. A'isha was a child of eight when she was betrothed to Muhammad and eighteen when he died. After his death she became a leader of the community. Muhammad had no sons who lived past early childhood. Thus his succession passed through his daughter Fatima, who is honored as the mother of the descendants of the Prophet.

Noura points out that Muslim law grants many rights to women. Noura: "By Qur'anic prescription, women have the right to own businesses, to initiate legal action, and to buy and sell property—and Allah gave women these rights centuries before Western women gained them. Married women have the right to their own income; they can start a business with it; they can put it into the bank or buy jewelry with it; they can do anything they want with it. Women are guaranteed the right to inherit under Qur'anic law, and if the portion decreed for sons is larger than that for daughters, it's because sons are required to care for the unmarried women of their families, and daughters aren't required to support themselves. Under Islam, married women keep their maiden names; children alone take fathers' names."

In Noura's view, Islam's separate women's sphere accords women authority. Noura enjoyed the community of women she found in Saudi Arabia, and she also liked the Saudi Arabian separate banks, businesses, and universities for women. Egypt, more modernized than Saudi Arabia, doesn't have many separate women's institutions, so my visit there couldn't provide me with an experience identical to Noura's in Makkah. But one day in Alexandria, Noura took care that we caught a woman-only tram, for she wanted me to experience this gender separatism. On this conveyance, with only women around me, I must admit that, liberated from male sexual stares, I felt a sense of freedom as well as closeness to the women around me.

In Muslim countries, women's authority is preeminent in the private sphere of the home. Noura: "In Islam, the power of the 'mother' dominates the home. Muslim children are taught to honor their mother first of all. Muslims will give their paychecks to their parents and forego marriage in order to support them; they will do anything for their mothers. When you marry you serve your mother-in-law; as you age and your children grow up and marry, you are the one who is served. Even urban professional women regard their families as the center of their lives. They live with husbands or families: single men and women living alone are considered anomalous, even dangerous."

According to Noura, Muslim doctrine supports a basic equality between the genders. "By Qur'anic prescription women and men are equal before Allah; no mythology exists about Eve bringing evil into the world. In contrast to Christian dogma, sexual pleasure is considered integral to marriage. In Arabic the word Allah has neither a masculine nor a feminine connotation." Noura's God isn't a gendered being; in fact, if anything, the feminine element in the godhead predominates over the masculine. (Scholars point out that attributes centering on mercy and benevolence predominate in the ninety-nine names of Allah.) "Did you see the pictograph of the goddess Nut holding up the world?" Noura asked me that when I returned to Alexandria from visiting Luxor and the Valleys of the Kings and Queens. "Muslims say," she told me, "that paradise is under the feet of the mother."

"What about cliterodectomy, polygamy, and men's ability to divorce wives with ease?" I asked Noura. "The best-known Middle Eastern feminist text in the West is Nawal El Saadawi's 1980 *The Hidden Face of Eve*. El Saadawi, an Egyptian, criticized Muslim countries severely for oppressing women. Even in Egypt Saadawi found widespread incest, a flourishing double standard, and much discrimination against women in law and society." Noura responded that cliterodectomy is an ancient practice that predated Islam and that neither the Qur'an nor Muslim law upholds. Polygamy, she asserted, is permitted but discouraged in the Qur'an, under the injunction that "one would be better for you if you but knew." Noura: "If a man must marry more than one woman, he is required by Islamic law to treat every wife exactly equally to the best of his ability. A woman may stipulate in her marriage contract that she has the right of divorce if her husband takes another wife. Muslims regard Western divorce and remarriage as simply 'serial polygamy,' which may be much more harmful to children and to women's dignity than the occasional polygamous relationship in which a woman keeps her status and children keep their father near."

As to the other charges against Islam, Noura has no illusions that, in specific situations, human actions can undermine her religion's purity. "I am not a sociologist," she responded when I posed Saadawi's criticisms to her. But she is a social feminist who, like Jehan Sadat, supports social reforms for women. One of Noura's mentors is Doctora Zahira Abdeen, an Egyptian woman who has founded schools, child wellness clinics, and medical clinics for women in Cairo and elsewhere.

Can Western feminism accommodate Noura's Islamic beliefs? Or are the differences too great for any rapprochement? Philosopher Marilyn Frye characterizes Western feminism as kaleidoscopic, as continually growing and multiplying. Over the decades of my own involvement with feminism, I have witnessed the emergence of many varieties: liberal, socialist, psychoanalytic, spiritual, postmodern, ecofeminist. Feminism is a protean ideology, extending from the right to the left of the political spectrum, and its varieties have often developed as critiques of major ideologies and interpretative schools, such as Marxism, Freudianism, and postmodernism. Feminism is not defined by one set of doctrines. At its best, it includes the voices of many women with many points of view. I honor those voices.

One constant has remained throughout the varieties of feminism. That constant is the division between "difference" feminists, who see men and women as fundamentally different, and "sameness" feminists, who view men and women as the same. In fact, the sameness feminists have adopted the position that each gender can shift in its composition when influenced by changing social, cultural, and historical factors. Recently, the "sameness" feminists seem to have carried the day. Their charge that the "difference" feminists are "essentialists" has been widely accepted by academic feminists. By viewing men and women as different, so their criticism goes, difference feminists play into bifurcated and conservative gender stereotypes.

I think that this criticism is overdrawn. I fear that, in the rush to view the sexes as the same, masculine qualities of power and aggression will become the norm, while caring and sensitivity, defined as feminine, will be downplayed. This tendency exists in much contemporary popular culture, with women in movies and television dramas displaying a violence equal to that of men. Moreover, as a feminist historian I celebrate "maternalist" social reform. In the United States women often pioneered in social reform independently from men, using their position as mothers as justification. (I do not regard these qualities as genetically determined but rather as socially constructed.) I respect the influence women's separate associations have had in my own life, and I remember that the many women's institutions and businesses that second wave feminism inspired created both an economic base and a greater self-confidence for women. In my positive interpretation of women's separate sphere my ideas intersect with those of Noura.

Noura and I want to understand each other. We both want to find a way to translate our values into an idiom the other can accept. How do I deal with her view that husbands should have final authority in families, with wives assuming domestic responsibility? How do I reconcile this stance with my belief that giving ultimate power to men promotes unfair gender hierarchies? Our conversation encounters difficulties here. From my perspective as a Western feminist, Noura is performing "double duty" in working full-time and caring for her home. Yet from her Muslim perspective she is privileged to be able to work, and her job neither reduces her duty to care for her family nor requires that her husband assist her in the home. Besides, she adds, she is not required to work. By Muslim law, her husband is responsible for family support. If they have decided that she will earn money, that's a private matter between the two of them. To Noura the authority of the father is necessary to preserve order and to insure the continuation of the *ummah*. At Lama families broke apart. Children's lives were disoriented, and adults suffered hurts. By Noura's Muslim beliefs, families stay together under the rule of the father, with considerable allowance given for consultation and co-ordination. It is not a dictatorship, Noura asserts. She calls her ideal family "a ship with a captain."

Noura and I disagree about spousal responsibility at home, and we also disagree about "veiling."[1] Noura has followed the Muslim dress code for over twenty years. Covering her body and her head is by now second nature: she would feel strange if not dressed this way. She considers this dress necessary because in her opinion the power of sexuality makes it impossible for a man and a woman to be alone or even on the streets together without risking sexual arousal. This dress insures that the physical body is hidden and sexuality is contained. Moreover, Noura believes that women can't easily prevent themselves from manipulating men through sexuality. Noura: "I went through a long period in my life of a tremendous amount of sexual showing off. I think most of us have. Sometimes it's subtle and sometimes it's not so subtle. I found myself gratified by being attractive to men, and then I came to understand that that was a waste of time unless I intended to follow through and have multiple love affairs. I was really being a hypocrite and a tease."

Noura dislikes the term "veiling," which implies restricting women. According to her, the Egyptian "scarf," the head covering with face uncovered, fulfills Qur'anic requirements. Even though she didn't mind wearing the abayah in Saudi Arabia (and she even found it liberating), she contends that completely covering the face isn't necessary.

"Why should women alone wear confining clothing, and not men?" I asked Noura. "Isn't this an unfair distinction between the genders?" She answered that the Qur'an also injoins men to constrain their sexuality by wearing loose clothing. For this reason, she said, men throughout the Middle East wear robes on the streets, as well as turbans, fezs, or gutras (a

---

[1] I use the terms "veiling" and "veils" because of their widespread popular usage. I place them in quotation marks because of their ambiguity. Noura greatly dislikes the terms.

scarf) on their heads. No less than women, according to Noura, they cover their sexuality.

Egyptian women love gold, silver, and bright colors, in fabrics and decorations that would be considered gaudy in the United States. The women's bazaar in Alexandria (a separate women's space) is filled with these colorful clothes and accessories as well as with revealing lingerie. But these goods are for private consumption in the home. In public spaces women increasingly cover their bodies and wear scarves, even though in cities such as Cairo and Alexandria their clothing may be more Western than traditional. When Noura gave her lecture on the United States to a class at a local Alexandria university, the male students sat together on one side of the central aisle and the woman students on the other; the women wore drab dresses covering their bodies, with scarves over their hair.

The scarf has little to do with fashion. It's a sign of piety and of rebellion against Western modernity. In her insightful book on the women's "veiling" movement in Turkey, Nilüfer Göle asserts that the return to the "veil" symbolizes the reconstruction of a common identity and community (*ummah*) among Muslims as well as a politics of identity among women. According to Göle, women employ their bodies as "political sites of resistance to the homogenizing forces of Western modernity." In Turkey the Islamist movement draws its female recruits primarily from university students and professional women. Their espousal of Muslim traditionalism has given them the confidence to work as journalists and politicians as well as to make films and write novels which express their new point of view. "The point of the scarf," Noura contends, "is to surrender to Allah's command in an outward form and to accept modesty out of inner conviction." When Noura puts on her scarf, tying it carefully so that not a strand of her hair shows, she puts on, symbolically, the whole of Islam. "I feel guilty not wearing the scarf," a young Muslim woman confessed to me in Alexandria. "I'm just not as devout a Muslim as I would like to be."

I understand why Noura covers her head; if I were to profess Islam, I might do the same. But understanding Noura's position doesn't mean that I agree with it. I don't like male comments on my appearance in public spaces, but I don't view sexuality as overpowering; and I worry about the implications of a theology and politics so firmly wedded to separation between the sexes. As Göle contends, the romanticization of tradition in the new Islamist movements could produce a totalitarian conception of religion, identity, and the state, under which women could be denied freedom (to adopt modernity) under the guise of being given freedom (to be traditional). Something of this sort seems to have happened in Iran.

At one of the talks I gave in Alexandria I criticized Western advertising and its media for objectifying women. A man in the audience vehemently disagreed. He argued that following fashion was fun for women and that advertising was essential to the growth of capitalism: in his view women were liberated, not downgraded, by advertising. As I searched for words to counter his attack, Noura stood up and defended me eloquently. She paraphrased and extended my position that advertising treats women as items for consumption, not as autonomous subjects, and that it violates women's right to their bodies. For a moment the interchange felt like our old debate partnership.

Noura and I can't reconcile all our beliefs. But I don't completely agree with friends of mine who are Jewish or Marxist and we respect our differences. Noura and I are both homemakers as well as involved in careers, and those similarities bring us together. We can happily discuss recipes, or health, or how to raise children, as well as current events or religion or a host of topics. I might tell her that the woman commentator who interviewed me on Alexandria's television station complained to me in private about having to do the household chores and care for her children when she came home from work, while her husband had no responsibility to help her. But Noura might point out to me that Western women often complain about having to work at the same time that they often express a desire to remain at home, taking care of their house and their children.

Noura's Islam is a religion of peace and toleration. To her the jihad, the command to do battle for Allah, refers to both warfare (the small jihad) and to the individual's internal struggle to overcome the *nafs*, or the ego, to find the one, to find Allah. This internal struggle is the real jihad. Her Islam accepts people of all creeds and colors in line with the religion's long history of toleration of other faiths. Her God isn't masculine. Her ideal male is Muhammad, a man of the people who welded together warring tribes and who preached a communal vision of charity and concern for others.

"One Ramadan," Noura remembers, "I made three different sets of circumnabulations around the Ka'abah. I went once with my husband, once with a Saudi Arabian princess, and once with a blind beggar."

We talked about these issues in Abiquiu, as we packed and made coffee and meals for anyone who appeared at the door. Visiting seemed constant, even though in a sense we were ourselves visitors, for we stayed there less than a week. We followed the Muslim imperative of hospitality, of welcoming strangers into your home. One evening a woman appeared who had been leading a camp at Lama on Murshid Sam's Dances of Universal Peace. We talked about Lama and Noura's having led the dances there and about my Sufi Order teacher in Los Angeles, who also leads the dances.

A professor of Islamic Studies at San Diego State University came by, and we discussed Sufism in the United States. Although she wore Western clothes and didn't "veil," she performed the Muslim evening prayer with Noura. Then a woman appeared who was conducting a seminar on Islam at Dar-al-Islam for high school teachers, under the auspices of the National Endowment for the Humanities. We spoke about similar work I had done on other subjects for the Endowment. It seemed so strange and so ordinary. There I was on a remote mesa in New Mexico, at an Islamic community, discussing familiar subjects with individuals whose lives had capriciously connected with mine.

The people who now live at Dar-al-Islam seemed distant. They didn't help us dismantle the contents of Noura's house, and they didn't lend a hand even when we had to load a large truck to move her possessions. I felt sorry for my friend, for the dissolution of her dream. The community still existing at Abiquiu seemed a pale version of the original. The buildings had Noura's and Nuridin's energy in them. They had brought those buildings into being; they had had to let them go.

Unexpectedly, the shaykh who had so influenced Fran in Jerusalem happened to be there, on a tour of Muslim communities in the United States. His beard was no longer red; with the passing of nearly twenty years it had become pepper and salt. Speaking publicly to the community he praised its women, and he urged them to realize their potential. I was surprised by his message, although by this point in my association with Noura I should have realized that others within Islam share her views on gender. I liked the shaykh's manner, for he seemed gentle and kind. Speaking in Arabic, Noura introduced me to him. He turned to me and said in English: "There is only one Sufism; you must be a Muslim to be a Sufi; other versions are heresy." Politely, I didn't respond.

If I had answered him I would have replied that although Islam has influenced me, I remain a Western woman, still devoted to Western feminism. Professing the Muslim faith doesn't appeal to me: I don't choose to submit to Islamic law or practice. My vision remains ecumenical; I honor the spirituality in all religions. I like doing *dhikr* and the Dances of Universal Peace, and I like my gnostic classes. I especially like the Sufi Order Universal Worship Service. (Because my Sufi Order group includes many feminist women, texts from feminist spirituality are often included in the readings from world religions.) I follow the teachings of Murshid Sam and Pir Vilayat Khan.

When I try to connect with a sense of the divine I look for a force within myself. That force seems composed of the compassion of my childhood faith, now mixed with the idea of divine and human love as interconnected, which I have learned from my Sufi Order teachers. For most of my life I rejected the spiritual side of my nature, just as I rejected my childhood. I no longer reject that part of myself. Feminist spirituality opened me to acknowledging it again; finding Fran brought me to the Sufi Order and its ecumenicism. Following my mentors, I view the spiritual force within me as connected to humanity and to the universe. The journey for me is inward as much as outward.

A renowned Sufi text is the *Conference of the Birds*, written by the Persian poet Jellaludin Attar in the twelfth century. The poem tells the story of the quest of thirty birds (*simourgh* in Persian) for Simourgh, the Divine Bird. They fulfill the quest when they realize that they themselves are the Divine Bird and that the real journey is inward, not outward:

> Pilgrim, pilgrimage and Road
> Was but Myself toward Myself, and your
> Arrival but Myself at my own Door. . . .

Although I belong to the Sufi Order, I haven't taken a new name, and I don't intend to do so. I changed my name once in my life, when I married my first husband. That change, I now realize, was part of a process of taking on a new self connected to rationality and intellectualism. It took me many years to adjust to that name, and I don't want to go through that process again. I won't follow Noura to her ultimate life resolution in Islam. Yet is my spiritual commitment so different from hers? No less than mine, her path is internal; no less than me, she strives to access a divine force within herself. She supports Islamic universalism; she honors other religions. Our external practices may differ, but she is a Sufi who has showed me the way along which I have traveled.

As we sat one evening after dinner, I told Noura about my initiation into the Sufi Order in the West at a weekend retreat in Phoenix, led by Pir

Vilayat Khan. I described how he had moved me as he spoke during those two days of the retreat. Like Fran many years before, I was drawn to his intellect, his sophistication, and his poetic spirituality, which he articulated as a series of visions. Seated in a tent, many individuals in the audience remained in the lotus position throughout the many hours that Pir Vilayat spoke. The Pir, now in his seventies, himself remained in that position. We observed silence during the retreat, and I liked that silence. I liked not having to talk while immersed in spiritual work.

During those two days in Phoenix, Pir Vilayat explored many ideas about transcendence. He explained to us that the uplifting emotions we experience when listening to music—or thrilling to a painting, a beautiful day, or a lover—are akin to the sense of ecstasy that is the mystic's goal. He played Bach's B-minor Mass, a favorite piece of his. He told us that the sense of transcendence he experienced when listening to it had helped him over the years to cope with the death of his sister during the Second World War. A French resistance fighter, she was killed by the Nazis. For a long time he worked with the names of Allah, explaining many of these attributes. He showed us how to pronounce and use them in meditating and how to re-create ourselves through those terms of grandeur, humility, and sensitivity. The names, he said, represent states of emotion within us.

A heart with two wings constitutes the Sufi Order logo. The heart is love, Pir Vilayat said. The wings are independence and indifference; they enable your soul to fly. He counseled us to strive for detachment, to look on ourselves as rays of divine light. "There is a polish for everything," said the prophet Muhammad, "and the polish for the heart is the remembrance of God." That is the meaning for me, I finally realized, of the paradox of Islam, of its message of finding freedom through submission. It means that we come to terms with our conditioning and that we find freedom through re-creating ourselves according to divine wisdom. And we find that wisdom with the aid of texts and teachers and the arts of worship and experience. I no longer believe, with Freud, that the "oceanic feeling" I experience is only an illusion. I respond to William James, the famed psychologist and Harvard professor, brother to Henry and Alice. He believed in the truth of the testimony he gathered in the 1900s about the experience of spiritual ecstasy from scores of contemporaries and historical figures.

In Abiquiu Noura and I sigh over our children. How similar they are to us and yet how different. There is my daughter who, a graduate student at USC, shudders at the thought of being an academic like her parents—

although she edits my books. My son, now at Yale, is immersed in the dramatic arts and determined to become a Shakespearean actor. Noura's oldest son is a building contractor oriented toward the Sufi Order. Her younger son is a Muslim who works with computers. Her oldest daughter died tragically some years ago. The two daughters of Noura's marriage to Nuridin are both still in the enchanted years of childhood. Noura and Nuridin are raising them as Muslims, while they attend an elite school in Alexandria and listen to Noura's stories of her childhood in a far-off land.

We talk of my new love, a professor of history at UCLA whom I met two months before, by chance at a party, and whom I am going to marry. How can I explain this sudden romance? I can only laugh and say: life always plays tricks; everything always changes just when one least expects it. People die unexpectedly; one meets men with whom one falls passionately in love, just as quickly to fall out of it. Against all odds, a young woman from the hinterlands without much of an education is admitted to a leading graduate school, marries a scion of a wealthy family, and winds up in a center of academic feminism, becoming one of the founders of the field of women's studies. Her best friend from high school does it all differently, eventually becoming a Muslim. And here they are together in Abiquiu after a separation of thirty years, in the midst of a New Mexico desert, calmly discussing their lives as though they were as regular as anyone's.

I spoke to Noura of my writing on aging and my view that true maturity only comes with middle age. I didn't grow up completely until I was in my fifties, until I endured a breakdown that was like a rebirth. Then I was ready to find a new spiritual path and a new human love that might last. In India it's not an unknown Hindu practice for middle-aged men and women, with their children grown, to leave their families and take to the road, often as mendicants, to shore up their spiritual practice and to find through such wandering an intensified life experience. In my own way I have taken a new path. Yet at the same time I have been wandering in a circle. Not until I came home and not until I found Fran could I declare that wandering at an end.

I look around Noura's house in Abiquiu, and I understand much more about her. The unity of her life, reflected in the furnishings and decoration of her house, reflects a lifetime learning a religion and an aesthetic different from that of the modern West. And just how different is Noura from Fran? She seems calmer, less frenzied, but no less intense. She is faithful to the practices of her religion, and she uses the phrase "inshallah" (God willing) all the time. But she is just as prone as ever to run off on an adventure, just as willing to stay up late talking, just as involved in a myriad of activities as she always was. The balance between us has shifted: I'm not the shy person of our youth, and I often lead in our interactions now. I wouldn't now be so rash as to be indifferent if she introduced me to a psychic astrologer; in fact, I would welcome such an introduction. I like the spare furnishings and the oriental rugs in her house, for I gave up stainless steel furniture and signed lithographs by famous artists years ago. And if Noura were to beckon me to go through a door marked no admittance, I'm sure my automatic reaction would be to restrain her—but then, as always, I would follow after.

Through my mind runs a verse by Jelalludin Rumi, the founder of the Mevlevi Order in Turkey in the thirteeth century C.E. Like Ibn al-Arabi, who was his friend, Rumi is considered one of the greatest Sufi writers. He is revered in Turkey as Shakespeare is in England. At my wedding I would read from poems by Rumi, and I would be married in a Sufi ceremony based on the Universal Worship Service. There would be readings from the texts of major world religions to celebrate my new love and my taking on of a new life partner. Fran didn't attend this second wedding of mine, but I can assure you that she was there in spirit. The verse in my head seems to express better than I could what my life has become and what I hope for the future:

> *And He is with you* means He is searching with you.
> He is nearer to you than yourself. Why look outside?
> Become like melting snow; wash yourself of yourself.
> With love your inner voice will find a tongue
> Growing like a silent white lily in the heart.

I still suffer attacks of shyness. I still sometimes fear abandonment and feel a sense of imminent catastrophe. But those negative emotions in me are now echoes of what they once were. Finding Fran, reliving my life and hers, separately and together, has been a voyage of discovery for me. What impact have I had on Noura? I think I have spurred her to review and renew her commitment to Islam and to articulate her own feminist position. I have given her support during a difficult time in her life, and I have helped her to bring to the surface distant memories and discontents and to understand them. Through me she can see what might have happened to her if she followed that alternative road of Lydia's and my imagination that pointed to a brilliant career in mainstream society.

Noura and I don't live near each other, and we don't see each other often, but we phone and e-mail and keep close. There is nothing quite like being with someone who knew you as a child and who shared your adolescent dreams. I look at Noura and I see Fran—in her smile, her gestures, her speech. That vision is exciting to me.

Prologue: Abiquiu, New Mexico (August 1994)

Page 1: The best biographies of Muhammad in English are Karen Armstrong, *Muhammad: A Biography of the Prophet* (San Francisco: HarperCollins, 1992) and Martin Lings, *Muhammad: His Life From the Earliest Sources* (Cambridge, UK: Islamic Text Society, 1983).

1: On the Muslim home and Muslim decorative arts more generally, see Seyyed Hossein Nasr, *Islamic Art and Spirituality* (Albany: State University of New York Press, 1989), pp. 37–38, and passim.

2: For calligraphy as the "most sacred form of Muslim art," see Seyyed Hossein Nasr, "The Quar'an as the Foundation of Islamic Spirituality," in Nasr, ed., *Islamic Spirituality: Foundations* (New York: Crossroads, 1987), p. 5.

4: For the stereotypical, distorted version of Islam, cf. Betty Mahmoody (with William Hoffer) *Not Without My Daughter* (New York: St. Martin's, 1987), and the popular movie made from the book. As a corrective see Jehan Sadat, *A Woman of Egypt* (New York: Simon and Schuster, 1987). For a brief overview of Islam, see Annemarie Schimmel, *Islam: An Introduction* (Albany: State University of New York Press, 1992).

5: On Sufism, cf. Nasr, *Islamic Spirituality*, and Anne Marie Schimmel, *Mystical Dimensions of Islam* (Chapel Hill: University of North Carolina Press, 1975). An excellent introduction to Sufism, particularly its varieties in the United States, is contained in *Gnosis: A Journal of the Western Inner Traditions* (Winter 1994). For an interesting secularized version of Islamic mysticism, see Kabir Edmund Helminski, *Living Presence: A Sufi Way to Mindfulness and the Essential Self* (New York: Jeremy P. Tarcher, 1992). With regard to the divisions in Islam between Sunnis and Shiites, most Sufis are Sunnis. The word "sufi" derives from the Arabic "suf," meaning wool, referring to the rough woolen garments that early ascetic and contemplative Muslims wore. But Arabic words can have multiple roots and meanings: some say the word "sufi" derived from the word meaning "purity" or from the word for "line," referring to the people who prayed directly in a line behind the prophet. On the derivation of the word, cf. Schimmel, p. 14, and Laleh Bakhtiar, *Sufi: Expressions of the Mystical Quest* (London: Thames and Hudson, 1976).

5: The best introduction to mysticism in general remains William James, *The Varieties of Religious Experience: A Study in Human Nature* (New York: Vintage, 1990). For Christian mysticism as contemplation, see F. C. Happold, *Mysticism: A Study and an Anthology* (London: Penguin, 1963).

6: For scholarly articles I have written on biography and autobiography, see Lois W. Banner, "Autobiography and Biography: Intermixing the Genres," *a/b: Auto/Biography Studies* 8 (Fall 1993): 12–38; Banner, "The Irony of Memory: Finding a Los(t) Angeles," *Pacific Historical Review* 35 (Spring 1994): 1–18.

6: The classic dismissal of communalism and spirituality is Christopher Lasch, *The Culture of Narcissism: American Life in an Age of Diminishing Expectations* (New York: Norton, 1979). For a representative critique of feminist spirituality, especially goddess worship, by a mainstream feminist writer, see Carol Tavris, *The Mismeasurement of Women* (New York: Simon and Schuster, 1992), pp. 71–79.

7: For critiques of second wave feminism, cf. Elizabeth Fox-Genovese, *Feminism Without Illusions: A Critique of Individualism* (Chapel Hill: University of North Carolina Press, 1991), and *Feminism Is Not the Story of My Life: How Today's Feminist Elite Has Lost Touch with the Real Concerns of Women* (New York: Nan A. Talese, 1996).

Chapter 1: The House on Hillcrest

11: On the history of Inglewood, I have used Glenn S. Dumké, *The Boom of the Eighties in Southern California* (San Marino, Cal.: Huntingtom Library, 1944); Lloyd P. Hamilton, ed., *Inglewood Community Book* (Inglewood, Cal.: Arthur Carson, 1949); Roy Rosenberg, *History of Inglewood: Narrative and Biographical* (Inglewood, Cal.: Arthur H. Cawston, 1938); W. W. Robinson, *Ranchos Become Cities* (Pasadena, Cal.: San Pasquel Press, 1939); Gladys Waddingham, *The History of Inglewood* (Inglewood, Cal.: Historical Society of Centinela Valley, 1994); Constance Zillgott, *Men Who Have Made Inglewood*, pamphlet, Inglewood Public Library, 1924; Historical Society of Centinela Valley, *Centinela Valley Heritage*, pamphlet, Inglewood Public Library, n.d.

13: "finest example": Hamilton, p. 10.

14: For English models of my house on Hillcrest, see James Chambers, *The English House* (New York: Norton, 1985).

14: On Los Angeles architecture, see Reyner Banham, *Los Angeles: The Architecture of Four Ecologies* (New York: Harper and Row, 1971), and Sam Hall Kaplan, *Los Angeles Lost and Found: An Architectural History of Los Angeles* (New York: Crown, 1987). In locating my family in time and space, I have also found helpful Kevin Starr, *Material Dreams: Southern California Through the 1920s* (New York: Oxford, 1990).

15: On split-level suburbia as the 1950s prototype, cf. Clifford Clark, *The American Family Home, 1800–1960* (Chapel Hill: University of North Carolina Press, 1986).

16: On Missouri Synod Lutheranism, see in particular Alan Graebner, *Uncertain Saints: The Laity in the Lutheran Church-Missouri Synod, 1900–1970* (Westport, Conn.: Greenwood, 1975).

17: The passages I quote are from the King James version of the Bible, which is the text I memorized in elementary school.

18: The "American Gothic" painting by Grant Wood is located in the Art Institute of Chicago.

18: "grandest homes": Waddingham, p. 44.

21: "My elders had learned German": Until World War I, many Lutheran churches conducted their services in German. Anti-German sentiment during the war generally prompted ending the practice. See Graebner, *Uncertain Saints*. My mother's confirmation certificate, dated June, 1919, and issued in Spokane, is written in German.

21: My great-grandmother Lena was raised in Minnesota near a Sioux reservation. In 1862 these Sioux, angry at their treatment, went on a rampage against whites in the area. Thus Lena's memory of hiding in the cellar may be accurate. See Richard O'Connor, *The German Americans: An Informal History* (Boston: Little, Brown, 1968), pp. 191–205.

23: Bruce Barton, *The Man Nobody Knows: A Discovery of the Real Jesus* (Indianapolis, Ind.: Bobbs-Merrill, 1924), intro., n.p.

26ff: My knowledge of Charlie's checkered employment and the details of the Silas Reid story come from the documents in United States of America, Territory of Alaska, Third Judicial Division, "Silas Reid Case," National Archives, Washington, D.C., document file #142–932. For an interpretation of these events, curiously omitting Charlie's central role, see Claus-M. Naské, "The Short and Unhappy Judgeship of Silas Hinckle Reid," in "A History of the Alaska Federal District Court System, 1884–1959, and the Creation of the Court System," unpub. mss., Anchorage Law Library, Anchorage, Alaska.

26: On the Alaska gold rush, I have used Pierre Berton, *The Klondike Fever: The Life and Times of the Last Great Gold Rush* (New York: Knopf, 1967); William Bronson, *The Last Grand Adventure* (New York: McGraw-Hill, 1977); Melanie J. Mayer, *Klondike Women: True Tales of the 1897–1898 Gold Rush* (Athens: Ohio University

Press, 1989); Morgan Murray, *One Man's Gold: A Klondike Album* (Seattle: University of Washington Press, 1967); and Archie Satterfield, *Chilkoot Pass: The Most Famous Trail in the North* (Anchorage: Alaska Northwest Books, 1973).

27: On Valdez, see Lone E. Johnson, *The Copper Spike* (Anchorage: Alaska Northwest Books, 1975), pp. 6–18. On the saloons and dance halls in Valdez, see Ella Higginson, *Alaska: The Great Company* (New York: Macmillan, 1908), p. 267; and Mss. Minutes, Valdez City Council, 1900–1910, City Hall, Valdez, Alaska. On Charlie's double-dealing, see also Commissioners' Court, 3rd Division, Book of Docket Entries, Civil, Sept. 1906, Valdez, Alaska: H. R. Leslie, Plaintiff v. C. E. Parkes, et al., defendants. Complaint filed, September, 1906. (The Valdez county courthouse contains the docket record.)

28: On Nellie Melba, see in particular Joseph Wechsberg, *Red Plush and Black Velvet: The Story of Melba and Her Times* (Boston: Little, Brown, 1961).

28: On the early Alaska court system, see Jeannette Paddock Nichols, *Alaska* (New York: Russell and Russell, 1963), pp. 147–292. On the Alaska judges as "czars," see Higginson, p. 349.

29: James Wickersham's manuscript diary is in the Alaska State Archives, Juneau, Alaska. An excerpted published version, omitting his comments on the Reid Affair, is James Wickersham, *Old Yukon: Tales—Trails—and Trials* (Washington, D.C.: Washington Law Book Co., 1938).

29: A report of the Grand Jury findings is contained in the *Valdez Daily Prospector*, Nov. 11, 1909.

29: On the large numbers of young men in Alaska and the small numbers of women, cf. Florence Lee Mallinson, *My Travels and Adventures in Alaska* (Seattle: Seattle-Alaska Publishing Co., 1914).

29: A record of Charlie's (and Lillian's) employment in Spokane is contained in *Polk's Spokane City Directory*, 1910, 1913–1915, 1917, 1919–1920.

Chapter 2: Melba

32: On women concert pianists and the importance of Leschetizsky, see Christine Ammer, *Unsung: A History of Women in American Music* (Westport, Conn.: Greenwood, 1980), pp. 55, 259.

33: In *Women Who Made Inglewood* (Inglewood, Cal.: Instant Print, 1996), n.p., Gladys Waddingham remembers my mother for her "spectacular piano concerts," contending that in the later ones before her death as many as twenty pianos were played simultaneously. In actuality, I think that Mrs. Waddingham's memory of the number of pianos is somewhat inflated.

34: On the third position in birth order, cf. George Edington and Bradford Wilson, *First Child, Second Child* (New York: McGraw-Hill, 1981). In *Born to Rebel: Birth Order, Family Dynamics, and Creative Lives* (New York: Pantheon, 1996), Frank

J. Sulloway contends that third children in birth order are often the family rebels. That interpretation also holds true in my case.

36: Until I read recent revisionist accounts of women in the 1950s written by a group of younger scholars in women's history who view that decade as a time of opportunity, my structuring of my memories for that decade involved mostly repression for women. My analysis of the impact of working women on me (of which I was not entirely conscious at the time) has been influenced by this new school, including their articles in Joanne Meyerowitz, ed., *Not June Cleaver:Women and Gender in Postwar America, 1945–1960* (Philadelphia:Temple University Press, 1994); and the roundtable session "Not Betty Crocker: 'Other' Women in the Postwar United States, 1945–1960," Berkshire Conference of Women Historians, June 13, 1993.The writing of these women has enabled me to structure my memories from a different perspective. In *Homeward Bound:American Families in the Cold War Era* (NewYork: Basic, 1988), ElaineTyler May stresses female containment in the 1950s, as does Benita Eisler in her still interesting *Private Lives: Men andWomen of the Fifties* (NewYork: FranklinWatts, 1986).

36: On women in the advertising business, see Roland Marchand, *Advertising and the American Dream: MakingWay for Modernity, 1920–1940* (Berkeley: University of California Press, 1985), pp. 33–35: "By the late 1920s, women probably played a more influential role in advertising than any other industry—with the possible exceptions of publishing, movies, and department store retailing, although they were usually copywriters, not account executives, and they were usually hired to present the women's point of view."

37: "Missouri Synod wouldn't allow women": Bible passages about wives submitting to their husbands were not stressed by Missouri Synod Lutheran ministers in Southern California in the 1940s and 1950s, although such passages would be stressed in the 1970s, after the appearance of the feminist movement. Conversation with Laurie Pintar, longtime Missouri Synod church member, September 1995.

37: My analysis of the "female sphere" of the 1950s has been influenced by Carroll Smith-Rosenberg, "The FemaleWorld of Love and Ritual: Relations Between Women in Nineteenth-Century America," *Signs: Journal ofWomen in Culture and Society* 1 (Autumn 1975): 1–29.There is no scholarly analysis of this phenomenon during the 1950s.

39: Camille Paglia makes a similar argument about beauty as power in *Sexual Personae: Art and Decadence from Nefertiti to Emily Dickinson* (New Haven:Yale University Press, 1990).

39: On the history of the American cult of personality, cf. Warren I. Susman, *Culture as History:The Transformation of American Society in the Twentieth Century* (New York: Pantheon, 1973). Susman does not discuss its implications for gender.

40: On bridge, see Charles Goren, *Bridge is My Game: Lessons of a Lifetime* (Gar-

in *Post-Romantic Literature* (New York: Columbia University Press, 1990), pp. ix-xiv; 1–7.

76: On Arthur Rackham, see Fred Gettings, *Arthur Rackham* (New York: Macmillan, 1975).

83: On T. E. Lawrence, see Lawrence James, *The Golden Warrior: The Life and Legend of Lawrence of Arabia* (London: Weidenfeld and Nicolson, 1990); on Richard Burton, see Fawn Brodie, *The Devil Drives: A Life of Sir Richard Burton* (New York: Norton, 1967); on Isabelle Eberhardt, see Annette Kobak, *Isabelle Eberhardt* (London: Chatto and Windus, 1988).

Chapter 5: Differences

90: "adolescent girls from indulgent families": cf. Erika Endrijonas, "No Experience Required: American Middle-Class Families and Their Cookbooks, 1945–1960," unpub. Ph.D. diss., 1995, University of Southern California.

93: "for professional training": see Richard Candida Smith, *Utopia and Dissent: Art, Poetry, and Politics in California* (Berkeley: University of California Press, 1995).

100 ff: On Anglicanism, I have consulted David L. Holmes, *A Brief History of the Episcopal Church* (Valley Forge, Pa.: Trinity, 1993); my own experiences in attending Episcopal churches in Los Angeles over the last ten years; and Elizabeth Davenport, an ordained Episcopal priest and the former Episcopal Chaplain at USC.

101: Murray's collection of Whittier's poems is Augustus T. Murray, *A Selection from the Religious Poems of John Greenleaf Whittier, with an Interpretative Essay* (Philadelphia: Friends' Book Store, 1934).

Chapter 6: Alma Mater (1956–1960)

109: On the loyalty oath controversy, see David P. Gardner, *The California Loyalty Oath Controversy* (Berkeley: University of California Press, 1967), and Ellen Schrecker, *No Ivory Tower: McCarthyism and the Universities* (New York: Oxford University Press, 1986), pp. 117–25.

109–110: On existentialism, the major work I read was Walter Kaufman, ed., *Existentialism from Dosteyevsky to Sartre* (New York: New American Library, 1956); on the New Criticism, Cleanth Brooks, *The Well-Wrought Urn: Studies in the Structure of Poetry* (New York: Reynal and Hitchcock, 1947); on functionalism, Talcott Parsons, *Essays in Sociological Theory* (Glencoe, Ill.: Free Press, 1949).

111: " 'oceanic feeling' and Freud": see Sigmund Freud, *Civilization and Its Discontents* (Garden City, New York: Doubleday, Anchor, 1958), pp. 1–13.

113: On Lipton and the Venice Beats, see John Alfred Maynard, *Venice West: The Beat Generation in Southern California* (New Brunswick, N.J.: Rutgers University Press, 1991).

114: Todd Gitlin, in *The Sixties: Years of Hope, Days of Rage* (New York: Bantam, 1987), p. 67, notes the importance of "red diaper" babies, as does Sara Evans, in *Personal Politics: The Roots of Women's Liberation in the Civil Rights Movement and the New Left* (New York: Knopf, 1979), pp. 119–20.

114: For the argument that liberal parents produced radical children, cf. Kenneth Keniston, *The Uncommitted: Alienated Youth in American Society* (New York: Dell, 1970).

118: "Stanford professors toward moderation": Wallace Sterling, long-term president of Stanford, drafted the statement issued by the Association of American Universities, composed of the presidents of the thirty-seven leading universities in the United States and Canada, reprobating any universities that allowed communists to remain on their faculties. Sterling's position was based on his belief, common in universities at the time, that because members of the Communist Party presumably had to follow the party line they couldn't be objective in their teaching (Schrecker, p. 188).

118: On the importance of Quakerism to college pacifism and protest, see Susan Lynn, *Progressive Women in Conservative Times: Racial Justice, Peace, and Feminism, 1945 to the 1960s* (New Brunswick, N.J.: Rutgers University Press, 1992).

119: The ghost catcher story, which Noura told me, is also contained in the textbook for the course, written by Fran's professor. See Frederick Spiegelberg, *Living Religions of the World* (Englewood Cliffs, N.J.: Prentice-Hall, 1956), pp. 778–79.

121: For the argument that servicemen stationed in the Far East brought Zen into the United States, see Rick Fields, *How the Swans Came to the Lake: A Narrative History of Buddhism in America* (Boulder, Col.: Shambhala, 1981). See also Hal Bridges, *American Mysticism: From William James to Zen* (New York: Harper and Row, 1970).

121: "master who gives": Paul Reps, *Zen Flesh, Zen Bones* (Hammondsworth, UK: Penguin, 1971), p. 101.

122: "caution in identifying": see Margaret Guenther, "Faust: The Tragedy Re-Examined," in Susan L. Cocalis and Kay Goodman, eds., *Beyond the Eternal Feminine: Critical Essays on Women and German Literature* (Stuttgart: Akademischer Verlag Hans-dieter Heinz, 1982), pp. 75–98; and Sandra M. Gilbert and Susan Gubar, *The Madwoman in the Attic: The Woman Writer and the Nineteenth-Century Literary Imagination* (New Haven: Yale University Press, 1979), p. 67.

123: Hans's questioning has not been uncommon among physicists. For a contemporary examination, see in particular Fritjof Capra, *The Tao of Physics: An Exploration of the Parallels Between Modern Physics and Eastern Mysticism* (Boulder, Col.: Shambhala, 1975).

123: On Theosophy, see K. Paul Johnson, *The Masters Revealed: Madame Blavatsky and the Myth of the Great White Lodge* (Albany: State University of New York Press, 1994). On Krishnamurti, cf. Mary Lutyens, *The Life and Death of Krishnamurti*

(London: Murray, 1990); Lutyens, ed., *The Krishnamurti Reader* (New York: Penguin, 1954); Hillary Rodrigues, *Insight and Religious Mind: An Analysis of Krishnamurti's Thought* (New York: Peter Lang, 1990); and Jacob Needleman, *The New Religions* (New York: Crossroad, 1984), pp. 145–66. On the esoteric revival of the late nineteenth century, cf. Janet Oppenheim, *The Other World: Spiritualism and Psychical Research in England, 1850–1914* (Cambridge: Cambridge University Press, 1985).

124: On Zen Buddhism in the U.S., see William Barrett, ed., *Zen Buddhism: Selected Writings of D. T. Suzuki* (Garden City, N.Y.: Doubleday, 1956); Alan Watts, *Beat Zen, Square Zen, and Zen* (San Francisco: City Lights, 1959); Helen Tworkov, *Zen in America: Five Teachers and the Search for an American Buddhism* (New York: Kodansha International, 1994); and Kenneth Kraft, *Zen: Teachers and Transition* (New York: Grove, 1988), especially Kraft, "Recent Developments in North American Zen," pp. 178–98.

Chapter 7: Going East (1960–1966)

127: Lisa Alther, *Kinflicks* (New York: New American Library, 1975); Erica Jong, *Fear of Flying* (New York: Holt, Rinehart, Winston, 1973); Lila Karp, *The Queen is in the Garbage* (New York: Vanguard, 1969); Kate Millett, *Flying* (New York: Knopf, 1974); Alix Kates Shulman, *Memoirs of an Ex-Prom Queen* (New York: Knopf, 1972). Quotes are from Millett, *Flying*, p. 237 and Karp, *Queen*, p. 17.

128: "women had long been admitted": cf. Rosalind Rosenberg, *Beyond Separate Spheres: Intellectual Roots of Modern Feminism* (New Haven: Yale University Press, 1982), p. 87.

129: On Columbia and doctorates to women, see Patricia Albjerg Graham, "Status Transitions of Women Students, Faculty, and Administrators," in Alice S. Rossi and Ann Calderwood, eds., *Academic Women on the Move* (New York: Russell Sage Foundation, 1973), p. 169; and Lindsey R. Harmon, *A Century of Doctorates: Data Analyses of Growth and Change* (Washington, D.C.: National Academy of Sciences, 1978).

129ff: My analysis of the situation in the History Department at Columbia is based on my own experience and on the answers I received to queries in letters I addressed to men who were professors there, including Alden Vaughan (May 23, 1993), Robert Cross (June 10, 1993), and William Leuchtenberg (June 31, 1993). I have also interviewed fellow graduate students in history. These included William Chafe, Linda Kerber, Regina Morantz-Sanchez, Carroll Smith-Rosenberg, and Barbara Sicherman. Gerda Lerner's experiences are contained in her *The Majority Finds Its Past: Placing Women in History* (New York: Oxford University Press, 1979).

129: On Beatrice Kevitt's editorial skill, see Stanley Elkins and Eric McKitrick, *The Hofstadter Aegis: A Memorial* (New York: Knopf, 1970), p. 308.

129: On the crisis in graduate education in history, see Committee on Graduate Education of the American Historical Association, *The Education of Historians in the United States* (New York: McGraw-Hill, 1962). According to Peter Novick, *The Noble Dream: The "Objectivity Question" and the American Historical Profession* (Cambridge: Cambridge University Press, 1988), p. 378: "The University of Chicago and the University of Pennsylvania accepted 90 percent of those who applied; Fritz Stern complained to an AHA (American Historical Association) committee that Columbia had 'large numbers of inferior students.' "

130: On the consensus school, cf. Marion J. Morton, *The Terrors of Ideological Politics: Liberal Historians in a Conservative Mood* (Cleveland: Case Western Reserve University Press, 1972); and David Noble, "The Reconstruction of Progress: Charles Beard, Richard Hofstadter, and Postwar Historical Thought," in Lary May, ed., *Recasting America: Culture and Politics in the Age of the Cold War* (Chicago: University of Chicago Press, 1989), pp. 61–75.

134: "dissertation on politics": *To the Hartford Convention: The Federalists and the Origins of Party Politics in Massachusetts, 1789–1815* (New York: Knopf, 1970).

134: "the new political history": see Allen G. Bogue, "The New Political History in the 1970s," in Michael Kammen, ed., *The Past Before Us: Contemporary Historical Writing in the United States* (Ithaca: Cornell University Press, 1980).

137: "artist Eva Hesse wrote": Randy Rosen and Catherine C. Brawer, eds., *Making Their Mark: Women Artists Move Into the Mainstream* (New York: Abbeville, 1988), p. 14.

139: "*Art News* featured": in "What is Pop Art: Interviews by G. R. Swanson," *Art News* (October 1963): 24ff.; (February 1964): 40ff.

139: "Kollwitz's work": see Martha Kearns, *Kaethe Kollwitz: Woman and Artist* (Old Westbury, N.Y.: Feminist Press, 1976).

140: "local feminist support groups were few": Surveying feminist commitment in 1964, Alice Rossi wrote that "there was practically no feminist spark among American women." Rossi, "Equality Between the Sexes," in Robert Jay Lifton, ed., *The Woman in America* (Boston: Houghton Mifflin, 1965), p. 99.

141: "genre and form": for confirmation of Fran's viewpoint about art history, see Eunice Lipton, *Alias Olympia: A Woman's Search for Manet's Notorious Model and Her Own Desire* (New York: Scribner, 1992), p. 97.

142: Judy Chicago and Miriam Shapiro: Elaine Hedges and Ingrid Wendt, *In Her Own Image: Women Working in the Arts* (New York: Feminist Press, 1980), p. 71.

142: "Not until the 1970s": cf. Norma Broude and Mary D. Garrard, eds., *The Power of Feminist Art: The American Movement of the 1970s, History and Impact* (New York: Abrams, 1994), pp. 90–139.

143 ff: The literature on Gurdjieff is large. I have found the following works the most informative: Jacob Needleman and George Baker, eds., *Gurdjieff: Essays and Reflections on the Man and His Teaching* (New York: Continuum, 1996); Kathleen

Riordan Spaeth, *The Gurdjieff Work* (Berkeley, Cal.: And/Or Press, 1976); Spaeth and Ira Friedlander, *Gurdjieff: Seeker of the Truth* (New York: Harper and Row, 1980); Kenneth Walker, *Gurdjieff: A Study of His Teaching* (London: Mandala, 1957); James Webb, *The Harmonious Circle: The Lives and Work of G. I. Gurdjieff, P. D. Ouspensky, and Their Followers* (New York: Putnam, 1980); Colin Wilson, *G. I. Gurdjieff: The War Against Sleep* (Wellingborough, UK: Aquarian, 1986). Gurdjieff's ideas influenced the development of recent self-realization systems such as EST, Arica, and the Diamond Path. On the recent popularity of the Enneagram, see Helen Palmer, *The Enneagram: Understanding Yourself and the Others in Your Life* (San Francisco: HarperSanFrancisco, 1991). Gurdjieff immortalized his early years of searching in his book, *Meetings with Remarkable Men*, which was made into a movie by Peter Brook, starring Terence Stamp.

144: Information on Mrs. March is contained in the above books and in Georgia Dullea, "Where Craftsmen Pursue Philosophy and an Almost Monastic Life," *New York Times*, Aug. 5, 1975.

Chapter 8: Feminism (1966–1982)

151: On the feminist history of Douglass College, see Margaret A. Judson, *Breaking the Barrier: A Professional Autobiography by a Woman Historian Before the Women's Movement* (New Brunswick, N.J.: Rutgers University Press, 1984).

151: "decrease in women faculty": see Judith P. Zinsser, *History and Feminism: A Glass Half Full* (New York: Twayne, 1993), p. 62.

153: Elaine Showalter's dissertation: *A Literature of their Own: British Women Novelists from Brontë to Lessing* (London: Virago, 1982); "gynocritics" is described in Showalter, ed., *The New Feminist Criticism: Essays on Women, Literature, and Theory* (London: Virago, 1985), especially Showalter, "Towards a Feminist Poetics," pp. 125–43.

154: My project on women as chefs was published as: "Why Women Have Not Been Great Chefs," *South Atlantic Quarterly* 42 (Spring 1973): 198–212. Like many other pioneers in the field of women's history, I was influenced in my early writing by Gerda Lerner's work, especially by "The Lady and the Mill Girl: Changes in the Status of Women in the Age of Jackson," *American Studies* 10 (Spring 1969): 5–15; and by "New Approaches to the Study of Women in American History," *Journal of Social History* 3 (Fall 1969): 53–62.

158: My narrative of the Berkshire Conference and its members draws from Judson, Zinsser, and Grace Larsen, "WAWH: The Early Years—Beginnings," in Marguerite Renner, ed., *Histories of the Western Association of Women Historians, 1969–1994* (Los Angeles: WAWH, 1994) and from my own memories. Mary Hartman and I edited the papers from the conference as *Clio's Consciousness Raised: New Perspectives on the History of Women* (New York: Harper and Row, 1974).

160: "modern field of women's history": Lise Vogel, "Telling Tales: Historians of Our Own Lives," *Journal of Women's History* 2 (Winter 1991): 91.

160: "number of organizations": Renner, and the pamphlet by Hilda Smith, Nupur Chaudhuri, and Gerda Lerner, *A History of the Coordinating Committee on Women in the Historical Profession—Conference Group in Women's History* ([?]: Coordinating Committee for Women in the Historical Profession–Conference Group in Women's History, 1989).

160: "women's studies programs": cf. Marilyn Boxer, "For and About Women: The Theory and Practice of Women's Studies in the United States," *Signs: Journal of Women in Culture and Society* 7 (Spring 1982): 661–95.

161: "published three articles": "Religion and Reform in the Early Republic: The Role of Youth," *American Quarterly* 33 (December 1971): 677–95; "Religious Benevolence as Social Control: A Critique of an Interpretation," *Journal of American History* 50 (June 1973): 23–41; "Presbyterians and Voluntarism in the Early Republic," *Journal of Presbyterian History* 50 (Fall 1972): 283–99. My dissertation on reform is "The Protestant Crusade: Religious Missions, Benevolence, and Reform in the United States, 1790–1840."

Chapter 9: Lama (1967–1971)

170: "critical of political radicals": with the exception of Theodore Roszak, *Making of a Counterculture: Reflections on the Technocratic Society and its Youthful Opposition* (Garden City, N.Y.: Doubleday, 1969), few of the works on the cultural radicalism of the sixties discern any connection between political radicalism and spirituality. Cf. William Braden, *The Age of Aquarias: Technology and the Cultural Revolution* (Chicago: Quadrangle, 1970); Timothy Miller, *Hippies and American Values* (Knoxville, Tenn.: University of Tennessee Press, 1991); and Steven M. Tipton, *Getting Saved from the Sixties: Moral Meaning in Conversion and Cultural Change* (Berkeley: University of California Press, 1982). Scholars writing from a religious studies perspective are more sympathetic. See Robert S. Ellwood, *The Sixties Spiritual Awakening: American Religion Moving from Modern to Postmodern* (New Brunswick, N.J.: Rutgers University Press, 1994).

170: For the historical context in 1968 and 1969 I have read through *Newsweek* magazine for those years.

172: For Luhan on Taos, see Mabel Dodge Luhan, *Edge of Taos Desert: An Escape to Reality* (New York: Harcourt, Brace, 1937), pp. 86, 99. For background on Luhan and Taos, see also Mabel Dodge Luhan, *Lorenzo in Taos* (New York: Knopf, 1932); Lois Palken Rudnick, *Mabel Dodge Luhan: New Woman, New Worlds* (Albuquerque: University of New Mexico Press, 1984); and Kay Aiken Reeve, *Santa Fe and Taos, 1898–1942: An American Cultural Center* (El Paso: Texas Western, 1982).

172: D. H. Lawrence describes his reaction to Taos in "New Mexico" and

"Taos," in Edward D. McDonald, ed., *Phoenix: The Posthumous Papers of D. H. Lawrence* (New York: Viking, 1936), pp. 100, 142.

173 ff: On communes I have used Richard Fairfield, *Communes USA: A Personal Tour* (Baltimore, Md.: Penguin, 1972); Hugh Gardner, *The Children of Prosperity: Thirteen Modern American Communes* (New York: St. Martin's, 1978); Delores Hayden, *Seven American Utopias: The Architecture of Communitarian Socialism, 1790–1975* (Cambridge, Mass.: MIT Press, 1975); Robert Houriot, *Getting Back Together* (New York: Coward and Geoghegan, 1971); Rosabeth Moss Kanter, *Commitment and Community: Communes and Utopias in Sociological Perspective* (Cambridge: Harvard University Press, 1972); Ron E. Roberts, *The New Communes: Coming Together in America* (Englewood Cliffs, N.J.: Prentice-Hall, 1971); Lawrence Veysey, *The Communal Experience: Anarchist and Mystical Counter-Cultures in America* (New York: Harper and Row, 1973); and Gilbert Zwicklin, *Countercultural Communes: A Sociological Perspective* (Westport, Conn.: Greenwood, 1983), p. 11.

Information on Lama is contained throughout these works, with specific chapters in Houriot, pp. 29–378; Roberts, pp. 63-65; Gardner, pp. 70–92; Fairfield, pp. 116–30. On Lama I have also used pamphlets and flyers from the Library, Lama pp. Foundation, and especially the video of Old Beans Week, Lama Foundation, June 1, 1990, including interviews of the past experiences of Chien, Ruth, Sara, Asha (Barbara von Briesen); Siddiq (Hans von Briesen); and Sakina von Briesen. See also Nuridin Durkee, "Embracing Islam," unpub. mss. autobiography, and Eliezer Sobel, "The Fire This Time," in *Yoga Journal* 131 (Nov./Dec. 1996): 84–91ff, and Nuridin's rejoinder in the April, 1997, issue of the *Yoga Journal*.

173: "intentional communities": *Intentional Communities: A Guide to Cooperative Living: 1990–91 Directory* (Evansville, Ind.: Fellowship for Intentional Community, 1990) lists 646 communities in 1990.

173: "mind-altering drugs": See Ram Dass's autobiography, contained as an introduction to *Be Here Now* (New York: Crown, 1994), n.p.

174: "Book of the Dead": see Timothy Leary, Ralph Metzner, and Richard Alpert, *The Psychedelic Experience: A Manual Based on the Tibetan Book of the Dead* (New Hyde Park, N.Y.: University, 1964).

174: In my discussion of mystical experiences, I have especially used James, *Varieties of Religious Experience*, p. 378. A discussion of Ibn Arabi's visions is contained in Seyyed Hossein Nasr, *Three Muslim Sages: Avicenna—Suhrawardi—Ibn Arabi* (Cambridge: Harvard University Press, 1964), p. 95.

175: "USCo": see "Luminal Music," *Time*, March 25, 1967, 78–80: "Brilliant strobe lights imprint patterns of whirling hexagons to induce the hallucinatory traumas that occur in some LSD trips."

182: For the life of Murshid Samuel Lewis, see Samuel L. Lewis, *Sufi Vision and Initiation: Meetings with Remarkable Beings*, ed. Neil Douglas-Klotz (San Francisco: Sufi Islamia/Prophecy Publications, 1986).

183: On Hazrat Inayat Khan, see Elisabeth de Jong-Keesing, *Inayat Khan:A Biography* (The Hague: East-West Publications, 1974).

183 fn.: On the Sufi orders in Egypt, see Valerie Hoffman, *Sufism, Mystics, and Saints in Modern Egypt* (Columbia, S.C.: University of South Carolina Press, 1995). See also Nasr, *Islamic Spirituality*, vol. 2, and J. Spencer Trimingham, *The Sufi Orders in Islam* (London: Oxford University Press, 1971).

184: "know that Allah": Samuel L. Lewis, *The Jerusalem Trilogy: Song of the Prophets* (Novato, Cal.: Prophecy Pressworks, 1975), p. 202.

184: "Dances of Universal Peace": *Spiritual Dance and Walk:An Introduction to the Dances of Universal Peace and Walking Meditations of Samuel L. Lewis* (Fairfax, Cal.: PeaceWorks, 1990).

185: On Ruth St. Denis, see Suzanne Shelton, *Divine Dancer:A Biography of Ruth St. Denis* (Garden City, N.Y.: Doubleday, 1981).

Chapter 10: Dar-al-Islam (1971–1990)

189: Natalie Goldberg describes her stay at Lama in *Long Quiet Highway:Waking Up in America* (New York: Bantam, 1993).

193ff: On Islamic mysticism, I have used Bakhtiar, *Sufi*; Hoffman, *Sufism, Mystics, and Saints*; Nasr, *Islamic Spirituality*; Schimmel, *Mystical Dimensions of Islam*; Nahid Angha, *Principles of Sufism* (Fremont, Cal.: Asian Humanities Press, 1991); Nathaniel P. Archer, ed., *The Sufi Mystery* (London: Octagon, 1980); Titus Burckhardt, *An Introduction to Sufism: The Mystical Dimension of Islam* (Wellingborough, UK: Aquarian, 1976); Martin Lings, *What Is Sufism?* (Cambridge, UK: Islamic Texts Society, 1993); and "Sufism: An Old Tradition for a New World," in "Collected Papers," Sufism Symposium, March 7–9, 1997, Fremont, Cal.

193: On Ibn Arabi, see Henri Corbin, *Creative Imagination in the Sufism of Ibn Arabi* (Princeton: Princeton University Press, 1969), and the many writings of William C. Chittick, summarized in Chittick, "Ibn Arabi and his School," in Nasr, *Islamic Spirituality*, vol. 1, pp. 49–80. For the intricacies of Sufi cosmology, see Seyyed Hossein Nasr, *An Introduction to Islamic Cosmological Doctrines* (Cambridge: Harvard University Press, 1964).

194: "seven hidden significations": Houston Smith, *The World's Religions: Our Great Wisdom Traditions* (San Francisco: HarperSan Francisco, 1991), p. 57.

194: "Sacred history in the Qur'an": Nasr, "Quar'an as Foundation of Islamic Spirituality," in Nasr, *Islamic Spirituality*, vol 1, p. 7. In his writing on the Qur'an, Nuridin Durkee extends Nasr's observation: "The floods, the exodus, the hijira, the battles, the angels descending and ascending, the entirety of the Qur'an is also an internal event and not only an historico-collective Revelation." See Durkee, "The Ritual of Qur'an as Spiritual Practice," in "Collected Papers," Sufism Symposium, p. 52.

194: "sounds and letters of Arabic": cf. Jean Carteins, "The Hidden Sciences in Islam," in Nasr, *Islamic Spirituality*, vol. 1; and Idries Shah, *The Sufis* (New York: Doubleday, 1964).

195: "power that separates true mysticism": Schimmel, p. 4.

195: "musical calligraphy": Frithjof Schuon, *Sufism: Veil and Quintessence* (Bloomington, Ind.: World Wisdom, 1981), p. 7.

197: *Seed* was published by Harmony, in New York City. It sold about 50,000 copies, according to Noura.

197: The Qur'an actually contains more than ninety-nine attributes of Allah. Pir Vilayat Khan writes that the number ninety-nine is based on a tradition established by a hadith. See Pir Vilayat Inayat Khan, *That Which Transpires Behind That Which Appears: The Experience of Sufism* (New Lebanon, N.Y.: Omega, 1994), p. 186.

198: Nurudin's book on Jerusalem was never published.

199: The conversion narrative is Muhammad Asad, *The Road to Mecca* (New York: Simon and Schuster, 1954).

207ff: On Dar-al-Islam, cf. William Tracy, "Dar-al-Islam: The Code and the Calling," *Aramco World* 39 (May/June 1988): 20–29. The current situation at the community is discussed in "For a Muslim Group, Desert Is Fertile Ground," in *New York Times*, May 5, 1996.

Epilogue: Abiquiu Revisited

211ff: On women in Islam, see Fatima Mernissi, *Islam and Democracy: Fear of the Modern World*, trans. Mary Jo Lakeland (Indianapolis, Ind.: Addison-Wesley, 1992); Naila Minai, ed., *Women in Islam: Tradition and Transition in the Middle East* (New York: Seaview, 1981); Valentine M. Maghadam, "Islamist Movements and Women's Responses in the Middle East," *Gender and History* 3 (Autumn 1981): 268–84; Minou Reeves, *Female Warriors of Allah: Women and the Islamic Revolution* (New York: Dutton, 1989); Judith Tucker, ed., *Arab Women: Old Boundaries, New Frontiers* (Bloomington, Ind.: Indiana University Press, 1993); and Judith Tucker, "Gender and Islamic History," in *Islamic and European Expansion: The Forging of a Global Order* (Philadelphia: Temple University Press, 1993). On women in Islamic religious doctrine, see Sachiko Murata, *The Tao of Islam: A Sourcebook on Gender Relationships in Islamic Thought* (Albany: State University of New York Press, 1992); and Barbara Freyer Stowasser, *Women in the Qur'an: Traditions and Interpretations* (New York: Oxford University Press, 1994).

215: Nawal El Saadawi, *The Hidden Face of Eve: Women in the Arab World*, trans. and ed., Sherif Hetata (Boston: Beacon, 1980).

215: "feminism as kaleidoscopic": Marilyn Frye, "Some Reflections on Separatism and Power," in Marilyn Persall, ed., *Women and Values: Readings in Recent Feminist Philosophy* (Belmont, Cal.: Wadsworth, 1986), p. 132. Conservative religious women in the United States are not without feminist views. See Carol Virginia Pohli, "Church Closets and Back Doors: A Feminist View of Moral Majority Women," *Feminist Studies* 9 (Fall 1983): 549–50, and Judith Stacey, *Brave New Families: Stories of Domestic Upheaval in Late Twentieth-Century America* (New York: Basic, 1990). Debra Kaufman has studied Jewish women who were radicals in the sixties and who have converted to orthodox Judaism. They find authority in a separate women's world, although their views on gender are not especially egalitarian. See Debra Renée Kaufman, *Rachel's Daughters: Newly Orthodox Jewish Women* (New Brunswick, N.J.: Rutgers University Press, 1990).

218ff: On "veiling," I have found especially useful Nilüfer Göle, *The Forbidden Modern: Civilization and Veiling* (Ann Arbor: University of Michigan, 1996).

221: poem by Attar, quoted by Maureen Clark: "From the Outside In," *Gnosis*, p. 17.

224: Rumi poem: "And He is With You," in *Love is a Stranger*, p. 35.